Augustinian-Cartesian Index

Other Titles of Interest from St. Augustine's Press

Zbigniew Janowski, *How to Read Descartes's Meditations*

Leszek Kolakowski, *My Correct Views on Everything*, edited by Zbigniew Janowski

Leszek Kolakowski, *The Two Eyes of Spinoza and Other Essays on Philosophers*, edited by Zbigniew Janowski

Leszek Kolakowski, *Religion: If There Is No God . . . On God, the Devil, Sin, and Other Worries of the So-Called Philosophy of Religion*

Leszek Kolakowski, *Husserl and the Search for Certitude*

Leszek Kolakowski, *Bergson*

Aristotle, *Aristotle – On Poetics*, translated by Seth Benardete and Michael Davis

Thomas Aquinas, *Disputed Questions on Virtue*

Francisco Suarez, *On Creation, Conservation, & Concurrence: Metaphysical Disputations 20–22*

William of Ockham, *Ockham's Theory of Terms: Part I of the Summa Logicae*

William of Ockham, *Ockham's Theory of Terms: Part II of the Summa Logicae*

Roger Bacon, *Roger Bacon's Philosophy of Nature*. Translation of *De multiplicatione specierum and De speculis comburentibus*

Rémi Brague, *Eccentric Culture: A Theory of Western Civilization*Plato, *The Symposium of Plato: The Shelley Translation*, translated by Percy Bysshe Shelley

Mario Enrique Sacchi, *The Apocalypse of Being: The Esoteric Gnosis of Martin Heidegger*

Roger Scruton, *An Intelligent Person's Guide to Modern Culture*

Roger Scruton, *The Meaning of Conservatism*

Roger Scruton, *On Hunting*

Roger Scruton, *Art and Imagination: A Study in the Philosophy of Mind*

Roger Scruton, *Aesthetic Understanding*

Josef Pieper, *Leisure, the Basis of Culture*

Josef Pieper, *Scholasticism: Personalities and Problems*

Josef Pieper, *The Silence of St. Thomas*

Peter Kreeft, *Socratic Logic: A Logic Text Using Socratic Method, Platonic Questions, and Aristotelian Principles*

Jacques Maritain, *Natural Law: Reflections on Theory and Practice*

Gabriel Marcel, *The Mystery of Being* (in two volumes)

Yves R. Simon, *The Great Dialogue of Nature and Space*

Jerome J. Langford, *Galileo, Science and the Church*

Augustinian-Cartesian Index

Texts and Commentary

Zbigniew Janowski

St. Augustine's Press
South Bend, Indiana
2004

Manufactured in the United States of America.

1 2 3 4 5 6 10 09 08 07 06 05 04

Library of Congress Cataloging in Publication Data
Janowski, Zbigniew.
Augustinian Cartesian index : texts and commentary / Zbigniew Janowski.
p. cm.
Includes bibliographical references and index.
ISBN 1-890318-10-8 (hardcover : alk. paper)
1. Augustine, Saint, Bishop of Hippo. 2. Descartes, René, 1596–1650. I. Title.
BR1720.A9 J36 2003
194 – dc21 2002151654

∞ *The paper used in this publication meets the minimum requirements of the American National Standard for Information Sciences – Permanence of Paper for Printed Materials, ANSI Z39.48-1984.*

St. Augustine's Press
www.staugustine.net

To

Jean-Luc Marion,

Leszek Kolakowski,

and in memory of

François Furet

Table of Contents

Appendixes

Preface to the French Edition

The history of this book is very short. In 1994, when I began writing my doctoral dissertation, *Cartesian Theodicy*, at the University of Chicago, I explained to Jean-Luc Marion that I had the intention of renewing the ancient thesis about the rapprochements between Descartes and St. Augustine. Not convinced that this was possible, he said: "Gilson did not entirely succeed; you are not going to either." Needless to say, such a remark from one of the greatest specialists on Descartes was not particularly encouraging. But the more I advanced in my topic, the more I was convinced that he had a good reason to say what he had said. After reading Léon Blanchet's *Les précédents historiques du "je pense, donc je suis,"* Etienne Gilson ironically remarked: "In the final analysis, although it is possible, as L. Blanchet would have it, that Descartes read St. Augustine, though there is *nothing* to warrant this." Nevertheless, in pursuing the comparisons between Descartes and St. Augustine, the "nothing" of Gilson was becoming more and more problematic. Dozens of pages of converging passages, some of them almost literal, could not be explained as a series of accidents. The direct influence of St. Augustine's works on Descartes began to appear to me indubitable, as it did to Jean-Luc Marion, who encouraged me to turn my findings into a book.

This work owes a great deal to several people. In the first place, I would like to express my gratitude to Jean-Luc Marion, who has always supported my Cartesian endeavors and helped me with his erudition and advice. Without his initiative and help, *The Augustinian-Cartesian Index* would never have seen the light of the day. I would also like to thank Vincent Carraud, who, in November 1996, invited me to the Université de Caen to give a lecture ("Saint Augustin autorise-t-il la doctrine des vérités éternelles?") where I voiced my ideas about the Cartesian-Augustinian connection for the first time. He suggested the prudent division of citations into certain and uncertain borrowings. The latter are marked in the *Index* as "Additions." I also owe a debt of gratitude to Miss Laurence Devillairs, who drew my attention to several passages that escaped my initial readings of Descartes and St.

Augustine. She also read the manuscript and corrected my French. I would like to thank Jean-François Courtine for accepting this book in his prestigious collection, and the Centre National du Livre for a fellowship that made the completion of this book possible. Finally, my thanks go to the Centre Raymond Aron at the École des Hautes Études en Sciences Sociales where I had the privilege to work on the *Index* during my stay in Paris.

Preface to the English Edition

The present work was intended as a literal translation from the French original. However, as I was working on it, I realized the considerable impact the works of Francis Bacon have had on the formation of Cartesian philosophy. Although *The Augustinian-Cartesian Index* is, as the title suggests, devoted to Augustine's influence on Descartes, it is at the same time a work that is primarily concerned with the study of the sources of Descartes's philosophy. The inclusion of an appendix on Bacon is only consistent with the character of such a work. (In Appendix 4, I have included most of the passages identified by André Laland in his seminal article, "Sur quelques textes de Bacon et de Descartes," in *Revue de Métaphysique et de Morale*, 1911. These are marked as XI–XVI.) Likewise, the inclusion of an appendix on Montaigne seemed to me justified. In contradistinction to St. Augustine or Bacon, Montaigne's influence on Descartes has been recognized for a long time. A number of passages have been identified by Cartesian scholars in the past. However, they are dispersed through learned books and journals, and have never been collected in a handy form for comparative purposes.

While working on *The Augustinian-Cartesian Index*, I was finishing my *Cartesian Theodicy: Descartes' Quest for Certitude*, in which I present an Augustinian reading of Descartes's *Meditations*. Although the topic and scope of the two works are different, I have included a few fragments from *The Cartesian Theodicy* in my commentary to the *Index*.

This work owes more than I can acknowledge to several friends: Jean-Luc Marion, Leszek Kolakowski, Daniel Garber, and Richard Watson. Red Watson urged me to translate *The Augustinian-Cartesian Index* into English. He also waded through the first rough version of the translation and corrected it. My friend Agnieszka Kolakowska polished this text and made it much more succinct than it was before. Jane Curran took the painstaking task of proofreading the *Index* proper. In writing the final sections on Bacon and Descartes and on Descartes and Montaigne, I received some feedback

from Marta Fattori, whose comments and seminal works on Bacon and Descartes were of invaluable help.

Among other friends who read some parts of this text and commented on it are: Giulia Belgioioso, Todd Breyfogle, Vincent Carraud, Emmanuel Faye, Chiaki Kagawa, Denis Kambouchner, Ryszard Legutko, Katia Mitova, Theo Verbeek, and my wife Catherine O'Neil. Finally, I thank my publisher Mr. Bruce Fingerhut for his patience in awaiting the final version of the manuscript.

Note on Abbreviations, Editions, and Translations

Throughout this text, I use abbreviations for authors, editions, and translations.

For example: "D VII – M VII: V, I, 25, T, I, 45" refers to a quotation from Descartes (D), in section VII of the Index, and from Montaigne (M), the French edition by Pierre Villey (V), volume number I, page number 25, English translation by E. J. Trenchmann.

The list of editions, translations, and abbreviations used in the text can be found below.

The names of authors are abbreviated as follows:

D – Descartes
A – Augustine
B – Bacon
T – St. Thomas Aquinas
S – Duns Scotus
M – Montaigne

Citations from Descartes's works are from Charles Adam and Paul Tannery (eds)., *Œvres de Descartes*, 2nd edition, 11 vols. (Paris: Vrin, 1974–1986). This is abbreviated to AT.

Citations in English from Descartes are from J. Cottingham, R. Stoothoff, D. Mardoch, and A. Kenny (eds.), *The Philosophical Writings of Descartes*, 3 vols. (Cambridge: Cambridge University Press, 1984–1995). This is abbreviated to CSM, with the exception of volume III, which is abbreviated to CSMK.

Citations in Latin from St. Augustine are from *Œuvres de Saint Augustin*, (Paris: Desclée de Brouwer, 1948–).

Citations in English from St. Augustine are from the following editions:

The Literal Meaning of Genesis, tr. by John Hammond Taylor, 2 vols. (New York: Newman Press, 1982).

On Order (*Divine Providence and the Problem of Evil*), tr. by Robert P. Russell, O.S.A. (New York: CIMA Publishing Co., Inc., 1948).

The Immortality of the Soul, tr. by Ludwig Schopp (Washington, D.C.: The Catholic University of America, 1947).

The Magnitude of the Soul, tr. by John J. McMahon (Washington, D.C.: The Catholic University of America, 1947).

On Free Will (*The Free Choice of the Will*), tr. by Robert Russell (Washington, D.C.: The Catholic University of America, 1968).

Against the Sceptics (*Answer to Skeptics*), tr. by Denis J. Kavanagh (New York: CIMA Publishing Company, 1948).

The Happy Life, tr. by Ludwig Schopp (New York: CIMA Publishing Company, 1948).

The City of God against the Pagans, tr. by Henry Bettenson (London: Penguin Books, 1972).

The Confessions, tr. by J. G. Pilkington, in *A Select Library of the Nicene and Post-Nicene Fathers*, vol. I. (New York: Charles Scribner's Sons, 1887).

Christian Doctrine, tr. by J. F. Show, in *A Select Library of the Nicene and Post-Nicene Fathers*, vol. II. (New York: Charles Scribner's Sons, 1887).

On the Trinity, tr. by Arthur West Haddan, in *A Select Library of the Nicene and Post-Nicene Fathers*, vol. III. (New York: Charles Scribner's Sons, 1887).

Of True Religion, tr. by John H. Burleigh, in *The Library of Christian Classics*, vol. VI, *Augustine: Earlier Writings* (London: SCM Press Ltd., 1953).

The Nature of the Good, tr. by John H. Burleigh, in *The Library of Christian Classics*, vol. VI, *Augustine: Earlier Writings* (London: SCM Press Ltd., 1953).

Citations from St. Thomas Aquinas are from the following editions:

Summa Contra Gentiles: On the Truth of the Catholic Faith (Garden City, N.Y.: Doubleday, 1957).

Summa Theologiæ, Latin Text and English Translation, Blackfriars edition (London and New York, 1964–).

Citations from Duns Scotus are to the following editions:

Ioannis Duns Scoti, "De Esse Dei," in *Opera Omnia*, vol. 2 (Vatican City: Typis Polyglottis Vaticanis, 1950).

Duns Scotus, *Philosophical Writings*, bi-lingual edition, translated by Allan Wolter (Indianapolis/Cambridge: Hackett Publishing Company, 1987).

Citations from Francis Bacon are from the following edition:

The Works of Francis Bacon, ed. by J. Spedding, D. L. Ellis and D. D. Heath (London: Longmans & Co. 1889–91).

Citations from Montaigne are from the following editions:

Montaigne, *Les Essais*, 3 vols. Pierre Villey ed. (Paris: Quadrige/PUF, 1999). Abbreviated to V.

Essais de Montaigne, ed. by M. Rat, 3 vols. (Paris: Éditions Garnier Frères, 1962). Abbreviated to EG.

Montaigne: Œuvres completes, ed. by Albert Thibaudet and Maurice Rat (Paris: Bibliotèque de la Pléiade, 1962). Abbreviated to PL.

The Essays of Montaigne, translated by E.J. Trenchmann, 2 vols. in one (Oxford: Oxford University Press, [1927]). All quotations in Appendix 3 and in the text following it are from this translation. Abbreviated to T.

The Essays of Michel de Montaigne, tr. and ed. with an introduction and notes by M. A. Screech (London: Allen Lane, The Penguin Press, 1987). Abbreviated to S.

Introduction

If you know something, it is entirely yours, even if you learned it from someone else.

Descartes to Beeckman, October 17, 1630

The more one is acquainted with the doctrine of St. Augustine, the more one will be disposed to embrace the philosophy of Descartes.

Mersenne to Voetius, December 13, 1642

The issue of Descartes's Augustinianism first appears in 1637, when, after the publication of the *Discourse on Method*, Marin Mersenne and Andreas Colvius rushed to inform Descartes that St. Augustine had also used the *cogito* in his writings. Several years later, in 1641, in his *Objections to the Meditations*, Antoine Arnauld pointed out a number of other similarities between elements of Descartes's metaphysics and St. Augustine's theology. He was the first Augustinian to notice them, but not the last: André Martin (alias Ambrosius Victor), Louis de la Forge, Claude Clerselier, Dom Robert Desgabet, Pierre-Sylvain Régis,[1] and many others did not fail to notice others.

What drew the Augustinians' attention in the first place, and made them adopt Descartes's philosophy, was the distinction between the body and the soul. In his Preface to Descartes's works, Clerselier wrote: "[Monsieur Descartes] very clearly explains the exact distinction between the Essence of Spiritual and Material things."[2] Louis de La Forge in his *Traité de l'esprit de l'homme* makes the same point,[3] and cites a long passage from *On the Trinity*

1 See *Cours entier de philosophie . . . selon les principes de M. Descartes*. La Métaphysique, Livre I, Partie II, chapt. XII ("Conformité des sentiments de saint Augustin avec la nature de l'esprit et de l'âme"), (Amsterdam, 1691), vol. I, pp. 148–53.

2 AT V, 633.

3 *Traité de l'esprit de l'homme. Latin edition, Lodovici de La Forge, M.D, Renati DesCartes Tractatus de Homine, et de Formatione Foetus*, Amsterdami, Apud Davidem Elsevirium,

to illustrate how close was Descartes's philosophy to St. Augustine's thought, at least in spirit. In the *Nouveaux Elémens de géométrie* (1682 ed.), Arnauld notes that Descartes, like St. Augustine, believes that the study of mathematics is the best method of detaching the soul from the body (*il semble qu'il n'y en ait guèrez de plus capables de détacher l'ame de cette application aux sens*), and concludes that the *nouvelle philosophie* can serve "to dispose one's soul to receive Christian truths."[4] In the same vein Nicolas Poisson, in his *Commentary to the Discourse on Method* (1670), stresses the common points between St. Augustine and Descartes. André Martin, the author of *Philosophia christiana* (1671) – a "learned collection" of the writings of St. Augustine, as Malebranche called it – had as much veneration for Descartes as for St. Augustine.[5] Daniel Pierre Huet, at one time a Cartesian and later an unforgiving enemy of the *nouvelle philosophie*, went so far as to refuse any originality to Descartes. In his *Censura philosophiae cartesianae* (1689) he states that "Cartesian Doubt" appears in *On Free Will* and *The City of God* (p. 203), and the "distinction between the soul and the body" in *On the Trinity* (p. 204), while the idea that "the soul knows itself" is present throughout the Augustinian corpus (p. 205).

Antoine Arnauld and Pierre Nicole are textbook examples of propagators of Cartesianism among the 17th-century Augustinians from Port-Royal. We must bear in mind, however, that the Port-Royal was neither the sole nor the most important seat of Cartesianism. "The good news Monsieur Descartes received at that time," writes Adrien Baillet, a biographer of Descartes, "concerned the success of his philosophy in France, and particularly among the Oratorian Fathers, who gave it universal approbation."[6] The author of the annals of the Oratory confirms this: "In 1628, Cardinal de Bérulle, having met M. Descartes at Bagui's, the papal nuncio's, asked him to expose his philosophical ideas in public, and at that time introduced him to

1677. See also A. Arnauld, *Examen d'un écrit qui a pour titre: Traité de l'essence du corps et de L'union de l'âme avec le corps, contre la philosophie de M. Descartes, Œuvres De Messire Antoine Arnauld*, vol. xxxviii.

4 In a letter to the Pope concerning the education of the Dauphin, Bossuet explains that "Philosophy consists first of making the soul aware of itself so that it can by degrees elevate itself to God. To become a perfect philosopher, man does not need to study anything but himself, nor does he need to leaf through a pile of books . . ." Quoted after Françisque Bouillier, *Histoire de la philosophie cartésienne* (Paris: Delgrave, 1868), vol. II, p. 244. As one can see from this letter, Cartesian attitude to philosophy was adopted by even the most conservative thinkers such as Bossuet only a few decades after Descartes's death.

5 *Revue de Fribourg* (1908), pp. 77–78.

6 *La Vie de Monsieur Descartes*, Livre VI (Paris: La Table Ronde, 1946), p. 196.

several Oratorian Fathers who later became his most zealous disciples. It is in that event that one should seek the first origins of Cartesianism in the Oratory."[7]

Many Oratorian Fathers propagated the *nouvelle philosophie* like Gospel. The attachment of the Augustinians to Descartes's philosophy was well expressed by the Calvinist Pierre Jurieu, who remarked that "the theologians of Port-Royal are as much attached to Cartesianism as they are to Christianity."[8] The Jesuit Pierre Daniel, author of a famous book *Voyage du Monde de M. Descartes* (1691, p. 285), reversed this perspective when he declared that "there are few Jansenists who are not Cartesians." Although our knowledge of the reception of Cartesian philosophy among Augustinians is far from complete, one can safely say that the Augustinians, and the Oratorians in particular, were much more predisposed to accept Descartes's philosophy than other religious orders. Of all the Oratorian colleges, the college in Angers embraced the *nouvelle philosophie* most ardently,[9] and became the most active center of Cartesianism.[10] Father André Martin (alias Ambrosius Victor) is credited with introducing Cartesianism to the Oratory.[11] In the preface to his *Philosophia christiana*, he announces that his intention is to substitute the true philosophy – the "philosophia christiana" of Descartes and St. Augustine – for the subtle and pitiful teachings of the school, which deserve only scorn and disgust. Bernard Lamy, a Jansenist, "in his first course at Angers attacked the Peripatetics."[12] He ended his career in 1675 in Saint-Martin de Miséré en Dauphiné, where he was sent into exile for teaching the philosophy of Descartes. Vincent Pellaut, a Jansenist whose theses were censured by the Sorbonne because they were "full of the opinions of Baius,"[13] also ended his career in exile, in 1677, in Brivé. In 1676, Father de

7 Archives Nationales MM 624 fol. 18v. Cited after Françis Ferrier, *La pensée philosophique du Père Guillaume Gibieuf: 1583–1650* (Lille: Atelier Reproduction de Thèses, 1976), vol. I, p. 120.

8 *La Politique du Clergé de France*, 2nd ed. (1681), p. 107. Cited also by Arnauld, *Apologie Pour Les Catholiques*, Chapt. V, in *Œuvres De Messire Antoine Arnauld*, vol. XIV, p. 615.

9 See Victor Cousin, *Fragments de philosophie moderne* (Paris, 1856), p. 22.

10 See Antoine Adam, *Du mysticism à la révolte*, pp. 289–91; Jacques Maillard, *L'Oratoire à Angers aux XVIIème et XVIIIème siècles* (Paris: Librairie C. Klincksieck [no date]), p. 188.

11 Louis Batterel, *Mémoires domestiques pour servir à l'histoire de l'Oratoire*, ed. by A. M. P. Ignold, 4 vols. (Paris, 1902–1905), vol. III, p. 518. This is the only work that contains complete information about Oratorian Fathers.

12 Letter of Malebranche's friend of Saumur or of Angers cited by François Girbal, *Bernard Lamy. Etude biographique et bibliographique* (Paris: PUF, 1964), p. 33.

13 Jacques Maillard, *L'Oratoire à Angers aux XVIIème et XVIIIème siècles, op. cit.*, p. 192.

Villecrose was summoned by the university to present his lecture notes, in which the examiners found "a number of Cartesian propositions."[14] Father Guillou, a Jansenist, publicly held up to ridicule the partisans of the philosophy of Aristotle and made a public avowal of his Cartesianism:

> How highly was esteemed the philosophy of Aristotle. . . . But also, how disdainful, useless, vain and incapable this philosophy turned out to be. Those who follow this philosophy today, called the Arabs, the Spanish, or, simply, Scholastics, are scarcely held in esteem. The old philosophy turns itself into dust . . . the labor and the study of Descartes awakes one's mind that is asleep in other men. . . . The philosophy of Descartes is in full brightness at the University of Paris from where it is propagated not only to other universities in the kingdom [of France], but to the entire world.[15]

In 1722, the university censured twelve propositions from Guillou's writings "as injurious to St. Thomas [Aquinas] and to all the other illustrious doctors, who have served the Church well, to numerous religious orders, and to the majority of the masters of the school, who for fifteen hundred years conserved the doctrine of Aristotle and continue to do so."[16] Similar things happened at Anjou, Saumur, and other Oratorian colleges.[17]

By 1678, Cartesianism was so widespread in the Oratorian colleges that a royal decree[18] was needed to curb the zeal of the apostles of the new faith. To save the Order from imminent ruin, its Superiors took matters into their own hands. They requested their professors to stop teaching *la nouvelle philosophie*. The Oratorian professors protested against this decision in a letter which reads: "if Cartesianism is a plague, there are two hundred of us here who are infected."[19] The prohibition does not seem to have worked mir-

14 *Ibid.*, p. 192.

15 Bibliothèque municipale d'Angers, manuscrit 1259 (1030). Cited in Jacques Maillard, *Ibid.*, pp. 193–94.

16 *Ibid.*, p. 194, note 169.

17 See L. de Lens, *La philosophie en Anjou*, 1873, and J. Dumont, *L'Oratoire et le cartésianisme en Anjou.*

18 The royal decree, of course, was not an expression of the king's personal sentiments. The Dauphin's tutor was the Cartesian Cordemoy, who obtained this position upon Bossuet's personal recommendation. One may safely assume that the king, probably without even comprehending the nature of the problem, signed the decree that was presented to him by the enemies of Cartesianism.

19 The letter is cited by Father Daniel in his *Voyage du monde de Descartes*, Part III. See also Ménage, *Menagina*, 1714 edition, vol. III, p. 262: "I saw a letter written in very good Latin from one of their young fathers asking permission to teach it [Cartesian philosophy] with two hundred other professors." See also Françisque Bouillier, *Histoire de la*

acles. In 1706 the General Assembly of the Jesuit Society in Rome passed a resolution that Descartes's philosophy should be combated as strongly as Jansenism.[20]

The enthusiastic reception of the *nouvelle philosophie* among the Augustinians raises the question of the nature of the relationship between Augustinianism and Cartesianism. Why was it almost exclusively the Augustinians who embraced the *nouvelle philosophie* as their own? Françisque Bouiller, in his monumental *Histoire de la philosophie cartésienne*, explains that "the fruits that the Church could expect from Descartes's philosophy was to install in the hearts of the philosophers the belief in the divinity and immortality of the soul. This is the principal cause of the attachment of Bossuet, Arnauld, and other great Cartesian theologians to Cartesianism."[21] "If it is impossible not to appreciate the vigor of theological Augustinism in the time of Descartes," Genviève Rodis-Lewis writes, "the essential object of the Saint's works [theology of grace] could mask, for those who knew them best, the originality of his philosophical argumentation."[22] Vincent Carraud, who meticulously analyzed Arnauld's reaction to the *Meditations*, observes that "it is very possible that the philosophical relevance of Cartesianism furnished [Arnauld] with a new occasion to read St. Augustine, in whose works several passages – in particular some that were not from the texts on grace that were customarily cited – now shone in a new light. This is the case precisely with the works to which Arnauld refers in the Fourth Set of Objections and which, it seems, are not those Saint-Cyran had keenly recommended that he read: *De libero arbitrio*, *De quantitate animae*, *Soliloquia*, and *De utilitate credendi*. Thus Cartesianism may have reactivated an interest in St. Augustine the philosopher and not merely the Doctor of grace."[23] Finally, according to Etienne Gilson, "[St. Augustine], this unsurpassed exponent of Christian wisdom, never had a philosophy for his theology."[24] This is precisely what

philosophie cartésienne (Paris: Delgrave, 1868), vol. II, pp. 9–10, and Jacques Maillard, *L'Oratoire à Angers aux XVIIème et XVIIIème siècles*, *op. cit.*, pp. 190 ff.

20 For details see Victor Cousin, *Oeuvres Philosophiques du Père André de la Compagnie de Jésus* (Paris: Adolphe Delahays Librairie, 1843), p. ccxxx.

21 Françisque Bouillier, *Histoire de la philosophie cartésienne* (Paris: Delgrave, 1868), vol. II, p. 231.

22 Geneviève Rodis-Lewis, "Augustinisme et cartésianisme," in *L'anthropologie cartésienne* (Paris: PUF, 1990), p. 45.

23 Vincent Carraud, "Arnauld: De l'occamisme au cartésianisme," in *Chroniques de Port-Royal: Antoine Arnauld (1612–1694). Philosophe, écrivain, théologien*, 44 (1995), p. 261. English translation in *Descartes and His Contemporaries*, edited by Roger Ariew and Marjorie Grene (Chicago: The University of Chicago Press, 1995), p. 112.

24 Etienne Gilson, *God and Philosophy* (New Haven: Yale University Press, 1941), p. 60.

Descartes accomplished: he created the first philosophy for the Augustinians. In categories and terms created by St. Augustine, Descartes provided a philosophy that not only satisfied the requirements of natural reason, but also responded to the requirements of Christian religion by establishing the existence of God and the immortality of the soul. Numerous passages in the *Meditations* must have sounded to the Augustinians as though the Saint himself were speaking through them.

* * *

It is not my goal in this work to recreate the conditions in which Descartes's philosophy was received among the 17th-century Augustinians. This has been done by many scholars.[25] Nor is it a study of the conceptual resemblances between Descartes's metaphysics and Augustine's theology. I am mainly interested in the question of how much the writings of St. Augustine contributed to the formation of Descartes's metaphysics. In short, did Descartes know the writings of St. Augustine, or was he merely influenced by the Augustinian tradition?[26]

25 Geneviève Rodis-Lewis "Augustinisme et cartésianisme," in *L'anthropologie cartésienne* (Paris: PUF, 1990); "Descartes – Cartésiens et anticartésiens Français," in *Histoire de la philosophie*, ed. by D'Yvon Beval (Paris: *Encyclopédie de la Pléiade*, 1973); Stephen Nadler, "Cartesianism and Port-Royal," in *Essays on Modern Philosophers From Descartes and Hobbes to Newton and Leibniz*, ed. by Vere Chappell (New York: Garland Publishing, Inc., 1992); Vincent Carraud, "Arnauld: De l'occamisme au cartésianisme," in *Chroniques de Port-Royal: Antoine Arnauld (1612–1694). Philosophe, écrivain, théologien* 44 (1995); Etienne Gilson, *The Unity of Philosophical Experience* (New York: Charles Scribner's Sons, 1937), pp. 125–98; François Girbal, *Bernard Lamy (1640–1715), Étude biographique et bibliographique* (Paris: PUF, 1964), et *L'affaire du P. André Martin à Saumur 1669–1675*; François Ferrier, *Un Augustinien de l'Oratoire* (Paris: Vrin, 1987); Louis Lescoeur, *La théodicé chrétienne d'après les Pères de l'église ou essai philosophique sur le Traité de Deo du P. [Louis] Thomassin, de l'Oratoire* (Paris: Charles Douniol, 1852). L. de Lens, *La philosophie en Anjou* (1873); J. Dumont, *L'Oratoire et le cartésianisme en Anjou*. Richard A. Watson, "Descartes and Cartesianism," in *Encyclopeadia Britannica*, vol. 15 (1989), and *The Breakdown of Cartesian Metaphysics* (Cambridge, Mass.: Hackett, 1998); Léon Blanchet, *Les antécédents historiques du "Je pense, donc je suis,"* (Paris: Alcan, 1920). See also number 135 (April/June 1982) of the *XVIIe siècle* devoted to St. Augustin, and *Chroniques de Port-Royal: Antoine Arnauld (1612–1694). Philosophe, écrivain, théologien* 44 (1995).

26 Etienne Gilson, *René Descartes. Discours de la méthode. Texte et commentaire* (Paris: Vrin, 1987), pp. 297–98.

27 Etienne Gilson, *La liberté chez Descartes et la théologie* (Paris: Felix Alcan, 1913). For criticism of Gilson's methodology, see Jean-Luc Marion, *Sur la théologie blanche de Descartes* (Paris: PUF, 1981), pp. 140–60. Alfred Espinas, *Descartes et la morale* (Paris: Éditions Bossard, 1925), vol. I, pp. 184–211; "Pour l'histoire du Cartésianisme," in

To some extent this work is a continuation of the pioneer work of Etienne Gilson, Alfred Espinas, and Jean Laporte,[27] who were the first Descartes scholars to raise the question of the relationship between Descartes's metaphysics and St. Augustine's theology. As time passed, the thesis of Augustinian "connections" in Descartes's philosophy was more or less abandoned for good.[28] Despite the occasional appearance of books and articles on St. Augustine and Descartes, more often than not studies of the famous *cogito*, not much has changed in Cartesian studies since Gilson. In fact, Gilson himself considered this problem insoluble and almost closed. "[W]e are never going to know to what degree Descartes could have been influenced, directly or indirectly, by St. Augustine or the Augustinian tradition."[29] "Whether Descartes was under the direct or indirect influence of St. Augustine's thought is a purely historical problem, to which a fully rigorous solution at the present stage of historical research is perhaps not possible."[30] Despite numerous attempts, the situation did not change for another fifty years. In 1978, in his *Cartésianisme et Augustinisme*, Henri Gouhier wrote: "Today our search for the link between Descartes and St. Augustine touches upon the issue of their mutual relationship. The main question naturally concerns the nature of this relationship, the main question being of possible borrowings."[31] Although the study of the connection between the two thinkers continued, our present knowledge of the real influence of St. Augustine's theology on the formation of Descartes's metaphysics remains almost at the point where Gilson began his search in 1913.[32]

One of the obstacles to determining Descartes's relationship with his predecessors is the lack of references to past or contemporary thinkers in his works. If their names come up in Descartes's writings, it is usually in a

Revue de Métaphysique et de Morale (1906); "L'idée initiale de la philosophie de Descartes," in *Revue de Métaphysique et de Morale* (1917). Jean Laporte, *Le rationalisme de Descartes* (Paris: PUF, 1950).

28 An instructive account of the place of Gilson's thesis in the development of Cartesian studies, and the Augustinian elements in it, can be found in Jean-Luc Marion's "L'instauration de la rapture: Gilson à la lecture de Descartes," in *Etienne Gilson et Nous: La philosophie et son histoire* (Paris: Vrin, 1979), pp. 13–34.

29 *René Descartes. Discours de la Méthode. Texte et commentaire* (Paris: Vrin, 1987), p. 298.

30 Etienne Gilson, "L'avenir de la métaphysique Augustinienne," *Revue de philosophie* (1930), p. 639.

31 Henri Gouhier, *Cartésianisme et Augustinisme au XVIIe siècle* (Paris: Vrin, 1978), p. 8.

32 In a recent work on the subject, *Descartes and Augustine* (Cambridge: Cambridge University Press, 1998, p. X), Stephen Menn completely ignores the question of the actual relationship between the two authors: "My judgment is that he [Descartes] simply read Augustine."

polemical context, or in correspondence, and often is accompanied by Descartes's remarking that the thinker under scrutiny is hardly worth reading. Secondly, Descartes created an image of himself as someone who did not like reading. On many occasions he claimed ignorance of the writings of others and displayed very little interest in what they had to say. If one contrasts Descartes with some of his contemporaries, such as Arnauld, Gassendi, or Hobbes, the last thing one could say is that Descartes possessed extensive knowledge of past philosophies. And if we contrast his writings with those of Suarez or Leibniz, who freely move among and quote from the ancients, the mediaevals, and their own contemporaries, Descartes indeed appears to be someone who stopped reading when he left La Flèche. This may in fact have been the case. But whatever the bulk of his reading in college, it must, beyond the slightest doubt, have been considerably greater than the references in his works imply. His claim that one can build a philosophy from the contents of one's mind by emptying it of all the opinions that one has acquired in one's lifetime persuaded Cartesian scholars that past philosophies are of no avail in explaining the origins of Descartes's metaphysics.

There is a further difficulty in establishing Descartes's acquaintance with St. Augustine: having identified those Augustinian themes which play a key role in Descartes's system (the *cogito* and the argument for the distinction between the mind and body), how can we tell for certain whether he really took them from St. Augustine's writings? Could it not be simply a coincidence? Philosophers sometimes arrive at similar intuitions and use the same examples without necessarily reading each other. One could argue that the *cogito* and the resulting distinction between the mind and the body constitute the only possible response to skepticism. Both St. Augustine and Descartes lived in times of all-pervasive skepticism and could have independently come up with similar solutions. With this observation one might consider the matter of possible borrowings as closed – were it not for the fact that the relationship between St. Augustine's theology and Descartes's metaphysics goes beyond the *cogito* and the distinction between the mind and body. No philosopher works in a vacuum of concepts and categories. Descartes said: *nemo ante me* ("no one before me"), but whatever he meant by this, he was preceded by twenty centuries of philosophical labor which, as Laberthonnière never tired of repeating, even his famous method of doubt could not fully annihilate. The building blocks of his philosophical edifice are not raw stones but bricks which have been worked upon, although some of them have been broken off from previous philosophical edifices. "Descartes's situation," Laberthonnière remarks, "is reminiscent of that of a man who finds himself in a place covered with ruins. But these ruins are like

ready-made stones at his disposal. He makes use of them. . . . The material is borrowed, but it is transformed, and yet it preserves its original look."[33] We can safely dismiss Descartes's own myth of his philosophy as an absolute beginning and see it merely as a rupture, however great, with the past.[34]

Another difficulty is that Descartes (1596–1650) came twelve centuries after St. Augustine (354–430), and several centuries after much meticulous philosophical labor by the Scholastic thinkers who transformed spoken Latin into a technical philosophical language. What is more, St. Augustine was not a philosopher in the technical sense of the word. His language is sometimes vague and lacks the precision characteristic of the Mediævals and of Descartes himself. What in St. Augustine sometimes occupies several or a dozen pages, in Descartes takes up no more than a paragraph, or a few lines; and vice versa: what in St. Augustine occupies no more than a page, a paragraph, or a sentence, assumes in Descartes the form of an elaborate argument.

* * *

In compiling this *Index* I have included only those passages from the writings of St. Augustine about which I could affirm with certainty or a high degree of probability that Descartes knew them. I have not included merely *conceptual* resemblances. For example, two of St. Augustine's works, *The Immortality of the Soul* and *The Magnitude of the Soul*, are devoted to the *nature* of the soul. Several passages from these works strongly *resemble* Descartes's considerations in the *Meditations*. In my commentary I argue that Descartes knew those works; however, when I could not find *exact* counterparts in the *Meditations*, I did not include these passages in the *Index*. I have included some of them in the section "Additions." On the other hand, if there is external evidence (which I present in my commentary) that a given passage from St. Augustine served Descartes as a source of *inspiration*, I have included it in the *Index*.

As far as I could, I have tried to let the passages from St. Augustine and

33 Labarthonnière, *Études sur Descartes*, in *Œuvres de Labarthonnière*, vol. II (Paris: Vrin, 1935), pp. 352–53.

36 For Descartes's debt to Mediæval thought see E. Gilson, *Études sur le rôle de la pensée médiévale dans la formation du système cartésien* (Paris: Vrin, 1984); *The Spirit of Modern Philosophy* (Notre Dame, Ind.: Notre Dame University Press, 1991); *La liberté chez Descartes et la théologie* (Paris: Félix Alcan, 1913); "La doctrine cartésienne de la liberté et la theologie," in *Bulletin de la Société Française de Philosophie* (19 March 1914); Henri Gouhier, *La pensée religieuse de Descartes* (Paris: Vrin, 1924). Vincent Mamus, *Saint Thomas D'Aquin et la philosophie cartesiénne: Êtudes de doctrines comparées*, 2 vols. (Paris: Librarie Victor Lecoffre, 1890).

Descartes speak for themselves. Sometimes, however, I offer my own interpretation of Descartes's metaphysics to support a certain thesis – for example, the thesis that Descartes read *The City of God* before 1640, even though all references to this work come after the publication of the *Meditations* in 1641. In all cases where my interpretation of Cartesian metaphysics significantly differs from that of other scholars, I include references to their works.

The *Index* is certainly not exhaustive, and there are surely passages in St. Augustine's writings that I have overlooked. The creation of an index that would be absolutely complete would require not only a perfect knowledge of Descartes's and St. Augustine's writings but an ability to access Descartes's mind and see *which* passages inspired him and *why*.

At the end of my commentary I present a chart of St. Augustine's works and offer tentative dates on which Descartes may have read them. This chart derives from the analysis of the development of Cartesian metaphysics that I present in the commentary.

I have divided the *Index* into two parts. The first contains borrowings and the second passages which it is almost certain that Descartes read but where there is no compelling evidence for this. The first part includes passages that are literal or almost literal quotations from St. Augustine. Possible borrowings are included in the section "Additions" that follow each section of the *Index*.

Because most of the borrowings from St. Augustine's writings are in the *Meditations*, the *Index* follows the numerical order of the *Meditations* (Meditation I, II, etc.) with successive page numbers referring to the Adam & Tannery edition. The reader will also find there the doctrine of the eternal truths (also called the doctrine of divine freedom) that Descartes formulated in his three famous letters of 1630 to Marin Mersenne. This inclusion is justified for two reasons. First, the doctrine occupies a central role in Cartesian metaphysics; second, the doctrine of human freedom in the Fourth Meditation is the logical consequence of the doctrine of divine freedom. There is reason to believe that the doctrine of the eternal truths formed part of the so-called "little treatise." I argue in my commentary that this was not, as it is usually assumed, an early work that Descartes never finished, but in all likelihood a draft of the *Meditations*. For reasons best known to himself Descartes did not include this doctrine in the *Meditations*, but, as I argue, there are traces of it in the *Meditations*, indicating, in my opinion, that originally the doctrine of the eternal truths was either a separate Meditation that preceded what is now known as the Fourth Meditation or was part of the Fourth Meditation.

The present arrangement of the *Index* has the advantage over, for example, a thematic one, in that it allows one to measure the extent to which Descartes remained under the influence of St. Augustine in writing his *Meditations*. I do, however, make some exceptions in this classification. For example, I include several passages from *The Principles of Philosophy* (1644) or from Descartes's letters in cases where I think a given passage from those writings is either more fully developed there than in the *Meditations* or supplements an argument presented in the *Meditations*.

First Part

Letter to the Sorbonne

SAINT AUGUSTINE

I A

1) Cujus [philosophiae] duplex quaestio est: una de anima, altera de Deo. Prima efficit ut nosmetipsos noverimus, altera, ut originem nostram. Illa nobis dulcior, ista charior, illa nos dignos beata vita, beatos haec facit; prima est illa discentibus, ista jam doctis.

***De Ordine*, II, xviii, 47.**

RENÉ DESCARTES

I D

1) Semper existimavi duas quaestiones, de Deo & de Anima, praecipuas esse ex iis quae Philosophiae potius quam Teologiae ope sunt demonstrandae . . .

***Meditationes, Epistola.* AT VII, 1.**

2) . . . nec ullam habere posse certam scientiam, priusquam suæ authorem originis agnoverit.

***Principiorum Philosopiæ*, I, 13. AT VIII, 10.**

SAINT AUGUSTINE

I A

1) To philosophy pertains a twofold question: the first treats of the soul; the second, of God. The first makes us know ourselves; the second, our origin. The former is the more delightful to us; the latter, more precious. The former makes us fit for happy life; the latter renders us happy. The first is for beginners; the latter, for the well instructed.

***On Order*, II, xviii, 47, p. 324.**

RENÉ DESCARTES

I D

1) I have always thought that two topics – namely God and the soul – are prime examples of subjects where demonstrative proofs ought to be given with the aid of philosophy rather than theology.

***Letter to the Sorbonne*. CSM, II, 3.**

2) [T]he possession of certain knowledge will not be possible until it [the mind] has come to know the author of its being.

***Principles of Philosophy*, I, 13. CSM II, 197.**

Sources for the Letter to the Sorbonne:

1. *On Order*, II, xviii, 47.

Second Part

First Meditation

SAINT AUGUSTINE

II A

1) [N]ec in eis visis hoc habetur, quae objiciuntur extrinsecus, ut in eo sic fallatur oculus, quemadmodum fallitur cum in aqua remus videtur infractus, et navigantibus turres moveri, et alia sexcenta quae aliter sunt quam videntur; quia nec per oculum carnis hoc cernitur.

***De Trinitate*, XV, xii, 21.**

III A

1) Nec illud potest Academicus adversus istam scientiam dicere. Furis fortassis et nescis; quia sanorum visis simillima sunt etiam visa surentium: sed qui furit vivit.

***De Trinitate*, XV, xii, 21.**

RENÉ DESCARTES

II D

1) Sed forte, quamvis interdum sensus circa minutia quaedam & remotiora nos fallant, pleraque tamen alia sunt de quibus dubitari plane non potest, quamvis ab iisdem hauriantur.

Med. I. AT VII, 18.

III D

1) Manus vero has ipsas, totumque hoc corpus meum esse, qua ratione posset negari? nisi me forte comparem nescio quibus insanis, quorum cerebella tam contumax vapor ex atra bile labefactat, ut constanter affeverent vel se esse reges, cum sunt pauperrimi, vel purpura indutos, cum sunt nudi, vel caput habere fictile, vel se totos esse cucurbitas, vel ex vitro conflatos; sed amentes sunt isti, nec minus ipse demens videre, si quod ab iis exemplum ad me transferrem.

Med. I. AT VII, 18–19.

SAINT AUGUSTINE

II A

1) And this again is not reckoned among those objects of sight that are presented from without, so that the eye may be deceived in it; in such way as it is when an oar in the water looks bent, and towers seem to move as you sail past them, and a thousand other things that are otherwise than they seem to be: for this is not a thing that is discerned by the eye of the flesh.

***On The Trinity*, XV, xii, 21. Vol. III, p. 211.**

III A

1) Nor can the Academic again say, in confutation of this knowledge: Perhaps you are mad, and do not know it: for what madmen see is precisely like what they also see who are sane; but he who is mad is alive.

***On The Trinity*, XV, xii, 21. Vol. III, p. 211. Cf. *Answer to Skeptics*, III, xi, 25, p. 196.**

RENÉ DESCARTES

II D

1) Yet although the senses occasionally deceive us with respect to objects which are very small or in the distance, there are many other beliefs about which doubt is quite impossible, even though they are derived from the senses.

Med. I. CSM II, 12–13.

III D

1) Again, how could it be denied that these hands or this whole body are mine? Unless perhaps I were to liken myself to madmen, whose brains are so damaged by the persistent vapors of melancholia that they firmly maintain they are kings when they are paupers, or say they are dressed in purple when they are naked, or that their heads are made of earthenware, or that they are pumpkins, or made of glass. But such people are insane, and I would be thought equally mad if I took anything from them as a model for myself.

Med. I. CSM II, 13.

IV A

1) Credo enim jam satis liquere quae per somnium et dementiam falsa videantur, ea scilicet quae ad corporis sensus pertinent: nam ter terna novem esse, et quadratum intelligibilium numerorum, necesse est vel genere humano stertente sit verum.

Contra Academicos, **III, xi, 25.**

2) Et semper eodem modo est, Duo et quauor, sex. Item semper eodem modo est quod est, quod quatuor habent duo et duo; hoc auem non habent duo: duo igitur quatuor sunt. Est autem ista ratio immutabilis: igitur ratio.

De immortalitate animae, **I, ii, 2.**

3) septem autem et tria decem sunt; et non solum nunc, sed etiam semper; neque ullo modo aliquando septem et tria non fuerunt decem, aut aliquando septem et tria non erunt decem.

De libero arbitrio, **II, viii, 21.**

IV D

1) Nam sive vigilem, sive dormiam, duo & trias simul juncta sunt quinque, quadratumque non plura habet latera quam quatuor.

Med. I. AT VII, 20.

V A

1) A. –Ubi rogavi, utrum omne quod non latet sciatur: tu enim huic rogationi temere assensus es.
E.–Nam quid velles dicerem?
A.–Non continuo esse scientiam, si quid non latet: sed si per rationem non latet: cum autem per corpus non latet, sensum vocari, si per se ipsam

V D

1) Quae duo ita distinguo, ut persvasio sit, cum superest aliqua ratio quae nos possit ad dubitandum impellere; scientia vero sit persuasio a ratione tam forti, ut nulla unquam fortiore concuti possit.

A Regius, 24 mai 1640. AT III, 65.

IV A

1) I regard it as sufficiently plain that the things which are seen awry through sleep or derangement are things that pertain to the bodily senses, for, even if the whole human race were fast asleep, it would still be necessarily true that three times three are nine, and that this is the square of intelligible numbers.

Answer to Skeptics, **III, xi, 25, p. 197.**

2) It is always true that two and four make six. In the same way, it is always true that four is the sum of two and two. This relationship is immutable and such reasoning is not subject to change; therefore this relationship is rational.

The Immortality of the Soul, **I, ii, 2, p. 18.**

3) Seven and three are ten, not only now, but forever. And there has never been, nor will there be a time when seven and three were not ten.

On Free Will, **II, viii, 21, p. 130.**

IV D

1) For whether I am awake or asleep, two and three added together are five, and a square has no more than four sides.

Med. I. CSM II, 14.

V A

1) A.– When I asked you whether everything that one is aware of is known, you answered in the affirmative, without thinking.
E.– What, then, would you have me say?
A.– That knowledge is not had simply if one is aware of something, but

VD

1) [T]here is conviction when there remains some reason which might lead us to doubt, but knowledge is conviction based on a reason so strong that it can never be shaken by any stronger reason.

To Regius, 24 May 1640. Cf. Med. I. AT VII, 21 (l. 16–25).

non lateat corporis passio. An ignoras quibusdam philosophis et peracutis visum esse, ne id ipsum quidem quod mente comprehenditur, ad nomen adspirare scientiae, nisi tam firma comprehensio sit, ut ab ea mens nulla ratione queat dimoveri?

***De quantitate animae*, XXX, 58.**

2) Quod autem Atheus possit clare cognoscere trianguli tres angulos aequales esse duobus rectis, non nego; sed tantum istam ejus cognitionem non esse veram scientiam affirmo, quia nulla cognitio, quae dubia reddi potest, videtur scientia appelanda; cumque ille supponatur esse atheus, non potest esse certus se non decipi in iis ipsis quae illi evidentissima videntur, ut fatis ostentum est; & quamvis forte dubium istud ipsi non occurat, potest tamen occurrere, si examinet, vel ab alio proponatur; nec unquam ab eo erit tutus, nisi prius Deum agnoscat.

***Secundae Responsiones.* AT VII, 141.**

VI A

1) Illud tamen dubium esse non debet corporales imagines, quae spiritu cernuntur, non semper signa esse aliarum rerum sive in vigilantibus sive in dormientibus sive in aegrotantibus; mirum est autem, si aliquando extasis fieri potest, ut non illae corporalium rerum simultidines aliquid significent.

Cum autem spiritus bonus in haec visa humanum spiritum adsumit aut rapit, nullo modo illas imagines signa rerum aliarum esse dubitandum est, et earum, quas nosse utile est; Dei enim munus est. Discretio

VI D

1) Unde autem scio illum non fecisse ut nulla plane sit terra, nullum coelum, nulla res extensa, nulla figura, nulla magnitudo, nullus locus, & tamen haec omnia non aliter quam nunc mihi videantur existere? Imo etiam, quemadmodum judicio interdum alios errare circa ea quae se perfectissime scire arbitrantur, ita ego ut fallar quoties duo & tria simul addo, vel numero quadrati latera. . . . At forte noluit Deus ita me decipi, dicitur enim summe bonus. . . . Supponam igitur non optimum Deum, fontem veritatis, sed genium

only if that awareness results from exercise of reason. For, if that awareness comes through the body, that is sensation; if the awareness is direct, that is said to be an experience of the body. Do you not know that some philosophers, and very good thinkers, too, thought that not even what is grasped by the mind is worthy of the name of knowledge, unless that comprehension is so firm that the mind cannot be moved from it by any argument?

***The Magnitude of the Soul*, XXX, 58, p. 125.**

2) The fact that an atheist can be "clearly aware that the three angles of a triangle are equal to two right angles" is something I do not dispute. But I maintain that this awareness of his is not true knowledge, since no act of awareness that can be rendered doubtful seems fit to be called knowledge. Now since we are supposing that this individual is an atheist, he cannot be certain that he is not being deceived on matters which seem to him to be very evident (as I fully explained). And although this doubt may not occur to him, it can still crop up if someone else raises the point or if he looks into the matter himself. So he will never be free of this doubt until he acknowledges that God exists.

***Second Set of Responses*. CSM II, 101.**

VI A

1) But of one thing there should be no doubt: corporeal images seen in the spirit are not always signs of other things, whether they are seen in waking hours, in sleep, or in sickness; but it would be a strange thing if an ecstasy could ever take place without the likeness of bodily things in having a meaning. . . . But when a good spirit seizes or ravishes the spirit of a man to direct it to an extraordinary vision, there can be no doubt that the images are signs of other things which it is useful to know, for this is a gift of God. The

VI D

1) How do I know that he [God] has not brought it about that there is no earth, no sky, no extended thing, no shape, no size, no place, while at the same time ensuring that all these things appear to me to exist just as they do now? What is more, since I sometimes believe that others go astray in cases where they think they have the most perfect knowledge, may I not similarly go wrong every time I add two and three or count the sides of a square, or in some even simpler matter, if this is imaginable? But perhaps God would not have

sane difficilima est, cum spiritus malignus quasi tranquillius agit ac sine de calme aliqua vexatione corporis adsumto humano spiritu dicit quod potest. . . . Quapropter et cum visis corporalibus diabolus fallit, nihil obest, quod ludificantur oculi, si non erratur in veritate fidei et intellegentiae sanitate, quae docet Deus subditos sibi.

***De Genesi ad litteram*, XII, xiii, 27–28–xiv, 30.**

aliquem malignum, eudemque summe potentem & callidum, omnem suam industriam in eo posuisse, ut me falleret.

Med. I. AT VII, 21–22.

Additions

VII A

1) Unde etiam phantasias rerum corporalium per corpis sensum haustas, et quodam modo infusas memoriae, ex quibus etiam ea quae non visa sunt, ficto phantasmate cogitantur, sive aliter quam sunt, sive fortuitu sicuti sunt, aliis omnino regulis supra mentem nostram incommutabiliter manentibus, vel approbare apud nosmetipsos, vel improbare convincimur, cum recte aliquid approbamus aut improbamus.

***De Trinitate*, IX, vi, 10.**

VII D

1) Tamen profecto est visa per quietem esse veluit quasdam pictas imagines, quae non nisi ad similitudinem rerum verarum fingi potuerunt; ideoque saltem generalia heac, oculos, manus, totumque corpus, res quasdam non imaginarias, sed veras existere. Nam sane pictores ipsi, ne tum quidem, cum Sirenas & Satyricos maxime inusitatis formis fingere student, naturas omni ex parte novas iis possunt assignare, sed tantummodo diversorum animalium membra permiscent.

Med. I. AT VII, 19–20.

discernment of these experiences is certainly a most difficult task when the evil spirit acts in a seemingly peaceful manner. . . . So also when the Devil deceives us with corporeal visions, no harm is done by the fact that he has played tricks with our eyes, so long as we not deviate from the true faith or lose the integrity of intelligence, by which God instructs those who are obedient to Him.

The Literal Meaning of Genesis, **XII, xiii, 27–28–xiv, 30. Vol. II, pp. 196, 198.**

allowed me to be deceived in this way, since He is said to be supremely good. . . . I will suppose therefore that not God, who is supremely good and the source of truth, but rather some malicious demon of the utmost power and cunning has employed all his energies in order to deceive me.

Med. I. CSM II, 14–15.

Additions

VII A

1) Whence also, even in the case of the images of things corporeal which are drawn in through the bodily sense, and in some way infused into the memory, from which also those things which have not been seen are thought under a fancied image, whether otherwise than they really are, or even perchance as they are; – even here too, we are proved either to accept or reject, within ourselves, by other rules which remain altogether unchangeable above our mind, when we approve or reject anything rightly.

***On the Trinity*, IX, vi, 10. Vol. III, p. 129. 16.**

VII D

1) Nonetheless, it must surely be admitted that the visions which come in sleep are like paintings, which must have been fashioned in the likeness of things that are real, and hence that at least these general kinds of things – eyes, head, hands and the body as a whole – are things which are not imaginary but are real and exist. For even painters try to create sirens and satyrs with the most extraordinary bodies, they cannot give them natures which are new in all respects; they simply jumble up the limbs of different animals.

Med. I. CSM II, 13.

VIII A

1) Quasivero quoniam somno membra nostra marcescunt, idcirco animus fiat ulla ex parte debilior . . . et si quid intelligit, aeque dormienti ac vigilanti verum est. Nam, verbi gratia, si per somnium disputare sibi visus fuerit, verasque rationes secutus in disputando didicerit aliquid, etiam expergefacto eaedem incummutabiles manent . . .

De immortalitate animae, **XIV, 23.**

VIII D

1) Ce qu'il y a de singulier à remarquer, c'est que, doutant si ce qu'il venoit de voir étoit songe ou vision, non seulement il décida, en dormant, que c'étoit un songe, mais il en fit encore l'interprétation avant quc le sommeil le quittât.

Olympica, **AT X, 184.**

VIII A

1) Sleep somehow deprives the senses of feeling and in some way closes them off, so that the soul gladly yields to such change of the body . . . and, if the mind conceives something, it is equally true for it whether it sleeps or is awake. If, for example, someone during a dream has appeared to himself to be engaged in a discussion and, pursuing true principles, has learned something in this discussion, then these true principles also remain the same and unchangeable after his awakening.

***The Immortality of the Soul*, XIV, 23, pp. 42–43.**

VIII D

1) The curious point about this was that, being in doubt as to whether what he had just seen was a dream or a vision, not only did he decide while still asleep that it was a dream, but he even decided on the interpretation before waking up.

***Olympica* ("Descartes' Dream"), November 1619. Translated by John Cottingham, *Descartes* (Oxford: Basil Blackwell, 1986), p. 163.**

Sources for the Fourth Meditation:

1. *On the Trinity*, XV, xii, 21.
2. *On the Trinity*, XV, xii, 21.
3. *Against Skeptics*, II, xi, 25.
4. *The Immortality of the Soul*, I, ii, 2.
5. *On Free Will*, II, viii, 21.
6. *The Magnitude of the Soul*, XXX, 58.
7. *The Literal Meaning of Genesis*, XII, xiii, 27–28–xiv, 30.
8. *On the Trinity*, IX, vi, 10.
9. *The Immortality of the Soul*, XIV, 23.

Third Part

Second Meditation

SAINT AUGUSTINE

1X A

1) Nulla in his veris Academicorum argumenta formido dicentium: Quid si falleris? Si enim fallor, sum. Nam qui non est, utique nec falli potest; ac per hoc sum, si fallor. Quia ergo sum si fallor, quo modo esse me fallor, quando certum est me esse, si fallor? Quia igitur essem qui fallerer, etiamsi fallerer, procul dubio in eo, quod me novi esse, non fallor. Consequens est autem, ut etiam in eo, quod me novi esse, non fallar. Sicut enim novi esse me, ita novi etiam hoc ipsum, nosse me.

***De Civitate Dei*, XI, 26.**

2) Accademica philosophia sic invaluit, ut de omnibus dubitans multo miserius insaniret: his ergo exceptis quae a corporis sensibus in animum veniunt, quantum rerum remanet quod ita sciamus, sicut nos vivere scimus? in quo prorsus non metuimus, ne aliqua verisimilitudine forte fallamur, quoniam certum est etiam eum qui fallitur vivere; nec in eis visis hoc habetur, quae objiciuntur extrinsecus, ut in eo sic fallatur oculus, quemadmodum fallitur

ENÉ DESCARTES

IX D

1) Sed est deceptor nescio quis, summe potens, summe callidus, qui de industria me semper fallit. Haud dubie igitur ego etiam sum, si me fallit; & fallat quantum potest, nunquam tamen efficiet, ut nihil sim quamdiu me aliquid esse cogitabo. Adeo ut, omnibus satis superque pensitatis, denique statuendum sit hoc pronuntiatum, *Ego sum, ego existo*, quoties a me profertur, vel mente concipitur, necessario esse verum.

Med. II. AT VII, 25.

SAINT AUGUSTINE

IX A

1) In respect of these truths, I am not at all afraid of the arguments of the Academicians, who say, What if you are deceived? For if I am deceived, I am. For he who is not cannot be deceived; and if I am deceived, by this same token I am. If I am deceived, how am I deceived in believing that I am? for it is certain that I am if I am deceived. Since, therefore, I, the person deceived, should be, even if I were deceived, certainly I am not deceived in this knowledge that I am. And, consequently, neither am I deceived in knowing that I know. For, as I know that I am, so I know this also, that I know.

***The City of God*, XI, 26. Vol. II, p. 220.**

2) [T]he academic philosophy has so prevailed as to be still more wretchedly insane by doubting all things; – passing by, then, those things that come into the mind by the bodily senses, how large a proportion is left of things which we know in such manner as we know that we live? In regard to this, indeed, we are absolutely without any fear lest perchance we are being deceived by some resemblance of the truth; since it is certain, that he

RENÉ DESCARTES

IX D

1) But there is a deceiver of supreme power and cunning who is deliberately and constantly deceiving me; and let him deceive me as much as he can, he will never bring it about that I am nothing so long as I think that I am something. So after considering everything very thoroughly, I must finally conclude that this proposition, I am, I exist, is necessarily true whenever it is put forward by me or conceived in my mind.

Med. II. CSM II, 17.

cum in aqua remus videtur infractus, et navigantibus turres moveri, et alia sexcenta quae aliter sunt quam videntur; quia nec per oculum carnis hoc cernitur. Intiam scientia est qua nos vivere scimus, ubi ne illud quidem Academicus dicere potest: Fortasse dormis, et nescis, et in somnis vides. Visa quippe somniatium simillima esse visis vigilantium quis ignorat? Sed qui certus est de vitae suae scientia, non in ea dicit, Scio me vigilare; sed, Scio me vivere: sive ergo dormiat, sive vigilet, vivit.

***De Trinitate,* XV, xii, 21.**

X A

1) Quamobrem nec illud audiendum est, quod quidam putaverunt, quitum quoddam esse corpus unde sint animae, quod nec terra nec aqua sit nec aer nec ignis, sive iste turbulentior atque terrenus, sive ille caelestis

X D

1) Sed quid esset haec anima, vel non advertebam, vel exiguum nescio quid imaginabar, instar venti, vel ignis, vel aetheris,[1] quod crassioribus mei partibus esset infusum. De corpore vero ne dubitabam qui-

1 "*Anima* en bon latin signifie *aërum, sive oris halitium*; d'où ie croy qu'il a esté transferé *ad significandam Mentem*, & c'est pour cela que i'ay dit que *sœpe sumitur pro re corporea.*" AT, III, 362.

who is deceived, yet lives. And this again is not reckoned among those objects of sight that are presented from without, so that the eye may be deceived in it; in such a way as it is when an oar in the water looks bent, and towers seem to move as you sail past them, and a thousand other things that are otherwise than they seem to be; for this is not a thing that is discerned by the eye of the flesh. The knowledge by which we know that we live is the most inward of all knowledge, of which even the Academic cannot insinuate: Perhaps you are asleep, and do not know it, and you see things in your sleep. For who does not know that what people see in dreams is precisely like what they see when awake? But he who is certain of the knowledge of his own life, does not therein say, I know I am awake, but, I know I am alive; therefore, whether he be asleep or awake, he is alive.

***On the Trinity*, XV, xii, 21. Vol. III, p. 211.**

X A

1) Therefore, no attention should be paid to the opinion of those who said that the soul is from a fifth corporeal element, not earth or water or air or fire (whether earthly fire familiar to us, which is always in motion, or heavenly fire, which is pure and bright), but some other kind of being, without any established

X D

1) But as to the nature of this soul, either I did not think about this or else I imagined it to be something tenuous, like a wind or fire or ether, which permeated my more solid parts. As to the body, however, I had no doubts about it, but thought I knew its nature distinctly. If I had tried to describe the mental concep-

purus et lucidus, sed nescio quid aliud, quod careat usitato nomine, sed tamen corpus sit. Si enim qui hoc sentiunt hoc dicunt corpus, quod et nos, id est naturam quamlibet longitudine, latitudine, altitudine spatium loci occupantem, neque hoc est anima neque inde facta credenda est. Quidquid enim tale est, ut multa non dicam, in quacumque sui parte lineis dividi vel circumscribi potest: quod anima si pateretur, nullo modo nosse posset tales lineas, quae per longum secari non queunt, quales in corpore non posse inveniri nihilominus nouit.

De Genesi ad litteram, **VII, xxi, 27.**

dem, sed distincte me nosse arbitrabar ejus aturam, quam si forte, qualem mente concipiebam, describere tentassem, sic explicuissem: per corpus intelligo illud omne quod aptum est figura aliqua terminari, loco circumscribi, spatium sic replere, ut ex eo aliud omne corpus excludat; tactu, visu, auditu, gustu, vel odoratu percipi, necnon moveri pluribus modis, non quidem a seipso, sed ab alio quopiam a quo tangatur: namque habere vim seipsum movendi, item sentiendi, vel cogitandi, nullo pacto ad naturam corporis pertinere judicabam; quinimo mirabar potius tales facultates in quibusdam corporibus reperiri.

Med. II. AT VII, 26.

XI A

1) Quapropter non est quidem humanae animae natura nec de terra nec de aqua nec de aere nec de igne quodlibet; sed tamen crassioris corporis sui materiam, hoc est humidam quandam terram, quae in carnis versa est qualitatem, per subtiliorem naturam corporis administrat, id est per lucem et aerem. Nullus enim sine his duobus vel sensus in corpore est vel ab anima spontaneus corporis motus.

De Genesi ad litteram, **VII, xv, 21.**

XI D

1) Quid vero ex iis quae animae tribuebam? Nutriri vel incedere? Quandoquidem jam corpus non habeo, haec quoque nihil sunt nisi figmenta. Sentire? Nempe etiam hoc non sit sine corpore . . .

Med. II. AT VII, 27.

name, which is a body. If those who follow this opinion agree with us on the definition of a body, namely, any substance occupying space with its length, breadth, and height, the soul is not that and must not be thought to be made of that. For whatever is of that nature, to put the matter briefly, can be divided or circumscribed by lines in any of its parts. But if the soul were capable of this, it could not know of lines that cannot be found in the world of bodies.

***The Literal Meaning of Genesis*, VII, xxi, 27, vol. II, p. 21. Cf. letter 166.**

tion I had of it, I would have expressed it as follows: by a body I understand whatever has a determinable shape and a definable location and can occupy a space in such a way as to exclude any other body; it can be perceived by touch, sight, hearing, taste or smell, and can be moved in various ways, not by itself but by whatever else comes into contact with it. For, according to my judgment, the power of self-movement, like the power of sensation or of thought, was quite foreign to the nature of a body; indeed, it was a source of wonder to me that certain bodies were found to contain faculties of this kind.

Med. II. CSM II, 17–18.

XI A

1) Hence, the human soul is not made of earth or of water or of air or of fire; but it is through the more subtle elements, namely, light and air, that it governs its material and grosser body, that is, moist earth which has been made into flesh. For without the two subtle elements there is no sensation in the body or any spontaneous bodily movement under the direction of the soul.

***The Literal Meaning of Genesis*, VII, xv, 21, vol. II, p. 16.**

XI D

1) But what about the attributes I assigned to the soul? Nutrition or movement? Since now I do not have a body, these are mere fabrications. Sense-perception? This surely does not occur without a body . . .

Med. II. CSM, II, 18.

XII A

1) Auferamus enim ab hac consideratione ceatera quae multa sunt, quibus homo constat: atque ut haec quae nunc requirimus, quantum in his rebus possumus, liquido reperiamus, de sola menta tractemus. . . . Mens vero et spiritus non relative dicuntur, sed essentiam demonstrant. Non enim quia mens et spiritus alicujus hominis est, ideo mens et spiritus est. Retracto enim eo quod homo est, quod adjuncto corpore dicitur; retracto ergo corpore, mens et spiritus manet . . .

***De Trinitate*, IX, ii, 2.**

2) Jamvero cum ratiocinamur, animus id agit. Non enim id agit, nisi qui intelligit: nec corpus intelligit, nec animus, auxiliante corpore, intelligit; quia cum intelligere vult, a corpore avertitur.

***De Immortalitate animae*, I, i, 1.**

XII D

1) Nihil nunc admitto nisi quod necessario sit verum; sum igitur praecise tantum res cogitans, id est, mens, sive animus, sive intellectus, sive ratio, voces mihi prius significationis ignotae. Sum autem res vera, & vere existens . . .

Med. II. AT VII, 27.

XII A

1) For let us put aside from the inquiry all the other many things of a man consists; and in order that we may discover clearly what we are now seeking, as far as in such a subject is possible, let us treat of the mind (*mens*) alone. . . . But mind and spirit are not said relatively, but express essence. For mind and spirit do not exist because the mind and spirit of some particular man exists. For if we subtract the body from which is man, which is so called with the conjunction of body, the mind and spirit remain.

***On the Trinity*, IX, ii, 2. Vol. III, p. 126.**

2) When we reason, it is an act of our mind; for only that reason which understands can reason. Neither the body understands, nor the mind, aided by the body, understands, because, when the mind wishes to understand, it is turned away from the body.

***Immortality of the Soul*, I, i, 1, p. 16.**

XII D

1) At present I am not admitting anything except what is necessarily true. I am, then, in the strict sense only a thing that thinks; that is, I am a mind, or intelligence, or intellect, or reason – words whose meaning I have been ignorant of until now. But for all that I am a thing which is real and which truly exists.

Med. II. CSM II, 18.

XIII A

1) Non itaque velut absentem se quaerat cernere, sed praesentem se curet discernere. Nec se quasi non norit cognoscat, sed ab eo quod alterum novit dignoscat.

***De Trinitate*, X, ix, 12.**

2) Quapropter non est quidem humanae animae natura nec de terra nec de aqua nec de aere nec de igne quodlibet . . .

***De Genesi ad litteram*, VII, xv, 21.**

3) Nam neque ex terra, neque ex aqua, neque ex aere, neque ex igni, neque ex his omnibus, neque ex aliquibus horum conjunctis constare animam puto.

***De quantitate animae*, I, 2.**

XIII D

1) Quid praeterea? Imaginabor: non sum compages illa membrorum, quae corpus humanum appellatur; non sum etiam tenuis aliquis aer istis membris infusus, non ventus, non ignis, non vapor, non halitus, non quidquid mihi fingo . . .

Med. II. AT VII, 27.

XIV A

1) Sed quoniam de natura mentis agitur, removeamus a consideratione nostra omnes notitias quea capiuntur extrinsecus per sensus corporis; et ea quae posuimus, omnes mentes de se ipsis nosse certasque esse, diligentius attendamus.

***De Trinitate*, X, x, 14.**

XIV D

1) Itaque cognosco nihil eorum quae possum imaginationis ope comprehendere, ad hanc quam de me habeo notitiam pertinere, mentemque ab illis diligentissime esse avocandam, ut suam ipsa naturam quam distinctissime percipiat.

Med. II. AT VII, 28.

XIII A

1) Let it [soul] not therefore seek to discern itself as though absent, but take pains to discern itself as present. Nor let it take knowledge of itself as if it did not know itself, but let it distinguish itself from that which it knows to be another.

***On the Trinity*, X, ix, 12. Vol. III, 140.**

2) Hence, the human soul is not made of earth or of water or of air or of fire . . .

***The Literal Meaning of Genesis*, VII, xv, 21. vol. II, p. 16**

3) I do not think that the soul is composed either of earth or water or air or fire, or of all these together, or of any combination of them.

***The Magnitude of the Soul*, I, 2, p. 60.**

XIII D

1) What else am I? I will use my imagination. I am not that structure of limbs which is called a human body. I am not even some thin vapor which permeates the limbs – a wind, fire, air, breath, or whatever I depict in my imagination . . .

Med. II. CSM, II, 18.

XIV A

1) But since we treat of the nature of the mind, let us remove from our consideration all knowledge which is received from without, through the senses of the body; and attend more carefully to the position which we have laid down, that all minds know and are certain concerning themselves.

***On the Trinity*, X, x, 14. Vol. III, p. 141.**

XIV D

1) I thus realize that none of the things that the imagination enables me to grasp is at all relevant to this knowledge of myself which I possess, and that the mind must therefore be most carefully diverted from such things if it is to perceive its own nature as distinctly as possible.

Med. II. CSM II, 19.

XV A

1) Vivere se tamen et meminisse, et intelligere, et velle, et cogitare, et scire, et judicare quis dubitet? Quandoquidem etiam si dubitat, vivit: si dubitat unde dubitet, meminit; si dubitat, dubitere se intelligit; si dubitat, certus esse vult; si dubitat, cogitat; si dubitat, scit se nescire; si dubitat, judicat non se temere consentire oportere.

De Trinitate, **X, x, 14.**

XV D

1) Sed quid igitur sum? Res cogitans. Quid est hoc? Nempe dubitans, intelligens, affirmans, negans, volens, nolens, imaginans quoque, & sentiens.

Med. II. AT VII, 28.

XVI A

1) Nam si ex albo cera nigrum colorem ducat alicunde, non minus cera est, et si ex quadrata rotundam formam sumat, et ex molli durescat, frigescatque ex calida: at ista in subjecto sunt, et cera subjectum. Manet autem cera non magis minusve cera, cum illa mutentur. Potest igitur aliqua mutatio fieri eorum quae in subjecto sunt, cum ipsum tamen juxta id quod hoc est ac dicitur, nonmutetur.

At si eorum quae in subjecto sunt, tanta commutatio fieret, ut illud quod subesse dicebatur, dici jam omnino non posset; veluti cum calore ignis cera in auras discedit, eamque mutationem patitur, ut recte intelligatur mutatum esse subjectum, quod cera erat, et cera jam non est: nullo modo aliqua ratione quidquam eorum, quae in illo sub-

XVI D

1) Sumamus, exempli causa, hanc ceram . . . dura est, frigida est, facile tangitur, ac, si articulo ferias, emittet sonum; omnia deniquae illi adsunt quae requiri videntur, ut corpus aliquod possit quam distinctissime cognosci. Sed ecce, dum loquor, igni admovetur: saporis reliquiae purgantur, odor expirat, color mutatur, figura tollitur, crescit magnitudo, fit liquida, fit calida, vixtangi potest, nec jam, si pulses, emittet sonum. Remanetne adhuc eadem cera? Remanere fatendum est; nemo negat, nemo aliter putat. Quid erat igitur in ea quod tam distincte comprehendebatur? Certe nihil eorum quae sensibus attingebam; nam quaecunque sub gestum, vel odoratum, vel visum, vel tactum, vel auditum veniebant, mutata jam sunt:

XV A

1) Yet whoever doubts that he himself lives, and remembers, and understands, and wills, and thinks, and knows, and judges? Seeing that even if he doubts that he lives; if he doubts, he remembers why he doubts; if he doubts, he understands that he doubts; if he doubts, he wishes to be certain; if he doubts, he thinks; if he doubts, he knows that he does not know; if he doubts, he judges that he ought not to assent rashly.

***On the Trinity*, X, x, 14. Vol. 16, p. 149.**

XV D

1) But what then am I? A thing that thinks. What is that? A thing that doubts, understands, affirms, denies, is willing, is unwilling, and also imagines and has sensory perceptions.

Med. II. CSM II, 19.

XVI A

1) If, for example, wax somehow changes from a white to a black color, it remains, nonetheless, wax. It is also the same if it changes to a round form from a square, or from soft to hard, or from warm to cold. All these changes are within the subject, and wax, even though these qualities are changed. Therefore, a change of those qualities can occur in the subject, while the subject itself, in regard to its essence and its name, is not changed.

If, however, the change of those qualities in the subject be so great that that which was said to be subject can no longer be called so at all – as when, for instance, the wax through the heat of fire dissolves into the air and undergoes this change in such a manner that we

XVI D

1) Let us take, for example, this piece of wax . . . it is hard, cold and can be handled without difficulty; if you rap it with your knuckle it makes a sound. In short, it has everything which appears necessary to enable a body to be known as distinctly as possible. But even as I speak, I put the wax by the fire, and look: the residual taste is eliminated, the smell goes away, the color changes, the shape is lost, the size increases; it becomes liquid and hot; you can hardly touch it, and if you strike it, it no longer makes a sound. But does the same wax remain? Evidently none of these features which I arrived at by means of the senses; for whatever came under taste, smell, sight, touch or hearing has now altered – yet the wax remains.

jecto ideo erant quia hoc erat, remanere putaretur.

De Immortalitate animae, **V, 8.**

remanet cera. Fortasse illud erat quod nunc cogito: nempe ceram ipsam non quidem fuisse istam dulcedinem mellis, nec florum fragrantiam, nec istam albedinem, nec figuram, nec sonum, sed corpus quod mihi apparebat paulo ante modis istis conspicuum, nunc diversis. Quid est autem hoc praecise quod sic imaginor? Attendamus, & remotis iis quae ad ceram non pertinent, videamus quid supersit: nempe nihil aliud quam extensum quid, flexibile, mutabile. Quid vero est hoc flexibile, mutabile?

Med. II. AT VII, 30–31.

XVII A

1) Ergo incumbendum omnibus ratiocinandi viribus video, ut ratio quid sit, et quoties definiri possit sciatur, ut secundum omnes modos et de animae immortalitate constet. Ratio est adspectus animi, quo per seipsum, non per corpus verum intuetur; aut ipsa veri contemplatio, non per corpus; aut ipsum verum quod contemplatur. Primum illud in animo esse nemo ambigit: de secundo et tertio quaeri potest: sed et secundum sine animo esse non potest.

***De Immortalitate animae*, VI, 10.**

XVII D

1) Quaenam vero est haec cera, quae non nisi mente percipitur? Nempe eadem quam video, quam tango, quam imaginor, eadem denique quam ab initio esse arbitrabar. Atqui, quod notandum est, ejus percepcio non visio, non tactio, non imaginatio est, nec unquam fuit, quamvis prius ita videretur, sed solius *mentis inspectio*, quae vel imperfecta esse potest & confusa, ut prius erat, vel clara & distincta, ut nunc est, prout minus vel magis ad illa ex quibus constat attendo.

Med. II. AT VII, 31.

rightly conceive the subject to be changed, because it was wax, and is wax no longer – then in no way could anyone logically believe that there remains any of those qualities which were in that subject insofar as it was this subject.

***The Immortality of the Soul,* V. 8, pp. 25–26.**

Perhaps the answer lies in the thought which now comes to my mind; namely, the wax was not after all the sweetness of the honey, or the fragrance of the flowers, or the whiteness, or the shape, or the sound, but was rather a body which presented itself to me in these various forms a little while ago, but which now exhibits different ones. But what is meant here by "flexible" and "changeable"?

Med. II. CSM II, 20.

XVII A

1) Hence, I see that we have to devote all our reasoning power to the task of knowing what reason is, and in how many ways it may be defined, so that the immortality of the soul may be established according to all these ways. Reason is the vision of the mind by means of which it beholds the true, by itself and without the help of the body; or the contemplation itself of the true, without the aid of the body; or the true itself, which it beholds.

As to the first, no one will doubt that reason is in the mind; about the second and third there may be some question. But, the second, also, cannot be without the mind. With regard to the third, the important question arises whether the true itself, which

XVII D

1) But what is this wax which is perceived by the mind alone? It is of course the same wax which I see, which I touch, which I picture in my imagination, in short the same wax which I thought it to be from the start. And yet, and here is the point, the perception I have of it is a case not of vision or touch or imagination – nor has it ever been, despite previous appearances – but of purely mental scrutiny (*mentis inspectio*); and this can be imperfect and confused, as it was before, or clear and distinct as it is now, depending on how carefully I concentrate on what the wax consists in.

Med. II. CSM II, 21.

XVIII A

1) De tertio magna quaestio est, utrum verum illud quod sine instrumento corporis animus intuetur, sit per seipsum, et non sit in animo, aut possit esse sine animo. Quoquolibet modo autem se habeat, non id posset contemplari animus per seipsum, nisi aliqua conjunctione cum eo. Nam omne quod contemplamur, sive cognitione capimus, aut sensu aut intellectu capimus. Sed ea quae sensu capiuntur, extra etiam nos esse, sentiuntur, et locis continentur, unde nec percipi quidem posse affirmantur. Ea vero quae intelliguntur, non quasi alibi posita intelliguntur, quam ipse qui intelligit animus: simul enim etiam intelliguntur non contineri loco.

***De Immortalitate animae*, VI. 10.**

XVIII D

1) Atque ecce tandem sponte sum reversus eo quo volebam; nam cum mihi nunc notum sit ipsamet corpora, non proprie a sensibus, vel ab imaginandi facultate, sed a solo intellectu percipi, nec ex eo percipi quod tangantur aut videantur sed tantum ex eo quod intelligantur aperte cognosco nihil facilius aut evidentius mea mente posse a me percipi. Sed quia tam cito deponi veteris opinionis consuetudo non potest, placet hic consistere, ut altius haec nova cognitio memoriae meae diuturnitate meditationis infigatur.

Med. II. AT VII, 33–34.

Sources for the Second Meditation

1. *The City of God*, XI, 26.
2. *On the Trinity*, XV, xii, 21.
3. *The Literal Meaning of Genesis*, VII, xxi, 27.
4. *The Literal Meaning of Genesis*, VII, xv, 21.
5. *On the Trinity*, IX, ii, 2.
6. *The Immortality of the Soul*, I, i, 1.
7. *On the Trinity*, X, ix, 12.
8. *The Literal Meaning of Genesis*, VI, xv, 21.
9. *The Magnitude of the Soul*, I, 2.
10. *On the Trinity*, X, x, 14.
11. *On the Trinity*, X, x, 14.
12. *The Immortality of the Soul*, V, 8.
13. *The Immortality of the Soul*, V. 9.

the mind beholds without the aid of the body, exists by itself and is not in the mind, or whether it can exist without the mind.

Immortality of the Soul, **VI, 10, p. 27.**

XVIII A

1) With regard to the third, the important question arises whether the true itself, which the mind beholds without the aid of the body, exists by itself and is not in the mind, or whether it can exist without the mind. But, howsoever this may be, the mind could not by itself behold it, except through some kind of connection with the True. For, all we contemplate we grasp by cogitation or perceive through sense or intellect. And, all those things that perceived through one of the senses are sensed as existing outside of us and are contained in space, which, we affirm, makes possible their perception. Those things that are comprehended by the intellect, however, are comprehended as existing nowhere else but in the comprehending mind itself and, at the same time, as not contained in space.

Immortality of the Soul, **VI. 10, p. 27.**

XVIII D

1) I see that without any effort I have now finally got back to where I wanted to be. I now know that even bodies are not strictly perceived by the senses or the faculty of imagination but by the intellect alone, and that this perception derives not from their being touched or seen but from their being understood; and in view of this I know plainly that I can achieve an easier and more evident perception of my own mind than of anything else. But since the habit of holding on to old opinions cannot be set aside so quickly, I should like to stop here and meditate for some time on this new knowledge I have gained, so as to fix more deeply in my memory.

Med. II. CSM II, 22–24.

Fourth Part

Fourth Meditation

SAINT AUGUSTINE

XIX A

1) Mutabilitas enim rerum mutabilium ipsa capax est formarum omnium, in quas mutantur res mutabiles. Et haec quid est? Numquid animus? numquid corpus? numquid species animi vel corporis? si dici posset "nihil aliquid" et "est non est" hoc eam dicerem; et tamen iam utcumque erat, ut species caperet istas visibiles et conpositas.

***Confessiones*, XII, vi. 6.**

RENÉ DESCARTES

XIX D

1) . . . me tanquam medium quid inter Deum & nihil, sive inter summum ens & non ens ita esse constitutum . . .

Med. IV. AT VII, 54.

SAINT AUGUSTINE

XX A

1) sed malum sit aversio ejus [voluntas libera] ab incommutabili bono, et conversio ad mutabilia bona . . . motus iste, id est aversio voluntatis a Domino Deo, sine dubitatione peccatum est.

***De libero arbitrio*, II, xix, 53–xx, 54.**

2) omnia peccata hoc uno genere contineri, cum quisque avertitur a divinis, vereque manentibus; et ad mutabilia atque incerta convertitur.

***De libero arbitrio*, I, xvi, 35.**

RENÉ DESCARTES

XX D

1) ad quae cum [voluntas] sit indifferens, facile a vero & bono deflectit, atque ita & fallor & pecco.

Med. IV. AT VII, 58.

SAINT AUGUSTINE

XIX A

1) For the mutability of mutable things is itself capable of all those forms into which mutable things are changed. And this mutability, what is it? Is it soul? Is it body? Is it the outer appearance of soul or body? Could it be said, "Nothing were something," and "That which is, is not," I would say that this were it; and yet in some manner was it already, since it could receive these visible and compound shapes.

***Confessions*, XII, vi, 6. Vol. I, p. 177.**

XX A

1) Evil consists rather in the will's turning away from the changeless good and in the will's turning to goods that are changeable . . . the turning away of the will from the Lord is unquestionably a sin.

***On Free Will*, II, xix, 53–xx, 54, pp. 161–62. Cf. *The Immortality of the Soul*, VII, 12, pp. 29–30.**

2) All sins fall under this one class and occur when a man turns away from what is divine and truly abiding and turns to what is changing and uncertain.

***On Free Will*, I, xvi, 35, p. 106.**

RENÉ DESCARTES

XIX D

1) . . . I am, as it were, something intermediate between God and nothingness, or between supreme being and non-being.

Med. IV. CSM, II, 38.

XX D

1) Since the will is indifferent in such cases, it easily turns aside from what is true and good, and this is the source of my error and sin.

Med. IV. CSM II, 41.

3) Et quaesivi, quid esset iniquitas, et non inveni substantiam, sed a summa substantia, te deo, detortae in infima voluntatis perversitatem proicientis intima sua et tumescentis foras.

Confessiones, **VII, xvi, 22.**

4) Aversa enim a sapientia incommutabili stulte ac misere vivit, quae informitas est. Formatur autem conversa ad incommutabile lumen sapientiae, verbum Dei.[1]

***De Genesi ad Litteram*, I, v, 10.**

XXI A

1) Deus autem nulli debet aliquid, quis omnia gratuito praestat. . . . Omnia ergo illi debent, primo quidquid sunt, in quantum naturae sunt: deinde quidquid melius possunt esse si velint, quaecumque acceperunt ut velint; et quidquid oporet eas esse. Ex eo igitur quod non accepit, nullus reus est; ex eo vero quod non facit quod debet, juste reus est. Debet autem, si accepit et voluntatem liberam, et sufficientissimam facultatem.

***De libero arbitrio*, III, xvi, 45.**

XXI D

1) Nec vero etiam queri possum, quod non satis amplam & perfectam voluntatem, sive arbitri libertatem, a Deo acceprim; nam sane nullius illam limitibus circumscribi experior. . . . Neque enim habeo causam ullam conquerendi, quod Deus mihi non majorem vim intelligendi, sive non majus lumen naturale dederit quam dedit, quia est de ratione intellectus-finiti ut multa no intelligat, & de ratione intellectus creati ut sit finitus; estque quod agam gratias illi, qui mihi nunquam quicquam debuit . . .

Med. IV. AT VII, 56–60

1 *Immortality of the Soul*, XII. 19, p. 39: "[T]he mind can possess wisdom in turning toward the source of its being, and can lose it by turning away from it."

3) And I inquired what iniquity was, and ascertained it not to be a substance, but a perversion of the will, bent aside from Thee, O God, the Supreme Substance, toward these lower things, and casting out its bowels, and swelling outwardly.

***Confessions*, VII, xvi, 22. Vol. I, p. 111.**

4) For when it [creature] is turned away from changeless Wisdom, its life is full of folly and wretchedness, and so it is in an unformed state.

***The Literal Meaning of Genesis*, I, v, 10, vol. I, p. 24.**

XXI A

1) God, however, is a debtor to no one since He confers everything gratuitously. . . . All things, therefore, owe to Him, first of all, such existence as they have by their natures, next whatever further perfection they can achieve, if they so will, according to the will they have received, and according to what it is their duty to become, and for all that they ought to be. No one is at fault for what he has not received, but he is justly at fault for not doing as he ought. Now he has an obligation to do so if he has received free will and all the power that is needed.

***On Free Will*, III, xvi, 45, pp. 206–7.**

XXI D

1) I cannot complain that the will or freedom of choice which I received from God is not sufficiently extensive or perfect, since I know by experience that it is not restricted in any way. . . . I have no cause for complaint on the grounds that the power of understanding or the natural light which God gave me is no greater than it is, for it is in the nature of a finite intellect to lack understanding of many things, and it is in the nature of a created intellect to be finite. Indeed, I have reason to give thanks to Him who has never owed me anything.

Med. IV. CSM, II, pp. 39–42. Cf. St. Thomas, *Summa contra Gentiles*, II, 28 et 29 [9].

2) Reddis debita nulli debens, donas debita nihil perdens.

Confessions, **I, iv, 4. Vol. I, p. 46.**

XXII A

1) Tunc vero invisibilia tua per ea quae facta sunt intellecta conspexi, sed aciem figere non evalui, et repercussa infirmitate redditus solitis, non mecum ferebam nisi amantem memoriam et quasi olefacta desiderantem, quae comedere nondum possem.

Confessiones, **VII, xvii, 23.**

XXII D

1) [N]am, quamvis eam in me infirmitate, esse experiar, ut non possim semper uni & eidem cognitioni defixus inhaerere . . .

Med. IV. AT VII, 61.

Additions

XXIII A

1) Nunc vero usque adeo peccatum voluntarium est malum, ut nullo modo sit peccatum, si non sit voluntarium. . . . Postremo, si non voluntate male facimus, nemo objurgandus est omnino, aut monendus: quibus sublatis, christiana lex et disciplina omnis religionis auferatur necesse est. Voluntate ergo peccatur. Et quoniam peccari non dubium est, ne hoc quidem dubitandum video, habere animas liberum voluntatis arbitrium. Tales enim servos suos meliores esse Deus judicavit, nature: si ei servirent liberaliter. Quod nullo modo fieri posset, si non voluntate, sed necessitate servirent.

De vera religione, **XIV, 27.**

XXIII D

1) *Summam esse hominis perfectionem, quod agat libere, sive per voluntatem; & per hoc laude vel vituperio dignum reddi.* Quod vero latissime pateat voluntas, hoc etiam ipsius naturae convenit; ac summa quaedam in homine perfectio est, quod agat per voluntatem, hoc est libere, atque ita peculiari quodam modo fit author suarum actionum, & ob ipsas laudem mereatur. Non enim laudantur automata, quod motus omnes ad quos instituta sunt, accurate exhibeant, accurate exhibeant, quia necessario illos sic exhibent, laudatur autem eorum artifex, quod tam accurata fabricarit, quia non necessario, sed libere ipsa fabricavit. Eademque ratione, magis profecto

2) You repay us what we deserve, and yet You owe nothing to any.

Confessions, **I, iv, 4. Vol. I, p. 46.**

XXII A

1) And then I saw Thy invisible things understood by the things that are made [cf. St. Paul, Letter to the Romans, i. 20]. But I was not able to fix my gaze thereon[2]; and my infirmity being beaten back, I was thrown again on my accustomed habits . . .

***Confessions*, VII, xvii, 23. Vol. I, p. 112.**

XXII D

1) I am aware of a certain weakness in me, in that I am unable to keep my attention fixed on one and the same item of knowledge at all times . . .

Med. IV. CSM, II, 43.

Additions

XXIII A

1) But in fact sin is so much a voluntary evil that it is not sin at all unless it is voluntary. . . . Besides if it is not by the exercise of will that we do wrong, no one at all is to be censured or warned. If you take away censure and warning the Christian law and the whole discipline of religion is necessarily abolished. Therefore, it is by the will that sin is committed. And since there is no doubt that sins are committed, I cannot see that is can be doubted that souls have free choice in willing. God judged that men would serve Him better if they

XXIII D

1) *The supreme perfection of man is that he acts freely or voluntarily, and it is this which makes him deserve praise or blame.*

The extremely broad scope of the will is part of its very nature. And it is a supreme perfection in man that he acts voluntarily, that is, freely; this makes him in a special way the author of his actions and deserving of praise for what he does. We do not praise automatons for accurately producing all the movements they were designed to perform, because the production of these movements occurs necessarily. It is the designer who is praised for con-

2 As Françis Ferrier points out in his *La pensée philosophique du Père Guillaume Gibieuf: 1583–1650* (Lille: Atelier Reproduction de Thèses, 1976), vol. II, 12ff., Descartes' idea of rectifying a judgment is similar to Gibieuf's constant reminder to "adhere to God" (see *De Liberate Dei*, p. 44) – a Bérullian leitmotiv *par excellence*.

nobis tribuendum est, quod verum amplectamur, cum amplectimur, quia voluntarie id agimus, quam si non possemus non aplecti.

Principiorum Philosophiae, **I, 37. AT VIII, 18.**

XXIV A

1) Inluditur autem anima similitudinibus rerum non earum vitio, sed opinionis suae, cum adprobat quae similia sunt pro his, quibus similia sunt, ab intellegentia deficiens. Fallitur ergo in visione corporali, cum in ipsis corporibus fieri putat, quod fit in corporis sensibus. . . . In visione autem spirituali, id est in corporum similitudinibus, quae spiritu videntur, fallitur anima, cum ea, quae sic videt, ipsa corpora esse arbitratur vel, quod sibi suspicione falsaque coniectura finxerit, hoc etiam in corporibus putat, quae non visa coniectat. At vero in illis intellectualibus visis non fallitur. . . . Praestantior est enim visio spiritualis quam corporalis et rursus praestantior intellectualis quam spiritualis.

***De Genesi ad litteram*, XII, xxv, 52; XII, xxiv, 51.**

XXIV D

1) Ex quibus patet, cum dicimus *intellectus certitudinem sensum certitudine longe esse majorem . . .*

***Sextae Responsiones.* AT VII, 438.**

served Him freely. That could not be so if they served Him by necessity and not by free will.

***On True Religion*, XIV, 27. Vol. VI, p. 238.**

structing such carefully made devices, for in constructing them he acted not out of necessity but freely. By the same principle, when we embrace the truth, our doing so voluntarily is much more to our credit than would be the case if we could not do otherwise.

***Principles of Philosophy*, I, 37. CSM I, 205.**

XXIV A

1) But the soul is deceived by the images of things, *not because of any fault of these images* but because of its won erroneous opinion when through lack of understanding it confuses different objects because of their similarity. . . . But in the spiritual vision, namely, in the likeness of bodies seen by the spirit, the soul is deceived when it attaches some property of its own fancy and false conjecture to bodies that it has not seen but merely conjures up in imagination. But in the intuition of the intellect it is not deceived. . . . And so corporeal vision is inferior to the spiritual, and both are inferior to the intellectual.[3]

***Literal Meaning of Genesis*, XII, xxv, 52; XII, xxiv, 51. Vol. II, pp. 215, 214.**

XXIV D

1) It is clear from this that when we say "The reliability of the intellect is much greater than that of the senses" . . .

***Sixth Set of Replies*. CSM II, p. 295. See also: *Le Monde*, I. AT XI, 5–6.**

3 "But how can the intellect enjoy any certainty unless it has previously derived it from the senses when they are working as they should? How can it correct a mistake made by one of the senses unless some other sense first corrects the mistake? Owing to refraction, a stick which is in fact straight appears bent in water. What corrects the error? The intellect? Not at all; it is the sense of touch." *Sixth Set of Objections*. CSM II, 282. Cf. St. Augustine, *De vera religione*, XXXI, 53, et *De Trinitate*, IX, vi, 11). See also Leo W. Keeler, S.J., "St. Augustine on the Problem of Error," in *Thought: Fordham University Quarterly*, December 1933, pp. 400–430.

XXV A

1) [C]umque intellectus amplissimus sit quoniam intelligit omnia, voluntas etiam ipsa amplissima est, seseque ad omnia bonorum genera, atque ad Bonum ipsum universum extendit intellectus. . . . Spontanea ergo voluntate homo . . . neque ullo termino circumscripto, sed amplo, ac libero movetur arbitrio, quod tum ad singulat um ad universum bonum extenditur.

Cardinal Gasparis Contareni, *De libero arbitrio, Opera*, Paris, 1571, p. 599.

XXV D

1) Ex his autem percipio nec vim volendi, quam a Deo habeo, per se spectatem, causam esse errorum meorum, est enim amplissima, atque in suo genere perfecta; neque etiam vim intelligendi, nam quidquid intelligo, cum a Deo habeam ut intelligam. . . . Unde ergo nascentur mei errores? Nempe ex hoc uno quod, cum latius pateat voluntas quam intellectus, illam non intra eosdem limites contineo, sed etiam ad illa quae non intelligo extendo . . .

Med. IV. AT VII, 58.

XXV A

1) As intelligence is very ample because it understands everything. The will itself is also very ample and extends itself toward all the kinds of good and the universal Good itself. . . . A spontaneous human will . . . unconfined by anything, but free and with no limits, stretches itself no less to any good as it does to the universal good.

Cardinal Gasparis Contareni, *De libero arbitrio, Opera,* Paris, 1571, p. 599. This sentence is quoted by G. Gibieuf in his *De Libertate Dei,* p. 44.

XXV D

1) From these considerations I perceive that the power of willing which I received from God is not, when considered in itself, the cause of my mistakes; for it is both extremely ample and also perfect of its kind. Nor is my power of understanding to blame; for since my understanding comes from God. . . . So what then is the source of my mistakes? It must be this: the scope of the will is wider than that of the intellect; but instead of restricting it within the same limits, I extend its use to matters which I do not understand.

Med. IV. AT IX, 46.

Sources for the Fourth Meditation[4]:

1. *The Confessions,* XII, vi, 6.
2. *On Free Will,* II, xix, 53–xx, 54.
3. *On Free Will,* I, xvi, 35.
4. *The Confessions,* VII, xvii, 22.
5. *The Literal Meaning of Genesis,* I, v, 10.
6. *On Free Will,* III, xvi, 45.
7. *The Confessions,* VII, xvii, 23.
8. *On True Religion,* XIV, 27.
9. *The Literal Meaning of Genesis,* XII, xxv, 52.
10. Gasparis Contareni, *De Libero Arbitrio* and Gibieuf, *De Libertate Dei,* p. 44.

4 For a detailed discussion of Descartes' debt to Augustine in the Fourth Meditation, see my *Cartesian Theodicy: Descartes' Quest for Certitude* (Dordrecht: Kluwer Academic Publishers, 2000), pp. 125–30. See also, Stephen Menn, "Descartes, Augustine, and the Status of Faith," in *Studies in Seventeenth Century European Philosophy,* M. A. Stewart ed. (Oxford: Oxford University Press, 1998).

Fifth Part

Sixth Meditation

SAINT AUGUSTINE

XXVI A

1) [C]ur anima, si non tanti spatii magnitudinem habet quanti corpus est, ubique illius sentit cum tangitur? . . . Attende ergo: nam sensum puto esse, non latare animam quod patitur corpus. . . . Dic igitur quid patiatur corpus tuum cum me vides?

E. – Patitur omnino aliquid: nam oculi mei partes, nisi fallor, corporis mei sunt; qui si nihil paterentur, quomodo te viderem? . . . Igitur si omne quod videmus, sentimus, sentimus, et omne quod sentimus, patimur; patimur omne quod videmus. . . . Accipe caetera: nam credo absurdissimum et stultissimum videri tibi, si quis affirmet ibi te pati aliquod corpus, ubi non est ipsum corpus quod pateris. . . . At si tu vides, tu sentis; si tu sentis, tu pateris; nec potes ibi pati aliquid, ubi non es; ibi autem e vides, ubi ego sum. . . . Quid? illud quod per visum sentimus, possumusne non videre?

E. – Nullo modo.

A. – Aliud est ergo sentire, aliud cognoscere?

E. – Omnino aliud: nam sentimus fumum, quem videmus; et ex eo ignem, quem non videmus, subesse cognoscimus.

A. – Bene intelligis. Sed vides certe cum hoc accidit, corpus nostrum, id est oculos, nihil pati ex igne, sed ex fumo quem solum vident. Etenim

RENÉ DESCARTES

XXVI D

1) [Q]uamvis ad ignem accedens sentio calorem, ut etiam ad eundem nimis prope accedens sentio dolorem, nulla profecto ratio est quae suadeat in igne aliquid esse simile isti calori, ut neque etiam isti dolori, sed tantummodo in eo aliquid esse quodcunque demum sit, quod istos in nobis sensus caloris vel doloris efficiat.

Et quamvis etiam in aliquo spatio

SAINT AUGUSTINE

XXVI A

1) A. – [I]f the soul's magnitude has not the same spatial extent as that of the body? . . . Listen carefully, then, for I think that sensation is "a bodily experience the awareness of which the soul cannot escape."[1] . . . Tell me now, what does your body experience when you see me?
E. – It experiences something, to be sure, for my eyes are part of my body, if I mistake not; and if they experience nothing, how could I see you? . . .
A. – Therefore, when we see each other, you experience me and, conversely, I experience you.
E. – So I think. Reason forces me to this conclusion at once.
A. – Take the rest, for I believe it would appear very absurd and stupid to you, if anyone should declare that you there experience a body, where the body itself which you experience is not. . . . But, if you see, you perceive; if you perceive, you are acted upon; and you cannot there be acted upon where you are not. But you see me where I am; therefore, you are acted upon where I am. But, if you are not there where I am, I know not how you dare say that I am seen by you. . . . Is it possible for

RENÉ DECARTES

XXVI D

1) Although I feel heat when I go near the fire and feel pain when I go too near, there is no convincing argument for supposing that there is something in the fire which resembles the heat, any more than for supposing that there is something which resembles the pain. There is simply reason to suppose that there is some-

1 For an excellent account of this theory, see Vernon Bourke, *Augustine's Quest for Wisdom*, pp. 111–12.

videre, sentire; et sentire, pati esse, jam supra consensimus.
E. – Teneo et assentior.
A. – Cum ergo per passionem corporis non latet aliquid animam, non continuo sensus vocatur unus de quinque memoratis; sed cum ipsa passio non latet: namque ille ignis non visus, nec auditus, nec olfactus, nec gustatus, nec tactus a nobis, non tamen latet animam, fumo viso. Et cum hoc non latere non vocetur sensus, quia ex igne corpus nihil est passum . . .
E. – Intelligo, et optime video istud congruere ac favere illi definitioni tuae, quam ut meam mihi defendendam dedisti: nam ita memini esse abs te sensum definitium, cum animam non latet quod patitur corpus. Itaque illud quod fumus videtur, sensum vocamus; passi sunt enim eum oculi videndo, qui sunt corporis partes et corpora: ignem autem, ex quo nihil corpus est passum, quamvis cognitus fuerit, sensum non vocamus.

***De Quantitate animae*, XXII, 40; XXIII, 41, 42, 43; XXIV, 45.**

nihil sit quod moveat sensum, non ideo sequitur in eo nullum esse corpus: sed video me in his aliisque permultis ordinem naturae pervertere esse assuentum, quia nempe sensuum perceptionibus, quae proprie tantum a natura datae sunt menti significandum quaenam composito, cujus pars est commoda sint vel incommoda . . .

Med. VI. AT VII, 83.

us not to see the object that we perceive by means of sight?
E. – No, it is not possible.
A. – Therefore, to perceive with the sense is one thing; to know is another.
E. – Altogether different; for we perceive the smoke that we see, and from that we know the presence of the fire which we do not see.
A. – You understand rightly. But you certainly see that when this happens, our body, that is, our eyes, have no experience of the fire, but only of the smoke, which is all that they see. For, we have agreed before that to see is to perceive and to perceive is to be acted upon. . . . When, therefore, there occurs a bodily experience which makes the soul aware of something, the phenomenon is not for that reason called an activity of one of the five senses, but only when the soul is aware of the bodily experience itself. While, therefore, this awareness of the soul may not be called an activity of sense, because the body has no experience of the fire, yet it is called knowledge through sense, because the presence of the fire was suspected and established from an experience which the body had . . .
E. – I understand and see very well that this squares with and supports that definition of yours which you gave me to defend, for so I recall your definition of sensation as "a bodily experience the awareness of which the soul cannot escape."

thing in the fire, whatever it may eventually turn out to be, which produces in us the feelings of heat or pain.

And likewise, even though there is nothing in any given space that stimulates the senses, it does not follow that there is no body there. In these cases and many others I see that I have been in the habit of misusing the order of nature. For the proper purpose of the sensory perceptions given me by nature is simply to inform the mind of what is beneficial or harmful for the composite of which the mind is a part . . .

Med. VI. CSM 57.

XXVII A

1) Intendit se anima in tactum, et eo calida, frigida, aspera, lenia, dura, mellia, levia, gravia sentit atque discernit. Deinde innumerabiles differentias saporum, odorum, sonorum, formarum, gustando, olficiendo, audiendo videndoque dijudicat. Atque in iis omnibus ea quae secundum naturam sui corporis sunt, adsciscit atque appetit; rejicit futique contraria.

De quantitate animae, **XXXIII, 71.**

XXVII D

1) Sed nova hic occurit difficultas circa illa ipsa quae tanquam persequenda vel fugienda mihi a natura exhibentur . . .

Med. VI. AT VII, 83.

XXVIII A

1) Moles quippe omnis quae occupat locum, non est in singulis suis partibus tota, sed in omnibus. Quare alia pars ejus alibi est, et alibi alia. Anima vero non modo universae moli corporis sui, sed etiam unicuique par-

XXVIII D

1) Adverto praeterea eam esse corporis naturam, ut nulla ejus pars possit ab alia parte aliquantum remota moveri, quin possit etiam moveri eodem modo a qualibet ex iis quae interjacent, quamvis illa remo-

Therefore, the seeing of smoke we call a sensation, for the eyes experienced that by seeing, and the eyes are parts of the body and corporeal, but the fire, of which the body had no experience, although the presence of the fire is known, we do not call an object of sensation.

***The Magnitude of the Soul,* XXII, 40; XXIII, 41, 42, 43; XXIV, 45; pp. 104, 105, 106, 107, 109, 110.**

XXVII A

1) The soul applies itself to the sense of touch; through it it feels and distinguishes hot and cold, rough and smooth, hard and soft, light and heavy. Then it distinguishes between unnumbered differences of taste and smell and sound and shapes, by tasting, smelling, hearing, and seeing. And in all these it comes to know and seek what suits the nature of its body; it rejects and shuns what is unsuited.

***The Magnitude of the Soul,* XXXIII, 71, p. 138.**

XXVII D

1) But a further problem now comes to mind regarding those very things which nature presents to me as objects which I should seek out or avoid . . .

Med. VI. AT IX, 66.

XXVIII A

1) Each mass that occupies space is not in its entirety in each of its single parts, but only in all taken together. Hence, one part is in one place; another in another. The soul, however, is present at the same time and

XXVIII D

1) My next observation is that the mind is not immediately affected by all parts of the body, but only by the brain, or perhaps just by one small part of the brain, namely the part which is said to contain the "com-

ticulae illius tota simul adest. Partis enim corporis passionum tota sentit, nec in toto tamen corpore. Cum enim quid dolet in pede, adverti oculus, loquitur lingua, admovetur, manus. Quod non fieret, nisi id quod animae in eis partibus est et in pede sentiret, nec sentire quod ibi factum est absens posset. Non enim nuntio aliquo credibile est fieri non sentiente quod nuntiat: quia passio quae fit non per continuationem molis currit, ut ceteras animae partes quae alibi sunt latere non sinat, sed illud tota sentit anima quod in particula fit pedis, et ibi tantum sentit ubi fit. Tota igitur singulis partibus simul adest, quae tota simul senti in singulis. Nec tamen hoc modo adest tota, ut candor vel alia hujusmodi qualitas in unaquaque parte corporis tota est. Nam quod in alia parte corpus patitur candoris immutatione, potest ad candorem qui est in alia parte non pertinere. Quapropter secundum partes molis a se distantes, et ipse a se distare convincitur. Non autem ita esse in anima per sensum, de quo dictum est, probatur.

De immortalitate animae, **XVI, 25.**

tior nihil agat . . . cum sentio dolorem pedis, docuit me Physica sensum illum fieri ope nervorum per pedem sparsorum, qui, inde ad cerebrum usque funium instar extensi, dum trahuntur in pede, trahunt etiam intimas cerebri partes ad quas pertingunt, quemdamque motum in iis excitant, qui institutus est a natura ut mentem afficiat sensu doloris tanquam in pede existentis. Sed quia illi nervi per tibiam, crus, lumbos, dorsum, & collum transire debent, ut a pede ad cerebrum perveniant, potest contingere ut, etiamsi eorum pars, quae est in pede, non attingatur, sed aliqua tantum ex intermediis, idem plane ille motus fiat in cerebro qui fit pede male affecto, ex quo necesse erit ut mens sentiat eundem dolorem. Et idem de quolibet alio sensu est putandum.

Adverto denique, quandoquidem unusquisque ex motibus, qui fiunt in ea parte cerebri quae immediate mentem afficit, non nisi unum aliquem sensum illi infert, nihil hac in re melius posse excogitari, quam si eum inferat qui, ex omnibus quos inferre potest, ad hominis sani conservationem quam maxime & quam frequentissime conducit.

Med. VI. AT VII, 86–87.

entire, not only in the entire mass of its body, but also in each of its individual parts. For, it is the entire soul that feels the pain of a part of the body, yet it does not feel it in the entire body. When, for example, there is an ache in the foot, the eye looks at it, the mouth speaks of it, and the hand reaches for it. This, of course, would be impossible, if what of the soul is in the parts did not also experience a sensation in the foot; if the soul were not present, it would be unable to feel what has happened there. For, it would be incredible of a messenger to announce a fact, the occurrence of which he had not experienced. The sensation which occurs does not run through the mass of the body by continuation in such fashion as not to remain unnoticed by other parts of the soul which are elsewhere, but the entire soul feels what is going on in the particular part of the foot and feels it only there where it occurs. Hence, the entire soul is present, at one and the same time, in the single parts, and it experiences sensation as a whole, at one and the same time, in the single part.

And yet, it is not present as a whole in such a manner as the whiteness or any other quality of this kind is present as a whole in each single part of the body. For, what the body, through a change of this whiteness, experiences in one part cannot be extended to the whiteness in the other part. hence mon sense." Every time this part of the brain is in a given state, it presents the same signals to the mind, even though the other parts of the body may be in a different condition . . . when I feel pain in my foot, physiology tells me that this happens by means of nerves distributed throughout the foot, and that these nerves are like cords which go from the foot right up to the brain. When the nerves are pulled in the foot, they in turn pull on inner parts of the brain to which they are attached, and produce a certain motion in them; and nature has laid it down that this motion should produce in the mind a sensation of pain, as occurring in the foot. But since these nerves, in passing from the foot to the brain, must pass through the calf, the thigh, the lumbar region, the back and the neck, it can happen that, even if it is not the part in the foot but one of the intermediate parts which is being pulled, the same motion will occur in the brain as occurs when the foot is hurt, and so it will necessarily come about that the mind feels the same sensation of pain. And we must suppose the same thing happens with regard to any other sensation.

My final observation is that any given movement occurring in the part of the brain that immediately affects the mind produces just one corresponding sensation; and hence the best system that could be devised is that it should produce the

Additions

XXIX A

1) Et si figurarum omnium planarum illa optima est quae circulo effingitur, in qua ratio docuit nihil melius esse puncto atque potentius, quod, nullo dubitande, partibus caret, quid mirum si anima neque corporea sit, neque ulla aut longitidine porrecta, aut latitudine diffusa, aut altitudine solidata: *et tamen tantum valeat in corpore, ut penes eam sit regimen omninum membrorum, et quasi cardo quidam in agendo, cunctarum corporialum motionum*?

***De quantitate animae*, XIV, 23.**

XXIX D

1) Docet etiam natura, per istos sensus doloris, famis, sitis & c., me non tantum adesse meo corpori ut nauta adest navigio, sed illi artissime esse conjunctum & quasi permixtum, adeo ut unum quid cum illo componam. Alioqui enim, cum corpus laeditur, ego, qui nihil aliud sum quam res cogitans, non sentirem idcirco dolorem, sed puro intellectu laesionem istam perciperem, ut nauta visu percipit si quid in nave frangatur . . .

Med. VI. AT VII, 81.

XXX A

1) Quare tendere ad nihilum, est ad interitum tendere. Qui cur non cadat in animum, vix est dicere, in quem defectus cadit. Dantur hic cetera: sed

XXX D

1) Nempe imprimis hic adverto magnam esse differentiam inter mentem & corpus, in eo quod corpus ex natura sua sit semper divisibile,

the result that, since the parts of the mass are distant from each other, the mass itself is distant from itself. That this, however, does not apply to the soul is proved by the sense experience [in the foot] mentioned above.

The Immortality of the Soul, **XVI, 25, pp. 46–47.**

one sensation which, of all possible sensations, is most especially and frequently conducive to the preservation of the healthy man.

Med. VI. CSM II, 59–60.

Additions

XXIX A

1) And, if a circle is the best of all plane figures, and if in a circle nothing is more excellent or more important than a point, which beyond all doubt is without any parts – why should anyone be astonished that the soul, which is neither a body, nor extended in length, nor spread out in width, nor massed in depth, has, nevertheless, such power that it rules all the members of the body and presides over all the motions of the body for all the world as the director of its activity?

The Magnitude of the Soul, **XIV, 23, p. 84.**

XXIX D

1) Nature also teaches me, by the sensations of pain, hunger, thirst and so on, that I am not merely present in my body as a sailor is present in a ship, but that I am very closely joined and, as it were, intermingled with it, so that I and the body form a unit. If this were not so, I, who am nothing but a thinking thing, would not feel pain when the body was hurt, but would perceive the damage purely by the intellect, just as a sailor perceives by sight if anything in his ship is broken.

Med. VI. CSM II, p. 56. Cf. Aristotle, *De anima*, 413a 8, and St. Thomas, *Summa contra Gentiles*, I, 26; II, 57 [2].

XXX A

1) A trend toward nothing is a trend toward destruction. Why this destruction does not fall upon the mind, although it is subject to defect,

XXX D

1) The first observation I make at the point is that there is a great difference between the mind and the body, inasmuch as the body is by its

negatur esse consequens interire id quod tendit ad nihilum, id est ad nihilum pervenire. Quod in corpore quoque animadverti potest.

Nam quoniam quodlibet corpus pars est mundi sensibilis, et ideo quanto majus est locique plus occupat, tanto magis propinquat universo: quantoque id magis facit, tanto magis est. Magis enim est totum quam pars. Quare etiam minus sit cum minitur necesse est. Defectum ergo patitur cum minitur. Porro autem minitur, cum ex eo aliquid praecisione detrahitur. Ex quo conficitur ut tali detractione tendat ad nihilum. At nulla praecisio perducit ad nihilum. Omnis enim pars quae remanet, corpus est, et quidquid hoc est, quantolibet spatio locum occupat. Neque id posset, nisi haberet partes in quas identidem caederetur. Potest igitur infinite caedendo infinite minui, et ideo defectumpati atque ad nihilum tendere, quamvis pervenirenunquam queat.

Quod item de ipso spatio et quolibet intervallo dici atque intelligi potest. Nam et de his etiam terminatis, dimidiam, verbi gratia, partem detrahendo, et ex eo quod restat, semper dimidiam, minuitur intervallum, atque ad finem progreditur, ad quem tamen nullo pervenitur modo.

Quo minushoc de animo formidandum est? Est enim profecto corpore melior et vivacior, a quo huic vita tribuitur.

De immortalitate animae, **VII. 12.**

mens autem plane indivisibilis; nam sane cum hanc considero, sive meipsum quatenus sum tantum res cogitans, nullas in me partes possum distinguere, sed rem plane unam & integram me esse intelligo & quamvis toti corpori tota mens unita esse videatur, abscisso tamen pede, vel brachio, vel quavis alia corporis parte, nihil ideo de mente subductum esse cognosco; neque etiam facultates volendi, sentiendi, intelligendi & c. ejus partes dici possunt, quia una & eadem mens est quae vult, quae sentit, quae intelligit. Contra vero nulla res corporea sive extensa potest a me cogitari, quam non facile in partes cogitatione dividam, atque hoc ipso illam divisibilem esse intelligam: quod unum sufficeret ad me docendum, mentem a corpore omnino esse diversam, si nondum illud aliunde satis scirem.

Med. VI. AT VII, 85–86.

is hard to say. While we may concede here the foregoing premises, we deny the conclusion that that which is tending toward nothing perishes, i.e., that it actually reaches nothing. The correctness of our denial may also be observed in the body. Since each body is a part of the sensible world, the closer it approaches the volume of the universe, the larger it is and the more space it occupies, the more the body does this, the larger is the body. For, the whole is larger than the part. Wherefore, it is necessarily smaller when it is reduced. It suffers a defect, then, when it is reduced. A body is naturally reduced if something is taken away from it by way of cutting off. From this it follows that through such taking away it tends to nothing. But, no cutting off actually leads the body to nothing. For, each part that remains is a body and occupies, to the extent of its quantity, some space. This is only possible for the reason that it has parts, into which it may repeatedly be cut. Thus, there is no limit for a body being reduced by means of unlimited cuttings; hence it can suffer defects and tend toward nothing, though it is never able to reach nothing.

This can likewise be stated and conceived with regard to space itself and to any interval whatever. For, if one takes away, let us say, a half of such defined divisions, and again the half of the remainder, and so forth, the interval will more and more decrease, advancing toward a

very nature always divisible, while the mind is utterly indivisible. For when I consider the mind, or myself insofar as I am merely a thinking thing, I am unable to distinguish any parts within myself; I understand myself to be something quite single and complete. Although the whole mind seems to be united to the whole body, I recognize that if a foot or arm or any other part of the body is cut off, nothing has thereby been taken away from the mind. As for the faculties of willing, of understanding, of sensory perception and so on, these cannot be termed parts of the mind, since it is one and the same mind that wills, and understands and has sensory perceptions. By contrast, there is no corporeal or extended thing that I can think of which in my thought I cannot easily divide into parts; and this very fact makes me understand that it is divisible. This one argument would be enough to show me that the mind is completely different from the body, even if I did not already know as much from other considerations.

Med. VI. CSM II, 59.

limit which, however, it will by no means reach.

How much less, then, have we to fear this in regard to the mind. For, the mind is certainly better and more alive than the body, since it is the mind that gives life to the body.

***The Immortality of the Soul,* VII. 12, pp. 30–31.**

Sources for the Sixth Meditation:

1. *The Magnitude of the Soul,* XXII, 40; XXIII, 41, 42, 43; XXIV, 45.
2. *The Magnitude of the Soul,* XXXIII, 71.
3. *The Immortality of the Soul,* XIV, 25.
4. *The Magnitude of the Soul*, XIV, 23.
5. *The Immortality of the Soul,* VII. 12.

Sixth Part

The Doctrine of Eternal Truths

SAINT AUGUSTINE

XXXI A

Diximusne aliquid et sonuinus aliquid dignum Deo? Imo vero nihil me aliud quam dicere voluisse sentio: si autem dixi, non hoc est quod dicere volui. Hoc unde scio, nisi quia Deus ineffabilis est; quod autem a me dictum est, si ineffabile esset, dictum non esset? Ac per hoc ne ineffabilis quidem dicendus est Deus, quia et hoc cum dicitur, aliquid dicitur. Et fit nescio quae pugna verborum, quoniam si illud est ineffabile, quod vel ineffabile dici potest. Quae pugna verborum silentio cavenda potius quam voce pecanda est.

***De Doctrina Christiana,* I. vi. 6.**

RENÉ DESCARTES

XXXI D

1) Je reviens à votre lettre du vingt-troisième Décembre, à laquelle je n'ai pas encore fait réponse. Le passage de saint Augustin touchant ceci, à savoir que Dieu est ineffable, ne dépend que d'une petite distinction qui est bien aisée à entendre. *Non possumus omnia quæ in Deo sunt verbis complecti, nec etiam mente comprehendere, ideoque Deus est Ineffabilis & Incomprehensibilis; sed multa tamen sunt revera in Deo, sive ad Deum pertinent, quæ possumus mente attingere ac verbis exprimere, imo etiam plura quam in ulla alia re, ideoque hoc sensu Deus est maxime Cognoscibilis & Effabilis* (Nous ne pouvons pas embrasser par des mots, ni même comprendre par notre esprit, toutes les choses qui sont en Dieu, et, pour cela, Dieu est Ineffable et Incompréhensible. Pourtant, en réalité, beaucoup de choses sont en Dieu, ou se rapportent à Dieu, que nous pouvons atteindre par l'esprit et exprimer par des mots. Il y en a même beaucoup plus qu'en aucune autre chose. En ce sens et pour cette raison, Dieu est le plus Connaissable et le plus Dicible de tous les êtres).

A Mersenne, 21 Janvier 1641. AT III, 284.

SAINT AUGUSTINE

XXXI A

1) Have I spoken of God, or uttered His praise, in any worthy way? Nay, I feel that I have done nothing more than desire to speak; and if I have said anything, it is not what I desired to say. How do I know this, except from the fact that God is ineffable? But what I have said, if it had been ineffable, could not have been spoken. And so God is not even to be called "ineffable," because to say even this is to speak of Him. Thus there arises a curious contradiction of words, because if the ineffable is what cannot be spoken of, it is not unspeakable if it can be called ineffable. And this opposition of words is rather to be avoided by silence than to be explained away by speech.

***On Christian Doctrine*, I, vi, 6. Vol. II, p. 524.**

RENÉ DESCARTES

XXXI D[1]

1) I come back to your letter of 23 December, which I have not yet answered. The passage from Augustine relevant to the point at issue – namely that God is ineffable – depends merely on a small distinction which is very easy to understand. *Non possumus omnia quæ in Deo sunt verbis complecti, nec etiam mente comprehendere, ideoque Deus est Ineffabilis & Incomprehensibilis; sed multa tamen sunt revera in Deo, sive ad Deum pertinent, quæ possumus mente attingere ac verbis exprimere, imo etiam plura quam in ulla alia re, ideoque hoc sensu Deus est maxime Cognoscibilis & Effabilis* (We cannot encompass in words everything that is in God, or indeed grasp it in our minds, and hence God is ineffable and beyond our comprehension. But there are many things really in God, or which relate to God, which we are capable of reaching in our minds and expressing in words – many more, indeed, than in the case of any other thing. And so in this sense God can be known and spoken of to a very great extent.)

To Mersenne, 21 January 1641. CSMK II, p. 169.

1 The link between Sermon 117 and Descartes's letter of January 21, 1641, was suggested by Ms. Sandrine Dupuis, in her paper *Saint Augustin: Une théorie de la connaissance* (St. Augustine: A Theory of Cognition," pp. 94-95), written under the direction of Prof. Emmanuel Faye, at the Université de Paris X - Nanterre, in 1999.

XXXII A

1) Et tamen Deus, cum de illu nihil digne dici possit, admisit humanae vocis obsequium, et verbis nostris in laude sua gaudere nos voluit. Nam inde est, quod dicitur Deus. Nam enim re vera in strepitu istarum duarum syllabarum ipse cognoscitur: sed tamen omnes latinae linguae scios, cum aures eorum sonus iste tetigerit, movet ad cogitandam excellentissimam quamdam immortalemque naturam.

***De doctrina Christiana*, I, vi. 6.**

XXXII D

1) [C]ar l'existence de Dieu est la premiere & la plus eternelle de toutes les véritez qui peuvent estre, & la seule d'où procedent toutes les autres. Mais ce qui fait qu'il est aisé en cecy de se méprendre, c'est que la pluspart des hommes ne considerent pas Dieu comme un estre infini & incomprehensible, & qui est le seul Autheur duquel toutes choses dependent; mais ils s'arrestent aux syllabes de son nom, & pensent que c'est assez le connoistre, si on sçait que Dieu veut dire le mesme que ce qui s'appele *Deus* en latin, & qui est adoré par les hommes.

A Mersenne, 6 mai 1630. AT I, 150.

XXXIII A

1) Nos itaque ista quae fecisti videmus, quia sunt, tu autem quia vides ea, sunt. Et nos foris vidimus, quia sunt, et intus, quia bona sunt: tu autem ibi vidisti facta, ubi vidisti facienda.

***Confessiones*, XIII, xxxviii. 53.**

XXXIII D

1) Mais nous ne nous les devons point representer, pour connoistre l'immensité de sa puissance, ny concevoir aucune preference ou priorité entre son entendement & sa volonté; car l'idée que nous avons de Dieu nous apprend qu'il n'y a en luy qu'une seule action, toute simple & toute pure; ce que ces mots de S. Augustin expriment fort bien: *quia vides ea, sunt, etc.*, pour ce qu'en Dieu *videre* et *velle* ne sont qu'une mesme chose.

A Mesland, 2 mai 1644. AT IV, 119.

XXXII A

2) And yet God, although nothing worthy of His greatness can be said of Him, has condescended to accept worship of men's mouth, and has desired us through the medium of our own words to rejoice in His praise. For on this principle it is that He is called Deus (God). For the sound of those two syllables in itself conveys no true knowledge of His nature; but yet all who know the Latin tongue are led, when that sound reaches their ears, to think of a nature supreme in excellence and eternal in existence.

***On Christian Doctrine*, I, vi, 6. Vol. II, p. 524.**

XXXII D

1) [F]or the existence of God is the first and the most eternal of all possible truths and the one from which alone all others proceed. It is easy to be mistaken about this because most people do not regard God as a being who is infinite and beyond our grasp, the sole author on whom all things depend; they stick at the syllables of His name and think it is sufficient knowledge of him to know that "God" means what is meant by *Deus* in Latin and what is adored by men.

To Mersenne, 6 May 1630. CSMK III, pp. 24–25.

XXXIII A

1) We therefore see those things which Thou madest, because they are; but they are because Thou seest they are.

***Confessions*, XIII, xxxviii. 53. Vol. I, p. 207.**

XXXIII D

1) But if we would know the immensity of His power we should not put these thoughts before our minds, nor should we conceive any precedence or priority between His intellect and his will; for the idea which we have of God teaches us that there is in Him only a single activity, entirely simple and entirely pure. This is well expressed by the words of St. Augustine: "They are so because Thou see'est them to be so"; because in God *seeing* and *willing* are one and the same thing.

To Mesland, 2 May 1644. CSMK III, p. 235.

XXXIV A

1) Universas autem creaturas suas, et spiritales et corporales, *non quia sunt ideo novit; sed ideo sunt quia novit. Non enim nescivit quae fuerat creaturus. Quia ergo scivit, creavit; non quia creavit, scivit.*

***De Trinitate*, XV, xiii, 22.**

2) Nos itaque ista quae fecisti videmus, quia sunt, tu autem quia vides ea, sunt. Et nos foris vidimus, quia sunt, et intus, quia bona sunt: tu autem ibi vidisti facta, ubi vidisti facienda.

***Confessiones*, XIII, xxxviii. 53.**

3) . . . cum voluntas tanti utique conditioris conditae rei cuiusque natura sit. . . . Sucut ergo non fuit inpossibile Deo, quas voluit instituere, sic ei non est inpossibile, in quidquid voluerit, quas instituit, mutare naturas.

***De Civitate Dei*, XXI, viii, 2, 5.**

XXXIV D

1) Pour les veritez éternelles, ie dis derechef que sunt tantum verae aut possibiles, quia Deus illas veras aut possibiles cognoscit, non autem contra veras à Deo cognosci quasi independenter ab illo sint verae (elles sont vraies ou possibles seulement parce que Dieu les connaît comme vraies ou possibles; mais, par contre, je dis pas qu'elles sont connues par Dieu comme vraies à la façon de vérités existant indépendamment de lui) . . . en Dieu ce n'est qu'un de vouloir & de connoistre; de sorte que ex hoc ipso quod aliquid velit, ideo cognoscit, & ideo tantum talis res est vera (de cela même qu'il veut quelque chose, il connaît par là cette chose, et par là seulement une telle chose est vraie).

A Mersenne, 6 mai 1630. AT I, 149

2) Car il est ceratin qu'il est aussi bien auteur de l'essence comme de l'existence de créatures: or cette essence n'est autre chose que ces vérités éternelles.

A Mersenne, 27 mai 1630. AT I, 151.

XXXIV A

1) And with respect to all His creatures, both spiritual and corporeal, He does not know them because they are, but they are because He knows them.

***On the Trinity*, XV, xiii, 22. Vol. III, p. 212.**

2) We therefore see those things which Thou madest, because they are; but they are because Thou seest they are.

***Confessions*, XIII, xxxviii. 53. Vol. I, p. 207.**

3) . . . the will of the great Creator assuredly is the nature of every created thing. . . . So, just as it was not impossible for God to set in being natures according to His will, so it is afterwards not impossible for Him to change those natures which He has set in being, in whatever way He chooses.

***The City of God*, XXI, viii, 2, 5, pp. 980–82. Cf. Letter 205 (*Patrologia Latina* XXXIII, p. 943ff). See also *Œuvres . . .*, vol. 37, note 40, p. 800.**

XXXIV D

1) As for the eternal truths, I say once more that *sunt tantum verae aut possibiles, quia Deus illas veras aut possibiles cognoscit, non autem contra veras à Deo cognosci quasi independenter ab illo sint verae (they are true or possible only because God knows them as true or possible. They are not known as true by God in any way which would imply that they are true independently of Him)*. . . . In God, willing and knowing are a single thing in such a way that *ex hoc ipso quod aliquid velit, ideo cognoscit, & ideo tantum talis res est vera* (by the very act of willing something He knows it and is only for this reason that such a thing is true).

To Mersenne, 6 May 1630. CSMK III, p. 24.

2) For it is certain that [God] is the author of the essence of created things no less than of their existence; and this essence is nothing other than the eternal truths.

To Mersenne, 27 May 1630. CSMK, III, p. 25.

XXXV A

1) Creatoris namque potentia et omnipotentis atque omnitenentis virtus, caussa subsistendi est omni creaturae; quae virtus ab eis, quae creata sunt, regendis, si aliquando cesseret, simul et illorum cesseret species, omnisque natura concideret. Neque enim sicut structor aedium cum fabricaverit, abscedit, atque, illo cessante atque abscedente, stat opus eius; ita mundus vel ictu oculi stare poterit, si ei Deus regimen sui subtraxerit.

***De Genesi ad litteram*, IV, xii, 22.**

XXXV D

1) [M]ais que, s'il y avoit quelques cors dans le monde, ou bien quelques inteligences, ou autres natures, qui ne fussent point toutes parfaites, leur estre devoit dependre de sa puissance, en telle sorte quelles ne pouvoient subsister sans luy un seul moment.

***Discours de la Méthode*, IV. AT VI, 35–36.**

2) Nec dubium est, si Deus cessaret a suo concursu, quin statim omnia quae creavit in nihilum essent abitura, quia, antequam creata essent & ipsis concursum suum praeberet, nihil erant.

A Hyperaspistes. Août 1641. AT III, 429.

XXVI A

1) Sed multum est ac difficillimum capare, quomodo dicatur, Deo non temporaliter jubente, neque id temporaliter audiente creatura, quae contemplatione veritatis omnia tempora excedit, sed intellectualitater sibimet impressas ab incommutabili Dei sapientia rationes, tanquam intelligibiles locutiones, in ea, quae infra sunt, transmittente, fieri temporales motus in rebus temporalibus vel formandis vel administrandis.

***De Genesi ad litteram*, I, ix, 17.**

XXVI D

1) [L]es verités mathematiques, lesquelles vous nommés eternelles, ont esté establies de Dieu & en dependent entieremant, aussy bien que tout le reste des creatures . . . & elles sont toutes *mentibus nostris ingenitae* (*innées en nos esprit*) ainsy qu'un Roy imprimeroit ses lois dans le cœur de tous ses sugets, s'il en avoit aussy bien le pouvoir.

A Mersenne, 15 avril 1630. AT I, 145.

XXXV A

1) For the power and might of the Creator, who rules and embraces all, makes every creature abide; and if this power ever ceased to govern creatures, their essences would pass away and all nature would perish. When a builder puts up a house and departs, his work remains in spite of the fact that he is no longer there. But the universe will pass away in the twinkling of an eye if God withdraws His ruling hand.

***The Literal Meaning of Genesis*, IV, xii, 22. Vol. I, p. 117.**

XXXV D

1) But if there were any bodies in the world, or any intelligences or other natures that were not wholly perfect, their being would have to depend on God's power in such a manner that they could not subsist for a single moment without Him.

***Discourse on the Method*, IV. CSM I, p. 129.**

2) There is no doubt that if God withdrew His concurrence, everything which He has created would immediately go to nothing.

To Hyperaspistes. August 1641. CSMK III, 193. Cf. St. Thomas, *Summa Theologica* Ia, Q. 104, 1.

XXVI A

1) God's decree is not pronounced in time, and it is heard, but not in time, by a creature that transcends all time in the contemplation of truth. But when this creature transmits to beings of a lower rank the forms (*rationes*) which are, so to speak, *intelligible utterances impressed upon its intellect by the unchangeable Wisdom of God*, then there can be movements in the temporal order in beings subject to time that are to be formed and governed.

***The Literal Meaning of Genesis*, I, ix, 17. Vol. I, pp. 28–29.**

XXVI D

1) The mathematical truths which you call eternal have been laid down by God and depend on Him entirely no less than the rest of His creatures . . . They are all *mentibus nostris ingenitae* (*inborn in our minds*) just as a king would imprint his laws on the hearts of all his subjects if he had enough power to do so.

To Mersenne, 15 April 1630. CSMK III, p. 23.

2) A. – [S]i tibi aliquis diceret numeros istos non ex aliqua sua natura, sed ex iis rebus quas sensu corporis attingamus impressos esse animo nostro quasi quasdam imagines quorumque visibilium; quod responderes? an tu quoque id putas.

– E. Nullo modo id putaverim: non enim si sensu corporis percepi numeros, idciro etiam rationem partitionis numerorum vel copulationis sensu corporis percipere potui. Hac enim luce mentis refello eum, quisquis vel in addendo vel in retrahendo dum computat falsam summam renuntiaverit.

***De libero arbitrio*, II, viii, 21.**

2) – A. *But suppose I were to tell you that these numbers have not been impressed upon our mind* by any nature of their own but come from things which we grasp with the bodily senses and were a kind of sense-image of things visible, how would you reply? Or would you also be of the same opinion?

– E. I could never think of such a thing. Even if I could perceive numbers by the bodily senses, I could not on this account also perceive the nature of numerical division and addition by the bodily sense. It is by the light of the mind that I show a man to be wrong whose computation indicates an incorrect total either in addition or subtraction.

***On Free Will*, II, viii, 21, pp. 129–30.**

The works of St. Augustine used in the formation of the Doctrine of Eternal Truths:

1. *On Christian Doctrine*, I, vi, 6.
2. *On Christian Doctrine*, I, vi, 6.
3. *The Confessions*, XIII, xxxviii. 53.
4. *On the Trinity*, XV, xiii, 22.
5. *The Confessions*, XIII, xxxviii. 53.
6. *The City of God*, XXI, viii, 2.
7. *The Literal Meaning of Genesis*, IV, xii, 22.
8. *The Literal Meaning of Genesis*, I, ix, 17.
9. *On Free Will*, II, viii, 21.

Seventh Part

Varia

SAINT AUGUSTINE

XXXVII A

1) Sed de omnipotentia eius, qua tot et tanta facit incredibilia, iam multa diximus. Si volunt invenire quod omnipotens non potest, habent prorsus, ego dicam: *mentiri non potest* . . . eique nos credere praedicenti, quem neque inpotentem neque mentientem possumus credere.

***De Civitate Dei*, XXII, xxv; XXI, v, 2.**

2) . . . si qui forte mihi dicerent: unde scis illos libros unius veri et veracissimi dei spiritu esse humano generi ministratos?

***De Civitate Dei*, XXI, v. 2, p. 973.**

DESCARTES

XXXVII D

1) Pour ceux qui disent que Dieu trompe continuellement les damnés, et qu'il nous peut aussi continuellement tromper, ils contredisent au fondement de la foi et de toute notre créance, qui est que *Deus mentiri non potest* ce qui est répété en tant de lieux dans saint Augustin, saint Thomas et autres, que je m'étonne que quelque théologien y contredise . . .

A Mersenne, 21 avril 1641. AT III, 359–60.

SAINT AUGUSTINE

XXXVIII A

1) In poenis autem malorum et inextinquibilis ignis et vivacissimus vernis ab allis atque aliis aliter atque aliter est expositus. Alii quippe utrumque ad corpus, alii utrumque ad animum retulerunt; alii proprie ad corpus ignem, tropice ad animum vermem, quod esse credibilius videtur.

***De Civitate Dei*, XX, xxii.**

DESCARTES

XXXVIII D

1) Et quamvis vulgo Theologi affirment damnatos igne inferni torqueri, non ideo tamen censent ipsos *decipi per falsam ideam ignis torquentis sibi a Deo inditam*, sed potius ab igne vere torqueri, quia . . .

***Sextae Responsiones*. AT VII, 428.**

SAINT AUGUSTINE

XXXVII A

1) As for God's omnipotence, I have said a great deal about this already. But if our friends want to discover something that the Almighty cannot do, here they have it: *God cannot lie!* . . . for we cannot believe that God is impotent, or that God is a liar.

***The City of God*, XXII, xxv, p. 1077; XXI, v, 2, p. 973. Cf. XXII, xxx.**

2) I ought to pay no attention to people who asked me how I could be sure that the Scriptures were delivered to mankind by the Spirit of the one true God who can tell no lie.

***The City of God*, XXI, v. 2, p. 973.**

DESCARTES

XXXVII D

1) Those who say that God continually deceives the damned, and that He might similarly be continually deceiving us, contradict the foundation of faith and all our belief, which is that *God cannot lie*. This is stated over and over again in so many places in St. Augustine, St. Thomas and others[1] that I am surprised that any theologian denies it.

To Mersenne, 21 April 1641. CSMK III, 179. Cf. *Sixth Set of Replies*, CSM II, 428.

XXXVIII A

1) In the punishment of the wicked, on the other hand, the unquenchable fire and the undying worm are differently explained by different authorities. Some people, in fact, refer both to the body; others refer both to the soul. Yet others refer the fire to the body in the literal sense, and this interpretation seems more credible.

***The City of God*, XX, xxii, p. 313.**

XXXVIII D

1) And although the theologians commonly say that the damned are tormented by the fires of hell, they are "deceived by the false idea of a tormenting fire which God has implanted in them"; rather they think that the damned are tormented by real fire.

***Sixth Set of Replies*. CSM II, 289.**

1 In a letter to Mersenne, December 1640 (AT III, 261; CSMK III, 161), Descartes says: "I shall look at St. Anselm at the first opportunity." In St. Anselm's *Proslogion*, VII, we read: "Or, if Thou canst not be corrupted, and canst not lie, nor make what is true, false . . ."

XXXIX A

1) Non ergo tunc simul omnia, et dies et nespera et mane, sed singillatim per ordinatem, quem scriptura commemorat. Au etiam tunc simul omnia, quoniam non secundum temporum moras, sicut siunt dies isti, cum oritur et occidit sol et in locum suum redit, ut rurus oriatur, sed secundum potentiam spiritualem mentis angelicae cuncta quae voluerit simul notitia conprehendente. . . . Mens vero angelica pura caritate inharens verbo Dei, posteaquam illo ordine creata est, ut praecederet cetera, prius ea vidit in verbo Dei facienda, quam facta sunt; si prius in eius fiebant cognitione, cum Deus dicebat, ut fierent, quam in sua propria natura: quae itidem facta in eis ipsis etiam cognovit minore utique notitia, quae respera dicta est . . .

***De Genesi ad litteram,* IV, xxxi. 48–xxxii. 49.**

2) Nunc, quoniam de sanctae civitatis exortu dicere institui et prius quod ad sanctos angelos adtinet dicendum putavi, quae huius civitatis et magna pars esret eo beatior, quod numquam peregrinata, quae hinc divina testimomia suppetant, quantum satis videbitur, Deo largiente explicare curabo. Ubi de mundi constitutione sacrae litterae loquuntur, non evidenter dicitur, utrum vel quo ordine creati sint angeli; sed si praetermissi non sunt,

XXXIX D

1) Quantum autem ad Genesin attinet, forsan illa creations narratio, quae ibi habetur, est metaphorica, ideoque Theologis relinquenda; nec tum sumi debet creatio tanquam sex diebus distincta, sed tantum hoc ob nostrum concipiendi modum ita distingui dicidebet, quemadmodum Augustinus per cogitationes Angelicas illa distinxit.

***Responsiones Renati Des Cartes Ad Quasdam Difficultates Ex Meditationibus Ejus.* 16 April 1648. AT V, 169.**

XXXIX A

1) . . . can we say that these three moments were simultaneous? They were not subject to the slow passage of time, as in the case of our days with the rising and setting of the sun and the return of the sun to the place of its rising. Day, evening, and morning at creation took place in the spiritual power of the minds of angels, who without any effort grasped at one and the same time all that they wished. . . . But the minds of angels, united to the Word of God in pure charity, created before the other works of creation, first saw in the Word of God those works to be made before they were actually made; and thus those works were first made in the angels' knowledge when God decreed that they should come into being, before they were made in their own proper natures.

***The Literal Meaning of Genesis*, IV, 49, vol. I, p. 139.**

2) I have undertaken to treat of the origin of the Holy City, and I have decided that I must first deal with the subject of the holy angels. They form the greater part of that City, and the more blessed part, in that they have never been on pilgrimage in a strange land; and I shall be at pains to explain, with God's aid, the information given on this subject in the inspired testimonies of Scripture, as far as shall seem sufficient. When

XXXIX D

1) As far as Genesis is concerned, however, the story of the creation to be found there is perhaps metaphorical, and so ought to be left to the theologians. In that case, the creation should not be taken as divided into six days, but the division into days should be taken as intended purely for the sake of our way of conceiving of things. This was the way Augustine proceeded when he made the divisions of the thoughts of angels.

***Conversation with Burman*, 16 April 1648. CSMK III, 349.**

vel caeli nomine, ubi dictum est: In principio fecit Deus caelum et terram, vel potius lucis huius, de qua loquor, significati sunt. Non autemesse praetermissos hinc existimo, quod scriptum est, requievisse Deum in die septimo ab omnibus operibus suis quae fecit, cum liber ipse ita sit exorsus: In principio fecit Deus caelum et terram; ut ante caelum et terram nihil aliud fecisse videatur. Cum ergo a caelo et terra coeperit, atque ipsa terra, quam primitus fecit, sicut scriptura consequenter eloquitur, invisibilis et incomposita nondumque luce facta utique tenebrae fuerint super abyssum, id est super quandam terrae et aquae indistinctam confusionem (ubi enim lux est, tenebrae sint necesse est), deinde omnia creando disposita sint, quae per sex dies consummata narrantur: quo modo angeli praetermitterentur, tamquam non essent in operibus Dei, a quibus in die septimo requievit? . . . non mihi videtur ab operibus Dei absurda sententia, si cum lux prima illa facta est, angeli creati intelleguntur, inter sanctos angelos et inmundos fuisse discretum, ubi dictum est: Et divisit Deus inter lucem et tenebras; et vocavit Deus lucem diem et tenebrasvocavit noctem. . . . Inter illam vero lucem, quae sancta societas angelorum est inlustrationes veritatis intellegibiliter fulgens, et ei contrarias tenebras, id est malorum angelorum aversorum a luce iustitiae aeterrimas

the sacred writings tell of the making of the world, there is no explicit statement about whether the angels were created, or in what order they were created. But if they were not passed over in the narrative, they were referred to either under the name of "heaven," when it is said that "in the beginning God created heaven and earth," or, more probably, under the name of the "light," about which I have been speaking.

I do not think that the angels were passed over, for this reason: that the Scripture says that God rested on the seventh day from all the works that he had done, while the whole book starts with the statement: "In the beginning God made heaven and the earth itself," which he made first, was, according to the next statement in Scripture, "invisible and disordered" and, because light had not yet been created, "darkness was over the abyss," that is, over a kind of confused and indistinct mass of land and water — because there must needs be darkness where light does not exist; then all things were set in order by God's creative act, all the things that, in the narrative, were completed in the course of the six days. How, then, could the angels have been passed over, as though they were not among those works from which God rested on the seventh day? . . . Although this is true, I do not think it would be out of harmony with the ways of God's working to suggest that, assuming the

mentes, ipse dividere potuit, cui etiam futurum non naturae, sed voluntatis malum occultum aut incertum esse nont potuit . . . angeli creati sunt, si eos recte lux illa primum facta significat aut illud potius caelum . . .

De Civitate Dei, **XI, ix–XI, xix; XII, xvi.**

XL A

1) cum vult intellegere vel divina vel Deum vel omnio etiam se ipsam suasque considerare virtutes, ut aliquid veri certique conprehendat, ab hac ipsorum quoque oculorum luce se avertat eamque ad hoc negotium non tantum nullo adivmento, verum etiam nonnullo inpedimento esse sentiens se in obtutum mentis adollat . . .

De Genesi ad litteram, **VII, xiv, 20.**

XL D

1) Quamvis enim jam ante dictum sit a multis, ad res Metaphysicas intelligendas mentem a sensibus esse abducendam . . .

Secundae Responsiones. **AT VII, 13**

creation of the first light to refer to the creation of the angels, the distinction between holy and the unclean angels is described in the passage, "And God divided the light from darkness: and God called the light 'Day'; and he called the darkness 'Night'. . . ." I am assuming that we are right in taking "first created light" a referring to them, or, more probably, in so interpreting "heaven" in the statement, "In the beginning God created heaven and earth." For the angels did not exist before they were made; otherwise these eternal beings would be thought to be co-eternal with God, if they are said to have existed always . . .

***The City of God*, XI, ix–XI, xix, pp. 438, 450; XII, xvi, 1, pp. 490–91. Cf. XII, xvi, 1–3.**

XL A

1) But the soul itself is of a different nature, so that when it wishes to understand the divine or God, or simply to understand itself and consider its own virtues, it turns away from this light of the eyes in order to have true and certain knowledge, and recognizing that this light is no help for its purpose, in fact is even something of an obstacle, it raises itself up to the vision of the mind.

***The Literal Meaning of Genesis*, VII, xiv, 20. Vol. II, p. 16. See also footnote 32 in *Oeuvres de saint Augustin*, vol. 48, pp. 701–4.**

XL D

1) Admittedly, many people had previously said that in order to understand metaphysical matters the mind must be drawn away from the senses . . .

***Second Set of Replies*. CSM II, 94.**

2) Namque aliud esse ipsam, aliud haec eius corporalia ministeria, vel vasa vel organa vel si quid aptius dici possunt, hinc evidenter elucet, quod plerumque se vehementi cogitationis intentione avertit ab omnibus, ut prae oculis patentibus recteque valentibus multa posita nesciat.

De Genesi ad Litteram, **VII, xix, 26.**

3) Cuius erroris maxima causa est, quod homo sibi ipse incognitus. Qui tamen ut se noscat, magna opus habet consuetudine recendi a sensibus et animum in se ipsumconligendi atque in se ipso retinendi. Quod hi tantum adsequuntur, qui plagas quasdam opinionum, quas vitae cotidianae cursus infligit, aut solitudine invurunt aut liberalibus medicant disciplinis. Ita enim sibi animus redditus, quae sit pulchritudo universitatis, intellegit, quae profecto ab uno cognominata est idciroque illam videre non licet animae, quae in multa procedit sectarque aviditate animae, quae in multa procedit sectaturque aviditate pauperim, quam nescit sola segregatione multitudinis posse vitari. Multitudinem autem non hominum dico, sed omnium quae sensus adtingit.

De Ordine, **I, i–ii.**

2) We must distinguish the soul itself from its corporeal agents, whether vessels or organs or whatever else they may be called. The difference is evident from the fact that the soul is frequently concentrated in thought and turns itself away from everything, so that it is ignorant of many things which are present before the eyes when they are wide open and able to see.

***The Literal Meaning of Genesis*, VII, xix, 26. Vol. II, p. 20.**

3) The chief cause of this error is that man does not know himself. Now, for acquiring this self-knowledge, he needs a constant habit of withdrawing from things of the senses and of concentrating his thought within himself, and holding it there. This they alone succeed in doing who definitely mark out in solitude the impressions of opinion which the course of daily life has made, or correct them by means of the liberal branches of learning.

When the soul has returned to itself in this manner, it understands what is the beauty of the universe; this term is evidently derived from the word *unum* (*one*). Wherefore, the beholding of oneness is not granted to that soul which wanders toward many objects and eagerly pursues mental beggary, which, though it does not know it, it can only be avoided by keeping aloof from the multitude; and I mean, not just the

multitude of men, but of all things that the senses reach.

***On Order*, I, i–ii, p. 241.**

Works of St. Augustine cited in Varia.

1. *The City of God*, xxv.
2. *The City of God*, XXII, xxv.
3. *The City of God*, XXII, xxv.
4. *The Literal Meaning of Genesis*, IV, xxxi. 48–xxxii. 49.
5. *The City of God*, XI, ix—XI, xix; XII, xvi, 1.
6. *The Literal Meaning of Genesis*, VII, xiv, 20.
7. *The Literal Meaning of Genesis*, VII, xix, 26.
8. *On Order*, XII, xii, 26.
9. *On Order*, I, i–ii, 26.

Commentary

I

The question which naturally arises concerns the direct and real influence of St. Augustine on Descartes: had Descartes read the works of St. Augustine and did he use them in developing his metaphysics? To answer this question let us begin with another one: why did Descartes entitle his principal work, devoted to first philosophy (*philosophia prima*), "The Meditations"? With the exception of Marcus Aurelius's *Meditations*, the title is without precedent in the history of European thought.[1] According to Henri Brémond, "It was Cardinal Pierre de Bérulle [1575–1629] who established the meditative form in France, where it remained popular for many centuries to come."[2] According to other scholars, the *Spiritual Exercises* of St. Ignatius might have suggested the meditative structure to Descartes.[3] Without denying the influence of Cardinal de Bérulle nor that of St. Ignatius on Descartes (although the degree of this influence is not easy to determine), it must be said that these two explanations are not sufficient. They take into account merely the formal character of the *Meditations*, i.e., the similarity of structure between the

1 In the *Preface* to his *Proslogium*, St. Anselm says: "In my judgment, neither this work nor the other, which I mentioned above, deserved to be called a book, or to bear the name of an author; and yet I thought they ought not to be sent forth without some title by which they might, in some sort, invite one into whose hands they fell to their perusal. I accordingly gave each a title, that the first might be known as *An Example of Meditation on the Grounds of Faith*, and its sequel as, *Faith Seeking Understanding*." In 1597 Bacon published a short work entitled *Meditationes Sacræ* (vol. VII, 231–54).

2 Henri Brémond, *Histoire littéraire du sentiment religieux en France* (Paris: Librairie Bloud et Gay, 1925), vol. III, p. 110.

3 See Z. Vendler, "Descartes' Exercises," *Canadian Journal of Philosophy*, 19, 1989, pp. 193–224. Cf. Arthur Thomson, "Ignace de Loyola et Descartes: L'influence des exercices spirituels sur les œuvres philosophiques de Descartes," *Archives de Philosophie* 35 (1972), pp. 61–85.

4 For example, Z. Vendler identified the passages in the *Meditations* that have their

Exercises of St. Ignatius and the *Meditations*.[4] They consider meditations simply as a spiritual form, widespread in Descartes's time, and suppose that he might have been influenced by its popularity to choose it as the literary genera for his work. But this does not explain the connection between meditations and "first philosophy." What, then, made Descartes choose the meditative form for a work of first philosophy?

In the *Second Set of Responses to the Meditations*, Descartes explains the link between meditations and philosophy:

> Many people had previously said that in order to understand metaphysical matters the mind must be drawn away from the senses (*mentem a sensibus esse abducendam*); but no one, so far as I know, had shown how this could be done. The correct, and in my view unique method of achieving this is contained in my Second Meditation. But the nature of the method is such that scrutinizing it just once is not enough. Protracted and repeated study is required to eradicate the lifelong habit of confusing things related to the intellect with corporeal things, and to replace it with the opposite habit of distinguishing the two; this will take at least a few days to acquire.[5]

Descartes first mentions "the method" eleven years earlier in his correspondence with Mersenne. In his letter of April 15, 1630, Descartes tells Mersenne that he has discovered a "method" that permits him "to demonstrate mathematical truths in a manner more evident than the truths of geometry."[6] A year later, during the summer of 1630, Descartes returns to this topic in a letter to Villebressieu: in order to acquire knowledge of God and the soul, Descartes explains, one needs to "detach the mind from the senses."[7] In other

counterparts in the *Exercises*. See his "Descartes' Exercises," *Canadian Journal of Philosophy* 19 (1989), pp. 193–224.

5 *Responses to the Second Set of Objections* (AT, VII, 131; CSM II, 94).

6 To Mersenne, 15 April 1630 (AT I, 144; CSMK III, 22). Cf. letter to Mersenne, 25 November 1630 (AT I, 182; CSMK III, 29).

7 In his letter to [Silhon], May 1637, (AT I, 353; CSMK III, 55) Descartes does not use the expression "detachment" of the spirit from the body, but the idea is the same: "If you spend a sufficient time on this meditation, you acquire by degrees a very clear, dare I say intuitive, notion of intellectual nature in general. This is the idea which, if considered without limitation, represents God, and if limited, is the idea of an angel or a human soul." Cf. *Discourse on Method* (AT VI, 37; CSMI, 129); *Meditations* (AT VII, 12; CSM II, 9); letter to Mersenne, 27 February 1637 (AT I, 350; CSMK III, 53: "in my view they [the reasons concerning the existence of God] are obscure only for those who cannot *abducere mentem a sensibus*."); to Vatier, 22 February 1638 (AT I, 560; CSMK III, 86); to Reneri for Pollot, April or May 1638 (AT II, 37–38; CSMK III, 98).

words, in the "pre-philosophical state," we are under the influence of "our appetites and passions"; we are like children who imagine "the stars being very small . . . although astronomical arguments clearly show us that they are large indeed."[8] But "In later years the mind is no longer a total slave to the body."[9] Thus the task of philosophy consists in liberating one's soul from the influence of the passions of the body[10] by means of "long exercises and often repeated meditations."[11] In this way meditations, originally a form of reli-

8 *Principles*, I, article 72. There is a similar idea in St. Thomas. "In part, the above opinion arises from the custom by which from their earliest days people are brought up to hear and to call upon the name of God. Custom, and especially custom in a child, comes to have the force of nature. As a result, what the mind is steeped in from childhood, it clings to very firmly as something known naturally and self-evidently" (*Summa Contra les Gentiles*, I, 11[1]), and: "The second awkward effect is that those who would come to discover the abovementioned truth would barely reach it after a great deal of time. The reasons are several. There is the profundity of this truth, which the human intellect is made capable of grasping by natural inquiry only after a long training. Then there are many things that must be presupposed, as we have said. There is also the fact that, in youth, when the soul is swayed by the various movements of the passions, it is not in a suitable state for the knowledge of such lofty truth" (*Ibid*. I, 4).

9 *Principles*, I, article 72. According to Henri Gouhier, the idea of childhood in Descartes is a counterpart of Original Sin: "But for Plato this union is a sign of a fall, the soul is no longer by itself, its body is its prison. For Descartes, this union is in conformity with the order of nature and the early years of this union condemn the soul to imprisonment. Both here and there is the scandal of the human condition. In the eyes of Plato man begins with the sensible world; in the eyes of Descartes man begins with being an infant. . . . The mission of philosophy is to substitute man for infant . . . it is not history that assures the passage from infancy to adult age, but philosophy insofar as it is opposed to history. . . . The point is to get rid of 'the old man,' who in the Cartesian vision of the universe is nothing but an aged infant." "Le refus du symbolism dans l'humanisme Cartésien d'une philoophie sans rhétorique," in *Atti Congresso internationale di studi umanistici, Venezia, 1954* (Roma: Fratelli Bocca Editori, 1955), pp. 89–90. And: "Why is infancy a species of Original Sin in the order of cognition? Because it is the period in our lives during which our appetites govern us. The Spirit of a child is taken up by what it senses and its first judgments are dictated by sensations without the control of the intellect. . . . The age of reason arrives very late. This is the scandal of the human condition; it is scandalous that being reasonable commences with not being that which one is." "Le refus du symbolisme dans l'humanisme Cartésien," *Archivo di Filosofia* (1958), p. 71.

10 "In order to philosophize seriously and search out the truth about all the things that are capable of being known, we must first of all lay aside all our preconceived opinions, or at least we must take the greatest care not to put our trust in any of the opinions accepted by us in the past until we have first scrutinized them afresh and confirmed their truth." *Principles*, I, article 75.

11 A***, March 1638 (AT II, 37; CSMK III, 98).

gious exercise *par excellence*,[12] are transformed by Descartes into a method that gave rise to the *philosophie nouvelle*; and on this foundation Descartes builds his physics to "make us masters and proprietors of nature."[13]

In the same letter to Villebressieu (1631), Descartes makes a reference to a meeting that took place in the residence of the papal nuncio, Cardinal Bagui, in November 1628,[14] during which, as Descartes reminds his friend, he had already talked about his "fine rule or method."[15] Then, on July 18, 1629, Descartes wrote to the Oratorian Guillaume Gibieuf to inform him that he just had begun writing "a little treatise"[16] on Divinity.[17] So it seems that by

12 See Henri Brémond, *Histoire littéraire du sentiment religieux en France, ibid.*, vol. VIII ("La métaphysique des saints"). Cf. *L'inquiétitude religieuse* (Paris: Librairie Academic Perrin, 1932).

13 *Discourse on Method* (AT VI, 62; CSM I, 142–43).

14 Adrien Baillet in his biography of Descartes remarks: "Cardinal [de Bérulle], having no difficulty in recognizing the importance of the project, and judging it to be worthy of carrying out, he used his authority over Descartes's conscience to make sure that he undertake it. He made him realize that since God gave him intellectual powers, which He did not give to others, he should be aware that he would be answerable to this supreme judge of men for the wrong he would be doing in depriving men of the fruits of his meditations. He went so far as to assure him that with intentions so pure and intellectual powers so great, he would have God's blessing and God would certainly assure his success." *La vie de Monsieur Descartes* (Paris: La Table Ronde, 1946), pp. 73–74.

15 "You saw these two results of my fine rule or natural method in the discussion which was forced on me in the presence of the Papal Nuncio, Cardinal de Bérulle, Father Mersenne and all the great and learned company assembled at the Nuncio's palace to hear M. de Chandoux lecture about his new philosophy. I made the whole company recognize what power the art of right reasoning has over the minds of those who have no learning beyond the ordinary, and how much better founded, and more true and natural, my principles are than any of those which are currently received in the learned world. You were as convinced as everybody else, and you were all good enough to beg me to put them in writing and publish them." To Villebressieu, Summer 1631 (AT I, 213; CSMK III, 32).

Professor Richard Watson suggested to me that the letter to Villebressieu, or at least the part I just quoted, might not be authentic, but was written by Clerselier. The first thing that is striking about this letter is that it is written in a triumphant tone, as though Descartes already gained victory over the Schoolmen. Given the fact that in 1631 Descartes has not published anything, his enthusiasm would seem to be unfounded. If Villebressieu had been present during this meeting, why would Descartes remind him about the meeting in such a detailed way, unless the purpose of it was to create the impression on the reader that the official "sponsorship" of Descartes's project should go to the Oratorians. (Cf. Baillet's account of the same meeting, footnote 14 above.)

16 "I expect to put you to some trouble when I complete a little treatise that I am starting. I would not have told you it was under way unless I feared that the length of time

the time Descartes wrote to Gibieuf, the method, or, rather, its germ, had already been in existence at least since November 1628.

Let us now turn to the three famous letters of 1630 to Mersenne, in which Descartes explains the "fruits" of his method. In the first letter (15 April 1630), he states that eternal truths have been established by God and depend entirely on him: "to say that these truths are independent of God is to talk of Him as if He were Jupiter or Saturn and subject Him to the Styx and the Fates."[18] God is like a king who establishes laws in his kingdom; these laws, Descartes adds, are "*mentibus nostris ingenitæ* [innate in our minds] just as a king would imprint his laws on the hearts of all his subjects."

In the second letter (6 May 1630), Descartes says that eternal truths

> are true or possible only because God knows them as true or possible. They are not known as true by God in any way that would imply that they are true independently of Him. If men really understood the sense of their words they could never say without blasphemy that the truth of anything is prior to the knowledge God has of it. In God, willing and knowing are a single thing such that by the very fact of willing something he knows it . . . for the existence of God is the first and the most eternal of all possible truths and the one from which alone all others proceed.

And he adds:

> It is easy to be mistaken about this because most people do not regard God as a being who is infinite and beyond our grasp, the sole author on whom all things depend; they stick to the syllables of His name and think it sufficient knowledge of Him to know that "God" means what is meant by *Deus* in Latin and what is adored by men. Those who have no higher thoughts than these can easily become atheists; and because they perfectly comprehend mathematical truths and do not perfectly comprehend the truth of God's existence, it is no wonder they do not think the former depend on the latter.

it needs would make you forget your promise to correct it and give it the finishing touches; for I do not expect to complete it within two or three years, and perhaps in the end I shall decide to burn it, or at least not to let it out of my hands or those of my friends without giving it careful scrutiny. If I am not clever enough to produce something worth while, I shall at any rate try to be astute enough not to publish my shortcomings." To Gibieuf, 18 July 1629 (AT I, 17; CSMK III, 5–6).

17 To Mersenne, 15 April 1630 (AT I, 137; CSMK III, 23).

18 On the Jupiterian metaphor, see J.-L. Marion, *Questions cartésiennes II* (Paris: PUF, 1997), pp. 119–41.

Finally, in the third letter (27 May 1630), Descartes gives a definition of an eternal truth: "it is certain that he is the author of the essence of created things no less than of their existence; and this essence is nothing other than the eternal truths."[19] Whence he concludes: "if God did not exist these truths would nevertheless be true."[20]

The two questions raised here by Descartes are two sides of the same coin: on the one side, the relationship between the existence of God and that of truth; on the other, atheism as a threat to the existence of truth. Let us approach the first problem by comparing Aquinas's conception of God with that of Descartes as it emerges in the letters to Mersenne.[21]

For Aquinas, "God is of an infinite simplicity" (*Deus infinitatae simplicitatis est*).[22] However, despite the fact that God's nature is absolutely simple,[23] it is possible to make a distinction between intelligence, will, and power (*Sed haec omnia [intellectus, voluntas, vis] in Deo unum sunt*).[24] God, Aquinas says, "acts with a view to an end," and an agent acting for an end "must act by intellect and will."[25] "The will has for its object a good"[26]; intellect determines the will "by proposing its proper object, which is an end."[27] In other words, God is like an archer who directs the flight of the arrow "to a definite target . . . ; [since] God is the first agent, He acts not through any necessity of

19 To Mersenne, 27 May 1630 (AT I, 151; CSMK III, 25).

20 To Mersenne, 6 May 1630 (AT I, 150; CSMK III, 25). For a long time, Descartes commentators had been trying to identify the adversary of Descartes. According to E. Gilson it is Duns Scotus: "*si poneretur, per impossibile, quod Deus non esset, et quod triangulus esset, adhuc tres angulas resolveretur ut in natura trianguli*"; *Ordinatio, Prologus,* p. 2, q. 3, n. 98, [2] 16). Jean-Luc Marion has convincingly demonstrated that it is Suarez. For two passages in Suarez to which Descartes is responding, see Marion's *Sur la théologie blanche de Descartes* (Paris: PUF, 1981), pp. 59–62. See also Timothy Cronin, "Eternal Truths in the Thought of Descartes and of his Adversary," in *Journal of the History of Ideas*, 21, 1960. Most recently the relationship between Suarez and Descartes was analyzed by Claudia Lorena García, "The Falsity of Non-Judgmental Cognitions in Descartes and Suarez," in *The Modern Schoolman* 77, no. 3 (2000).

21 For Descartes's opposition to Suarez, see Jean-Luc Marion, *ibid.,* chap. IV. See also Timothy J. Cronin, *Objective Being in Descartes and Suarez* (Rome: Gregorian University Press, 1966); and "Eternal Truths in the Thought of Descartes and of his Adversary," in *Journal of the History of Ideas* 21 (1960).

22 *Summa Contra Gentiles,* I, 26.

23 *Summa Contra Gentiles,* I, 10.

24 *Summa Theologica,* Ia, Q. 19 Art. 5. Cf. Art. 2. According to Descartes "there is in God an absolute immensity, simplicity and unity which embraces all other attributes." *Responses to the Second Set of Objections* (AT VII, 137; CSM II, 98).

25 *Summa Contra Gentiles,* II, 23.

26 *Summa Contra Gentiles,* II, 23.

27 *Summa Contra Gentiles,* I, 72.

His nature, but through His intellect and will."[28] Because goodness is being, Aquinas goes on, and intelligence can will only that which is good, and because that which is good is also that which is not contradictory, God always wants that which is not contradictory. In short, the goodness of creation consists in its rationality. That God always acts rationally "[is] evident from the fact that the universe is not the result of chance, but is ordered towards good."[29] In other words, that God is a being who possesses will and intellect is evident from the fact that we can find His traces in the world: otherwise the ontological proof that leads from the creation to the creator would be impossible.

In casting doubt on the existence of the external world, Descartes excludes the possibility of construing a cosmological proof for the existence of God and by the same token of any knowledge concerning the origin of the world. To this Descartes could reply that although it is true that in his system one cannot determine whether the world originated by chance or was created by God, insofar as the human cognitive apparatus is part of the world, there must be a difference between the cognitive apparatus of a creature created by God and a creature that came into being by chance.[30] The difference is that the creature that originated by chance is subject to error as a matter of course.

28 *Summa Contra Gentiles*, II, 23 [5].

29 *Summa Contra Gentiles*, II, 23 [5].

30 Descartes's argument in the First Meditation suggests that this problem was not alien to him: "the less powerful they make my original cause, the more likely it is that I am so imperfect as to be deceived all the time" (*quo minus potentem originis meae authorem assignabunt, eo probabilius erit me tam imperfectum esse ut semper fallar*. AT VII, 21; CSM II, 14). Note that in this argument, he takes into account only the human cognitive apparatus, not the world as such. Furthermore, according to this argument, there is a (direct?) relationship between the cognitive apparatus of a creature, that owes its origin to chance, and the one which was created by God. Given that perfection does not consist in absolute cognitive infallibility, the question arises: do we have a means to "measure" this difference? To put it differently, given that God endowed us with nature which goes wrong "sometimes" (AT VII, 21), what is the difference between this nature and one that originated by chance? The question is extremely complicated, and Descartes seems to avoid it in his responses. The first response: "I cannot therefore deny that there may in some way be more perfection in the universe as a whole because some of its parts are not immune from error, while others are immune, than there would be if all the parts were exactly alike" (*Sed non ideo possum negare quin major quodammodo perfectio sit in tota rerum universitate, quod quadem ejus partes ab erroribus immunes non sint, aliae vero sint, quam si omnes plane similes essent*. Med. IV. AT VII, 61; CSM II, 42). The second response: "It is quite clear from all this that, notwithstanding the immense goodness of God, the nature of man as a combination of mind and body is such that it is bound to mislead him from time to time" (*Ex quibus omnio manifestum est, non obstante immensa Dei bonitate, naturam hominis ut ex mente & corpore*

Aquinas would not be entirely satisfied by such a response. The Scholastic order signifies a harmony of beings,[31] at the top of which is God; in Descartes's philosophy, order signifies a system of physical laws that rule the Cartesian *extensio*. "The world of St. Thomas remains populated by beings," says Etienne Gilson, "as it is in the case of the world of Aristotle; our science concerns *that which is*, and our supreme science, metaphysics, concerns by the same token the knowledge of that which is being as being."[32] To paraphrase Gilson, the world of Descartes is populated by machines; our supreme science, physics, concerns knowledge of physical laws.[33]

But is Descartes's conception of the world – defined as an agglomeration of matter subject to physical laws – the result of casting doubt on the existence of the external world, or rather of a conception of God as being without will or intellect? To put it differently: which comes first? Does the method of Universal Doubt follow from Descartes's conception of God, or vice versa? As the passage from *Summa Contra Gentiles* cited above makes clear, for Aquinas the fact that we can detect order in the universe implies the existence of a Creator who has both will and intellect. If this is the case, it seems that Descartes's conception of the universe, defined as an agglomeration of matter subject to the laws of physics, is the result of blurring the distinction between these two divine attributes. In introducing a non-Scholastic conception of God, Descartes not only created a different conception of the world, but also destroyed the Scholastic harmony of beings.[34]

compositi non posse non aliquando esse fallacem. AT VII, 88; CSM II, 61). These two responses are totally different. The first one is an analysis of human cognitive fallibility from the point of view of the totality of creation (Cf. St. Thomas, *Summa Contra Gentiles*, I, 70 [4]; St. Augustine, *On Free Will*, III, xi, 32); the other, from the point of view of the union of body and soul._

31 "There would not be a perfect likeness of God in the universe if all things were of one grade of being. For this reason, then, is there distinction among created things." St. Thomas, *Summa Contra Gentiles*, II, 45 [3].

32 Etienne Gilson, *L'être et l'essence* (Paris: Vrin, 1994), pp. 121–22.

33 For the transformation of metaphysics by Descartes, see Férdinand Alquié, *La Découverte métaphysique de l'homme chez Descartes*, Paris: PUF, 1950; Jean Laporte, *Le rationalisme de Descartes* (Paris: PUF, 1950), pp. 339–419; Vincent Carraud, "Descartes appartient-il à l'histoire de la métaphysique?" in *Lire Descartes Aujourd'hui*, Actes publié par Olivier Depré et Danielle Lories (Louvain-Paris: Bibliotèque Philosophique de Louvain, 47, 1997), pp. 153–71.

34 Several of Descartes's contemporaries were well aware of this transformation. Pascal's *chiquenaude* is probably the most famous expression of this anti-Cartesian sentiment: "I cannot for give Descartes: in his whole philosophy he would like to do without God; but he could not help allowing him a flick of the fingers to set the world in motion; after that he had no more use for God." "God created the world for two

According to Aquinas, there is another reason for thinking that God acts rationally: although divine reason is infinitely greater than that of man,[35] the principle of non-contradiction applies both to man and to God. Consequently, we know *a priori* that there are things that God cannot do. "It appears that the will of God cannot be of things that are impossible in themselves. For these have a contradiction in themselves, for example that man is an ass,[36] in which the rational and the irrational are included. For what is incompatible with something excludes some of the things that are necessary to it, as to be an ass excludes man's reason. . . . That which is of itself impossible is not an object of the intellect, because it is self-contradictory. . . . Therefore, that which is of itself impossible cannot be the object of the will."[37]

Nothing would have appeared to Descartes more "blasphemous" than such a conception of God. As Descartes explained to Mersenne in 1630, to subject God to human criteria, such as the criteria of rationality, "is to talk of him as if He were Jupiter or Saturn and to subject Him to the Styx and the Fates." The God of Descartes is not the archer of Aquinas (*nam sagittae motus est*), nor is he Ockham's "rational creator" (*Deus est rationabiliter operans*).[38] He is "a being who is infinite and beyond our grasp . . . whose power surpasses the bounds of human understanding . . ." He has neither intellect nor

reasons . . . one, to provide an idea of his greatness, the other to depict invisible things in the visible. M. Descartes has destroyed the one as well as the other." "The sun is a lovely piece of work," one says to him. "Not at all," he replies, "it is a mass of metal filings." . . . "The world is so big that one can get lost in it," he says, "but I regard it as a set of numbers." ". . . Descartes is like a thief who has killed another thief [Aristotle] and taken his booty from him." Le Maistre de Sacy, *Conversation with Fontaine*. And: "One can say that Cartesian philosophy in attempting to account for all the wonders of Nature in terms of simple movements, it narrows and limits, so to speak, the grandeur of the works of God, and it diminishes the admiration which one should have for them. This admiration is one of the principle exercises of piety, and one of the least of the ordinary ways to elevate oneself to know and love God," Du Vaucel.

35 *Summa Contra Gentiles*, I, 82.

36 *Summa Contra Gentiles*, I, 84.

37 *Summa Contra Gentiles*, I, 84. Cf. *Ibid.* I, 29 [2–3].

38 "Cuius ratio est quia, secundum beatum Augustinum ubi supra, propter hoc praecise ponendae sunt idea in Deo, quia Deus est rationbiliter operans. . . . Et quia illas aspicit in producendo, ideo dicitur rationabiliter operans quia perfecte scit, non tantum in univesali sed etiam in particulari et distinctissime, quid operatur. . . . Et ex hoc ipso quod Deus est Deus, Deus cognoscit omnia. Nec esset rationabiliter operans nisi cognosceret illa quae operatur." Guillemi de Ockham, *Scriptum in Librum Primum Sententiarum Ordinatio*, Liber I, Distinctio 35, Questio V. *Opera Philosophica et Theologica*. Editerunt Girardus I. Etzkorn et Franciscus E. Kelley (New York: St. Bonaventure University, 1979), vol. IV, *Opera Theologica.*, pp. 492, 504, 506.

will: in God, as Descartes says, quoting St. Augustine – against Aquinas[39] and Suarez – *velle* and *videre* are one and the same thing. "In God, willing, understanding and creating are all the same thing without one being prior to the other *ne quidem ratione* (*even conceptually*)."[40] Whereas for Aquinas "God acts by His intellect. But the intellect does not produce an effect except by means of the will . . . God acts by His will, not of natural necessity."[41] The *modus operandi* of Descartes's God is that of supreme legislator or absolute monarch. The act of creating eternal truths by imprinting them on man's mind is analogous to the act of laying down laws in a kingdom. God is the absolute sovereign who does not need to explain to His subjects why He has established some laws rather than others. Aquinas's God, unlike Descartes's, rules like a constitutional monarch. Because His actions must conform to the principle of non-contradiction, the laws in the Scholastic kingdom are intelligible to his subjects. They are like traces the king left on purpose so that his subjects can know that he exists and know his nature.[42] Descartes, on the contrary, thinks that the less the subjects know about the king the better, "provided of course that they do not get the idea that they have no king – they must know him enough to be in no doubt about that."[43]

Descartes no doubt considered his conception of God to have a certain

39 In the letter to Mersenne (25 December 1639; AT II, 630) Descartes writes: "I have here a *Summa* of St. Thomas and the Bible that I brought from France." Which *Summa* does Descartes have in mind? *Summa Theologica* or *Summa Contra Gentiles*? Numerous expressions in *Summa Contra Gentiles* suggest that Descartes read *Summa Contra Gentiles*. See Appendix I.

In his letter to Mersenne, 27 May 1630 (AT I, 152; CSMK III, 25), Descartes says: "I do not conceive them [eternal truths] as *emanating* from God like rays from the sun . . ." In *Summa Contra Gentiles*, III, 65, we read: "Furthermore, there are two positions regarding the origin of things: one, from faith . . . and the position of certain philosophers [Cf. Ibid., II, 31ff], that things have *emanated* from God eternally (. . . *res ab æterno a Deo fluxerunt*)." If Descartes took the idea of "emanation" from Aquinas, he must have read *Summa Contra Gentiles* before 1630. Also, the three divine actions – "willing, understanding and producing" – are the same which Aquinas lists in *Summa Contra Gentiles*, II, 10 [2]. See footnote 40 below.

40 To Mersenne, 27 May 1630 (AT I, 153; CSMK III, 25–26). In the *Summa Contra Gentiles*, II, 10 [2], Aquinas says: "From the foregoing it is clear, also, that the multifarious actions attributed to God, as understanding, willing, producing things, and the like are not diverse realities, since each of these actions in God is His very being, which is one and the same."

41 *Summa Contra Gentiles*, II, 23 [4].

42 St. Thomas, *Summa Contra Gentiles*, I, 4. Cf. E. Gilson, "The Essence of God," in *Elements of Christian Metaphysics* (Westport, Conn.: Greenwood Press, 1960), pp. 104–35.

43 To Mersenne, 15 April 1630 (AT I, 145; CSMK III, 23).

advantage over that of the Scholastics.[44] But what exactly did this advantage consist of? The core of Descartes's conception is the following: if God does not exist, the eternal verities would not be true, where the word "true" must be taken to mean "true in the absolute sense." That is why, according to Descartes, atheism inevitably leads to the rejection of the concept of Truth. The Scholastic solution clearly does not satisfy him. According to Aquinas, the eternal truths are necessary or true because they are part of the Divine mind, which is eternal.[45] Because the Scholastic proofs for the existence of God demonstrate merely that the object of faith is not contradictory,[46] an atheist can reject the existence of God without thereby denying the objective validity of mathematical verities or Truth as such.

Descartes's argument against atheists is as follows: if one conceives of God as the author of the very *nature* of mathematical truths, one cannot say that it is intrinsically or absolutely necessary that two plus two make four or that all radii of a circle be equal: if two plus two makes four and the radii of a circle are equal, it is only because God ordained them to be such.[47] In other words, because the concept of logical necessity is not a property of mathematical objects, let alone of human reason,[48] but rather of God, on whose existence everything depends, to deny the existence of God is to deny the intrinsic validity of mathematics, which is a paradigm of certitude. If there is no God, the eternal verities are nothing but rules that govern our cognitive processes; we can ascribe no objective validity to them.

Descartes returned to this question in 1641, in the *Responses to the Meditations*. This time his formulation of 1630 takes the form of a polemic against atheists:

44 Descartes never overtly criticized the Scholastics, let alone St. Thomas. However, in a letter to Voetius, he makes it clear that in contrast to St. Thomas's proofs for the existence of God, which can be considered of little value, his are "better." May 1643 (AT VIII, 176; CSMK III, 223).

45 St. Thomas, *Summa Theologica*, Ia, Q. 16, 7. "Il ne suffit pas de répondre avec le divin Thomas . . . dit Suarez, que, sans existence, ces énonciations ne sont vraies que dans l'entendement divin, mais non en soi," "il ne suffit pas dire que, ôtée l'existence des choses, cette connexion ne demeure que dans l'*exemplar* divin . . . , au sens de divin Thomas." *Disputatio Metaphysica*, XXXI, s. 12, n. 40, [1] 26, 294, et n. 46, [1] 26, 297–98. Citation after Marion, *op. cit.*, p. 44.

For Suarez's, and Vasques's criticism of the position of Thomas on this point, see Jean-Luc Marion, *Sur la théologie blanche de Descartes* (Paris: PUF, 1981), pp. 43–69. For a different position of Descartes's anti-Thomism, see my *Cartesian Theodicy, Descartes' Quest for Certitude* (Dordrecht: Kluwer Academic Publishers, 2000), pp. 86–97.

46 E. Gilson, *Elements of Christian Metaphysics* (Westport, Conn.: Greenwood Press, 1960).

47 *Responses to the Sixth Set of Objections* (AT VII, 436; CSM II, 294).

48 *Responses to the Second Set of Objections* (AT VII, 436; CSM II, 294).

> The fact that an atheist can be "clearly aware that the three angles of a triangle are equal to two right angles" is something I do not dispute. But I maintain that this awareness of his is not true knowledge. Now because we are supposing that this individual is an atheist, he cannot be certain that he is not being deceived on matters that seem to him to be very evident (as I fully explained). And although this doubt may not occur to him, it can still crop up if someone else raises the point or if he looks into the matter himself. So he will never be free of this doubt until he acknowledges that God exists (*Second Set of Replies*, AT VII, 141; CSM II, 101).[49]

The Cartesian definition of science as a conviction that cannot be shaken is a repetition of a fragment of *The Magnitude of the Soul*, XXX, 58 (p. 125):

> A. —When I asked you whether everything that one is aware of is known, you answered in the affirmative, without thinking.
> E.— What, then, would you have me say?
> A.—That knowledge is not had simply because one is aware of something, but only because that awareness results from an exercise of reason. For, if that awareness comes through the body, that is sensation; if the awareness is direct, that is said to be an experience of the body. Do you not know that some philosophers, and very good thinkers, too, thought that not even what is grasped by the mind is worthy of the name knowledge unless that comprehension is so firm that the mind cannot be moved from it by any argument?

Accordingly, "my" subjective feeling that something is evident cannot have any claims to Truth. Because human reason is not reliable, Truth must have its foundation in a Being that exists necessarily. This is the meaning of the expression "*Si Deus non esset, nihilominus istae veritates essent verae.*"

Let us now turn to the second question. What is the relationship between atheism and the existence of Truth? As I stress above, according to Descartes the existence of Truth depends on the existence of God. Accordingly, in denying the existence of God, an atheist also denies the existence of Truth. On this view, atheism is not only a moral fault but first and foremost a logical one, rooted in a misunderstanding of the idea of God ("Those who have no higher thoughts than these can easily become atheists"; 6 May 1630) Now, if atheism is a logical fault, the remedy for it must be sought in reason itself. This is what Descartes does in the *Meditations*.[50] He points out to atheists, "by philo-

49 *Responses to the Second Set of Objections* (AT VII, 436; CSM II, 294).

50 "I have always thought that two topics – namely God and the soul – are prime examples of subjects where demonstrative proofs ought to be given with the aid of philos-

sophical arguments," that God exists and that the soul is immortal, and he asks them to "lay down the spirit of contradiction."[51] The "spirit of contradiction" in this context means the futile hope of finding Truth without recourse to God. The apologetic character of the *Meditations* lies in the demonstration that the existence of Truth depends on the existence of God.

Let us reconsider Descartes's statement of 1630 – "those easily become atheists, because they perfectly comprehend mathematical truths, and do not perfectly comprehend the truth of God's existence" – in light of his reasoning in the *Meditations*. Descartes specialists usually place the "universal doubt" in the mainstream of the Skeptical tradition.[52] From a purely historical point of view, such an interpretation is correct, but it does not take into account the fact that Descartes is the first philosopher in the long history of European skepticism to have cast doubt on mathematics.[53] The argument on which the reasoning in the *Meditations* rests has nothing to do with skepticism, but rather with atheism. Descartes does not have any empirical reason to consider mathematical cognition as uncertain. What, then, incited him to cast doubt on it? The reason is of a *theological* nature: more precisely, it concerns the disparity between divine goodness and omnipotence and the fact that as God's creature I have a nature subject to deception.[54] Given that my senses deceive me, Descartes argues, I should suppose that mathematics is uncertain despite the fact that I have a psychological conviction ("*une assurance morale*") that it is certain. In this part of the *Meditations* Descartes introduces the hypothesis of a deceiving god (that St. Augustine introduces in *The Literal Meaning of Genesis*[55]):

ophy rather than theology . . . in the case of unbelievers, it seems that there is no religion, and practically no moral virtue, that they can be persuaded to adopt until these two truths are proved to them by natural reason." Dedicatory letter to the Sorbonne (AT VII, 1–2; CSM II, 1).

51 Dedicatory letter to the Sorbonne (AT VII, 6; CSM II, 6).

52 See, for example, Richard Popkin, *History of Scepticism* (New York: Harper and Row, 1964); Edwin Curley, *Descartes against the Skeptics* (Cambridge, Mass.: Harvard University Press, 1972).

53 Francisco Sanches tried to cast doubt on mathematics. See his letter to Colvius, in A. Moreira de Sá, *Francisco Sanches, Filosofo e Matemático*, (Lisboa, 1947), vol. 2. Reprinted in: Joaquim de Carvalho *Francisco Sanches, Opera Philosophica*, Nova edição (Coimbra, 1955), pp. 146–53. See also Joseph Moreau, "Doute et savoir chez Francisco Sanches," *Portugiesische forschungen des görresgesellschaft, 1ère série, Aufsätze zur portugiesischen kulturgeschichte*, vol. I (1960).

54 See my *Cartesian Theodicy. Descartes' Quest for Certitude* (Dordrecht: Kluwer Academic Publishers, 2000), chapter 2; and "How to Read Descartes' First Meditation," in *The Southern Journal of Philosophy* 35 (1997).

55 See Index: VI. Similar hypothesis is also in Plutarch (see *De Stoicorum repugnantis*, in

> And yet firmly rooted in my mind is the long-standing opinion that there is an omnipotent God who made me the kind of creature that I am. How do I know that He has not brought it about that there is no earth, no sky, no extended thing, no shape, no size, no place, while at the same time ensuring that all these things appear to me to exist just as they do now? What is more, because I sometimes believe that others go astray in cases where they think they have the most perfect knowledge, may I not similarly go wrong every time I add two and three or count the sides of a square, or in some even simpler matter, if that is imaginable.
>
> But perhaps God would not have allowed me to be deceived in this way because He is said to be supremely good. But if it were inconsistent with His goodness to have created me such that I am deceived all the time, it would seem equally foreign to His goodness to allow me to be deceived even occasionally; yet this last assertion cannot be made.[56]

Let us note that the structure of the second part of the hypothesis of the *deus deceptor* resembles the famous Epicurean argument: because there is evil, then God is either evil or impotent or both. Descartes's argument is analogous: because I have a nature which sometimes deceives me, God is either evil or impotent or both. In other words, the fact that I have a nature subject to deception is proof that I was not created by God.

The part that follows the hypothesis of the evil genius begins with a polemic against "some people" (*nonnulli qui*) who "would prefer to deny the existence of a God so powerful rather than believe that everything else is uncertain." But why should anyone "prefer" to deny the existence of God? One possible line of reasoning is that if a God so powerful does not exist, He cannot render mathematics (the subject of the preceding paragraph) doubtful. "But let us not oppose them for a moment," Descartes adds in the French version, "and assume that everything said about God is a fable." In other words, suppose that God does not exist. Descartes's next step is to turn the argument of "some people" back against them. One can deny the existence of God, but one needs to substitute some other cause of my coming into being for Him. There are three such causes: chance, necessity, and the continuous series of causes.[57] However, none of them is all-powerful, and "the

Plutarchi Chaeronensis, Quae Supersunt, Omnia Graece et Latine, ed. Iacobus Reiski, vol. 10, Lipsiae, 1878) and Cicero (see his *Academica*, II, xv, 47).

56 Med. I (AT VII, 21; CSM II, 14).

57 The three causes come from Cicero's *De Fato*. See chaps. XVII, X, XI. "Continuous series of causes" represents the position of Chryssipus, who, according to Cicero, "as an official arbiter, wanted to take the middle ground." *De Fato*, XVII, 39. It is likely that

less powerful the author of my nature, the more likely it is that I am always deceived."

Descartes's argument[58] is aimed not at skeptics but at atheists: those atheists (*nonnulli qui*) who do not realize that the existence of truth depends on the existence of God, and that there is a relationship between the power of the First Cause of our existence and our cognitive apparatus. Descartes's argument boils down to the following: if I do not owe my nature (i.e., cognitive constitution) to an all-powerful God, then I owe it to a cause that is not all-powerful (chance, fate, or a continuous series of causes). Since none of these causes is all-powerful, it is more likely that my nature is subject to deception. If God does not exist – Descartes tells the atheists – there is no cognitive certitude. In short, either God or cognitive nihilism.[59]

The argument of 1641, at least the part of it just quoted above, which links atheism to the conception of science, repeats the essential points of Descartes's letters to Mersenne of 1630. The polemic against "some people" in the First Meditation is an elaborated version of Descartes's position in those early letters, which suggests that this reasoning was probably part of the speech against the Pyrrhonists that Descartes gave at the papal nuncio's in 1628.

II

From the point of view of the chronology of the development of Descartes's philosophy, the doctrine of the eternal truths is inseparable from the discovery of the method (i.e., meditation); as a matter of fact, it follows from it. In conceptual order, the foundation of Truth is the doctrine of the eternal truths, which rests on the doctrine of God's incomprehensibility. How did Descartes

Descartes took this idea from the *Tusculanes*. Descartes's expression "fruits of philosophy" is a Ciceronian cliché.

58 See Z. Janowski, "How to Read the First Meditation," in *The Southern Journal of Philosophy* 35, no. 3 (1997), pp. 321–38. Cf. G.J.D. Moyal, "Veritas aeterna, Deo volente," *Les Études philosophiques* 4 (1987), according to whom *nonnulli qui* are atheist mathematicians (p. 470, 474); J.-M. Beyssade, "'Devenir athées': Sur un passage controversé de la Première Méditation," in *Archives de Philosophie* (Bulletin Cartésien, XX) 55 (1992), pp. 3–6; J.-L. Marion, *Questions Cartésiennes II, op. cit.*, pp. 119–41; R. Stoothoff, "Descartes' Dilemma," in *The Philosophical Quarterly* 39, no. 156.

59 Among contemporary philosophers who insists on this Cartesian motif, see Leszek Kolakowski. *Religion. If there is no God . . .* (Oxford: Oxford University Press, 1982); *Husserl and the Search for Certitude* (South Bend, Ind.: St. Augustine's Press, 2001); "Comment une vérité sans Dieu est-elle possible?" in *Le Genre humain*, vols. 7–8, pp. 75–80; *Metaphysical Horror* (London: Penguin, 2000); "The Death of Utopia Reconsidered," in *Modernity on Endless Trial* (Chicago: The University of Chicago Press, 1991).

arrive at this doctrine? We know that in the second part of the 1620s Descartes worked on several different projects. In 1627, he composed the *Regulae ad directionem ingeni*. The *Regulae* contains little of the metaphysics of the *Meditations*.[60] But if we look at the essential themes of *Discourse* IV (1637) and those of the *Meditations* (1641), we see that the germ of Cartesian metaphysics is in the three letters of 1630. Thus the most significant development of Descartes's thought must have taken place between the time of the *Regulae* (1627) and the beginning of the 1630s, or even in 1629 when Descartes informed Guillaume Gibieuf about his "work on Divinity," which he promised to send him so the Oratorian could pronounce his opinion on it.

The "little treatise," as Descartes called it, has never been found, so we can only speculate about its contents. We know, however, that it concerned the existence of God and the distinction between soul and body,[61] and that it contained the *cogito*.[62] Moreover, in 1629 Descartes defined the soul as a "thinking substance."[63] So it is natural to wonder whether the "little treatise" also contained the doctrine of the eternal truths. I will approach this question by trying to determine the relationship between the doctrine of the eternal truths and the metaphysics of the *Meditations*, which contains *all* the elements of the "little treatise" mentioned above._

According to Alexandre Koyré, the doctrine of the eternal truths is an aberration on Descartes's part, happily overcome by the time of the *Meditations*.[64] According to Henri Gouhier, "without doubt, one can read the *Discourse on Method*, the six *Meditations*, and the *Principles of Philosophy* without finding the doctrine of the eternal truths explicitly expounded."[65] Even if Gouhier is right in saying that this doctrine is not *explicitly* present in the *Meditations*, it is *implicitly* present – in three places in the *Meditations*, as I show below.

There is a direct relationship between the procedure that led Descartes to

60 According to Henri Gouhier, "At the time of the *Regulae*, that is, before Descartes left for Holland, the *cogito* had not been formulated." "Pour une histoire des Méditations Métaphysiques" in *Études d'histoire de la philosophie française* (New York: Georg Olms Verlag Hildesheim, 1976). Cf. J.-L. Marion's extensive discussion in his *Questions Cartésiennes* (Paris: PUF, 1991), pp. 37–73.

61 To Mersenne, March 1637 (AT I, 350–51).

62 See H. Gouhier, "Pour une histoire des Méditations Métaphysiques," in *Études d'histoire de la philosophie française* (New York: Georg Olms Verlag Hildesheim, 1976), p. 12. Cf. Geneviève Rodis-Lewis, "L'écho de la première métaphysique dans les *Méditations*," in *Le développement de la pensée de Descartes* (Paris: Vrin, 1997).

63 To Mersenne, March 1637 (AT I, 350–51).

64 A. Koyrè, *Essai sur l'idée de dieu et les preuves de son existence chez Descartes* (Paris: Édition Ernest Leroux, 1922), pp. 19–21.

65 H. Gouhier, *Cartésianisme et Augustinisme au XVIIe siècle* (Paris: Vrin, 1978), p. 157.

cast doubt on the existence of the external world and his conception of God. Let us note that the hypothesis of the deceiving God is inconceivable from the Scholastic perspective, and from the perspective of the philosophy of Aquinas in particular: because mathematical objects are "in" the divine mind, Aquinas could not say, like Descartes, that God could have arranged things so that I went wrong each time I added two plus three. The paragraph that follows the hypothesis of the deceiving god begins with the introduction of "some people" who "would prefer to deny the existence of a God so powerful." How powerful? Apparently powerful enough to cast doubt on mathematics. The introduction of "some people" is a response to the idea that God can do "anything." In short, what Descartes here calls an "old-standing opinion" (*vetus opinio*) is in fact his own opinion, and it is in this guise that he attempts to smuggle in his own conception of God and the doctrine of the eternal truths elaborated in the three letters to Mersenne in1630.

In the Second Meditation, after sending his meditator through the whirlpool of doubt, Descartes states: "I am a mind, or intelligence, or intellect, or reason." A Scholastic could not subscribe to such an epistemologically purifying procedure. The reason is simple: the soul in Scholastic thought is the *form* of the human body (*anima corporis forma*). If Cartesian man emerges victorious from the whirlpool of doubt it is only because his soul is *not* the substantial form of a body.[66] It seems that despite his emphatic declarations, Descartes did not begin his meditations from an epistemological absolute point zero. In demonstrating that he is a "thinking thing," he in fact demonstrates what the doctrine of the eternal truths requires, namely that the soul is not the form of a body.[67]

66 As I remark above, according to Descartes, there is no intrinsic or absolute necessity in the laws of mathematics, they are nothing but divine decrees. Thus, rationality is nothing but the rules of human thinking. This Cartesian decreetalism has far-reaching consequences. If we cannot imagine something, for example, a man who is an ass, it does not mean that God cannot accomplish it. If this is the case, the question arises: in what sense can one call the Cartesian soul a "substantial form"? If the Cartesian God has the power to put a rational soul in the ass's body, the union between the Cartesian soul and body cannot be substantial. The doctrine of the eternal truths not only excludes the substantial union between the body and soul, but also makes it impossible. (For substantial union in St. Thomas, see *Summa Contra Gentiles*, II, 56, 69–72, 90. See also E. Gilson, "L'innéisme cartésien et la théologie," in *Revue de Métaphysique et de Morale* 22 (1914), pp. 456–99).

67 Did Descartes realize that his conception of the soul was opposite to that of the Scholastics? In the dedicatory letter to the Sorbonne, Descartes makes reference to the Eighth Session of the Lateran Council, held under Leo X, the Pope ordered Christian philosophers (1) to demonstrate that soul is not mortal, to (2) and determine its nature. The text to which Descartes makes reference is the papal Bull *Apostolici*

According to this doctrine, God can do anything. Thus, to use an example from Aquinas, God can put a human soul in an ass's body. If He can do this, a soul cannot be the form of the body. In short, the doctrine of the eternal truths makes the substantial union impossible. Descartes retains the vocabulary of the School by calling the soul a "substantial form," but the term has completely lost its Scholastic content.[68]

Regiminis (19 December 1513): "Because in our days (and we painfully bring this up) the sower of cockle, ancient enemy of the human race, has dared to disseminate and advance in the field of the Lord a number of pernicious errors always rejected by the faithful, especially concerning the nature of the rational soul, namely, that it is mortal, or one in all men, and some rashly philosophizing affirmed that this is true at least according to philosophy, in our desire to offer suitable remedies against a plague of this kind, with the approval of this holy Council, we condemn and reject all who assert that [1] *the intellectual soul is mortal*, or [2] *is one in all men*, and those who cast doubt on these truths, because it [the soul] is not only truly in itself and essentially the form of the human body (*forma corporis*), as was defined in the canon of Pope CLEMENT V our predecessor of happy memory published in the (general) Council of VIENNE but it is also multiple according to the multitude of bodies into which it is infused, multiplied, and to be multiplied. . . . And because [3] *truth never contradicts truth*, we declare every assertion contrary to the truth of illumined faith to be altogether false; and, that it may not be permitted to dogmatize otherwise, we strictly forbid it, and we declare that all who adhere to errors of this kind are to be shunned and to be punished as detestable and abominable infidels who disseminate most damnable heresies and who weaken the Catholic faith." (*Enchiridion Symbolorum, Definitionum et Declarationum De Rebus Fidei Et Morum*, Henricus Denzinger ed., no. 738). In condemning the errors of the Averroists, Leo X renewed the edict of Clement V, *De Trinitate et fide catholica* (6 May 1312): "Porro doctrinam omnem seu positionem temere asserentem, aut vertentem in dubium, quod substantia animae rationalis seu intellectivae vere ac per se humani corporis non sit forma, velut erroneam ac veritati catholicae inimicam fidei, praedicto sacro approbante Concilio reprobamus: definientes, ut cunctis nota sitfidei sincerae veritas ac praecludantur universis erroribus aditus, ne ne subintrent, quod quisquis deinceps asserere, defendere seu tenere pertinaciter praesumpserit, quod anima rationalis seu intellectiva non sit *forma corporis humani per se et essentialiter*, tamquam *haereticus* sit censendus" (Denzinger, *ibid.*, no. 902). In his Letter to the Sorbonne, Descartes mentions only the errors the Bull condemns. What he does not mention, however, is the fact that Leo X invited all the proofs for the immortality of the soul as *humani corporis forma*.

The question arises: is Descartes's conception of the soul orthodox? If the *Apostolici Regiminis* represents the official Church doctrine, Descartes's conception of the soul is not orthodox. As a matter of fact, Descartes used the Bull for purposes contrary to those for which it was originally designed. In light of the *Apostolici Regiminis*, Descartes could have been accused of heresy. For a discussion of this problem, see my "Is Descartes' Conception of the Soul Orthodox?" in *Revue de Metaphysique et de Morale* no. 1 (2000).

68 Cf. St. Thomas, *Summa Contra Gentiles*, II, 44–101.

The Fourth Meditation is devoted to the theory of human freedom. This doctrine is a logical consequence of the doctrine of divine freedom[69] that Descartes formulated in 1630; so there are grounds for supposing that the "little treatise" also contained the theory of human freedom.

These three points in the *Meditations* follow from the doctrine of eternal truths formulated in 1630. My hypothesis contains three other suggestions. First, even if the doctrine of the eternal truths is not explicitly presented in the *Meditations*, it is present throughout that text insofar as it is Descartes's conception of God that lies behind the Universal Doubt. Second, the "little treatise" is an integral part of the *Meditations*. A fragment from a letter Descartes wrote to Mersenne after the publication of the *Discourse* supports this claim: "As for your second objection that I have not explained at sufficient length how I know that the soul is distinct from the body and that its nature is solely to think . . . eight years ago, however, I wrote in Latin the beginning of a treatise of metaphysics in which this argument is conducted at some length; if a Latin version of my present book is made, as is planned, I could have it included."[70] What does the word "beginning" refer to? Apparently to the beginning of the "little treatise," which Descartes for some reason either abandoned or did not finish editing. From the essential points of the metaphysics of the *Meditations* one can infer that the "beginning" covers roughly the first three Meditations. Besides, insofar as the conception of human liberty is the consequence of the conception of divine liberty, human liberty must have been part of the "little treatise."[71] There seems no reason to assume that the *Meditations* is a different work from the "little treatise." The *Meditations* is a revised version, but as far as the essential points of Cartesian metaphysics are concerned, they are the same work.

In his letter to Gibieuf of 1629, Descartes says that he would probably finish his treatise in about three years. This implies that he thought he had already worked out the greater part of his metaphysics. So why did he abandon the idea of publishing his work on "Divinity" in the first half of the

69 *Responses to the Sixth Set of Objections* (AT VII, 432; CSM II, 292).

70 To Mersenne, March 1637 (AT I, 350–51; CSMK III, 53).

71 The Fourth Meditation, which is devoted as much to truth and falsity as to human freedom, is badly organized. The first thing that strikes a reader of this Meditation is the fact that Descartes does not explain what freedom has to do with such categories as truth and falsity. The Fourth Meditation bears traces of heavy revisions of a piece that contained an elaborate discussion on human freedom in its original form. Because the conception of human freedom follows from, and is intelligible only in the context of the conception of divine freedom, however, it would appear that the "little treatise" contained one more Meditation, on Divine freedom, i.e., the doctrine of eternal truths, which probably was part of the present Fourth Meditation.

1630s? There are at least two explanations. First, the letter to Mersenne of March 1637 suggests that his metaphysics (i.e., the doctrine of eternal truths) might appear too shocking.[72] Before presenting it in its strictly philosophical form, in Latin, Descartes probably decided to try out a more popular version, written in the vernacular, in order to see how his philosophy would be received. After the publication of the *Discourse* in 1637, however, no revolution took place,[73] and Descartes realized that the "feeble minds" who had avidly devoured the doubts of the *Discourse* without realizing the consequences were capable of devouring it in greater quantity and in a more radical form. This time Descartes decided to supply them with a much stronger prescription – the Universal Doubt and the hypothesis of the evil genius. The effect, as one can judge from the reaction of Voetius, Triglandus and Revius,[74] was surprising. The drug had a much stronger effect than Descartes had anticipated. Had it not been for the intervention of the French ambassador Servien, Descartes would probably have been accused of blasphemy.

Descartes may have had another reason, of a more "political" nature, for not proceeding with the publication of his metaphysics. In 1630, his confidant Guillaume Gibieuf published *De Libertate Dei et creaturae*. Gibieuf's objectives were to refute the false conception of the "freedom of indifference" and establish the Augustinian thesis of God's liberty. The subtitle of the book was "*juxta doctrinam D. AUGUSTINI, D. Thomae, D. Bonaventurae, D. Scoti, Gandaunensis, Durandi, aliorumque veterum Theologorum.*" The name of St. Augustine stands out; it is printed in capital letters and occupies a whole line, thus giving the great Father of the Church (whom Gibieuf quotes throughout the book) an exclusive place among the rest. "I would not at all be surprised," Jansenius wrote about this book, "if the doctors rose up against the book of the Seminarist [Oratorian Gibieuf]."[75] Although

72 "I hope to put this in writing, within the next fortnight, in my treatise on physics; but I do not want you to keep it secret. On the contrary I beg you to tell people as often as the occasion demands, provided you do not mention my name. I should be glad to know the objections which can be made against this view." To Mersenne, 15 April 1630 (AT I, 146; CSMK III, 23).

73 See Daniel Garber, "Descartes, the Aristotelians, and the Revolution that did not Happen in 1637," in *The Monist* 71, no. 4 (1988), pp. 471–86. One cannot exclude the possibility that the *Discourse* was not read. Therefore, four years later, in publishing the *Meditations*, Descartes decided to invite people to respond to the *Meditations*.

74 See Theo Verbeek, *Descartes and the Dutch: Early Reactions to Cartesian Philosophy*, 1937–1650. (Carbondale: Southern Illinois University Press, 1992), and "Descartes and the Problem of Atheism: The Utrecht Crisis," in *Dutch Review of Church History* 71 (1991).

75 Letter to Saint-Cyran of 5 April 1630. Published by Jean Orcibal in *Les origines du*

Jansenius had certain reservations about the book on the grounds that it was too philosophical,[76] he thought it contained good things and promised Saint-Cyran to give it his "moderate approbation."[77]

Soon after the book's publication Gibieuf was attacked by two spokesmen of the Society of Jesus. In 1632 François Annat (1590–1670), confessor to Louis XIII, relentless critic of the Jansenists and architect of the "Five Propositions" which led to the condemnation of the doctrine of St. Augustine by the Papacy, published a malicious response to Gibieuf's theses, *Eugenii Philadelphi Romani exercitatio scholastica tripartita. Contra novem rationem tuendi physicas praemotiones liberorum agentium, eorumque libertatem exponendi, quam auctor operis De Libertate Dei et Creaturae nuper invexit.* Another Jesuit theologian and polemicist, Théophile Raynaud, author of the famous pamphlet *Calvinismus bestiarum religio*, accused Gibieuf of apostasy and Calvinism in his massive book *Nova Libertatis explicatio* (published anonymously in November 1632 and later condemned by the Holy Office).[78] Calvinism, argued Raynaud, is the religion of the *beasts*: it denies man liberty and thus likens him to animals. Philip Chalmers (known under his Latin name as Camerarius), who was the one originally commissioned to write the book, and was as much the object of Raynaud's attack as Gibieuf,[79] responded in 1634 with a book dedicated to Riccardi, *Antiquitatis de novitate victoria, sive justa deffensio promotionis physicae contra impetitiones pseudo Eugenii Philadelphi Romani.* Finally, in 1634 the Capucin Louis a Dola attacked Gibieuf's thesis on the cooperation of God with human actions. Despite their attempts to censure *De Libertate*, the Jesuits never succeeded in getting Gibieuf's book put on the index; it seems that they did succeed, however, in preventing it from being reprinted.[80]

How can we account for the Jesuits' panicked reaction against Gibieuf's book? The explanation lies in what the Augustinians and Molinists respectively considered to be the essence of human freedom. According to Gibieuf, who is concerned about whether man's liberty of indifference is absolute – in

Jansénisme. Vol. I. *Correspondance de Jansénius*, p. 456. For details of anti-Molinism of Gibieuf's account see Batterel-Ingold, *Mémoires domestiques pour servir à l'histoire de l'Oratoire* (Paris, 1902), vol. I, pp. 239–44.

76 Letter to Saint-Cyran of 21 September 1629 (Orcibal, *op. cit.*, p. 437).

77 Letter to Saint-Cyran of 21 September 1629 (Orcibal, *op. cit.*, p. 438).

78 For Raynauld's attack on Gibieuf, see *Th. Raynaudi Opera*, t. XVIII, pp. 9–14.

79 The subtitle of Annat's book is: "[C]um Appendice ad Guillelmum Camerarium Scotum Appendix: ad Camerarium" (pp. 325–64). Much of the contents of chapter III is devoted to the criticism of Chalmers.

80 Batterel-Ingold, *Mémoires domestiques pour servir à l'histoire de l'Oratoire* (Paris, 1902), vol. I, p. 245.

other words, whether it belongs to the *essence* of human freedom[81] – liberty of indifference is only "conditional," and "tempered" by its end.[82] Hence, Gibieuf concludes (and here he repeats St. Augustine verbatim), the more man becomes subject to God's will the more he is free.

Freedom of indifference was not discussed in a vacuum. It concerned the most fundamental theological problem: can we avoid sin without divine grace? According to St. Augustine and his seventeenth-century followers,[83] human will after the Fall is totally corrupt and cannot do good; it can incline itself only toward evil. It follows that, if human beings were to rely only on their own resources to do good, they would all deserve eternal damnation. In other words, as a result of Original Sin we are entirely at God's mercy, and insofar as man is capable of doing good, it is in fact thanks to God, who works in man and through man. Whatever good man is capable of is the result of God's grace. But a question remains: can grace be resisted? Augustine and his followers say no: God's grace works in man with the power of *necessity* and cannot be resisted. However, because the opposite of freedom is not necessity but compulsion (*vis externa*), there is no conflict between God's imposition of grace and human freedom. "The more human will is subject to divine grace," St. Augustine claims, "the more free it is."[84] In short, human freedom lies in man's submission to God's will. For the most part Gibieuf does nothing but reiterate or quote St. Augustine.[85]

The controversy between the Molinists and the Augustinians is easily translatable into philosophical language: If God's freedom is absolute, what is the nature and extent of human freedom? Gibieuf's answer is that God does not tend toward any end in order to be free; He is not subject to anything higher than Himself, and is not dependent on any principle.[86] God is

81 *De Libertate*, p. 68: "Hic duae quaestiones emergunt: una, utrum indifferentia libertatis sit indifferentia absoluta ad agendum & non agendum."

82 *De Libertate*, pp. 68–69: "Dico I. Indifferentia quae spectat ad liberum arbitrium creaturae, non est indifferentia absoluta ad agendum & non agendum, sed indifferentia conditionata & temperata per respectum ad finem."

83 See, for example, De Condren, *Sentiment du R. P. de Condren, second général de l'Oratoire, touchant l'impuissance et la faiblesse de la nature pour faire le bien*, Biblioteque Sainte-Geneviève. M 3209 (Y-f-in–8o. 7), p. 62.

84 St. Augustine, Letter 89: "Voluntas libera tanto liberior quanto divinae gratiae subjector."

85 *De Libertate*, p. iii: "Hanc autem explicandi rationem ex D. Augustini liquidissimis fontibus manifeste defluere, qui Libertatem tat majorem affirmat, quanto divinae Gratiae subjectior fuerit: qui magnam docet esse libertatem, quando possumus non peccare, maximam vero cum ne peccare quidem possumus: prorus Deo subjecti."

86 *De Libertate*, p. 69: "Quia enim Deus nec finem habet, nec principium, ac nullum

indifferent; in fact, His indifference is absolute.[87] Thus God's liberty consists first and foremost in His absolute sovereignty, which stems from His perfect *unity*.[88] God is not moved to action by any end.[89] He is limited neither by place nor by nature. In short, God is free because nothing, absolutely nothing, can limit or oppose Him.[90] Man, on the contrary, is free insofar as he does God's will.

According to Molina, human freedom is the power to "act or not act, or to do something or its opposite, and this faculty of acting or doing something or its opposite when all that is required for acting is given is called liberty."[91] It follows from this that if one is capable of doing good through one's own resources (and we all are, because God's grace, while necessary, is equally distributed), one can also be *indifferent* with respect to the choice between good and evil, right and wrong, and truth and falsity.

Nothing seems further removed from Descartes's doctrine than such a conception of liberty. "We are free not only when ignorance of what is good and true makes us indifferent; we are truly free – indeed most free – when a clear perception impels us to pursue some object."[92] In other words, we are truly free even when have no choice. Although the Cartesian conception of liberty does not sound particularly liberal, it is in perfect conformity with that of St. Augustine. "You are free when you are a slave; free from sin, a slave of justice" (*Eris liber, si fueris servus; liber peccati, servus justiciae*). Let us translate this into the language of Cartesian epistemology: "You are free when you are a slave: free from error, a slave of clear and distinct ideas." (*Eris liber, si fueris servus; liber errorum, servus idearum clarorum et distinctarum*). "I

proinde superiorem cuius directioni subdatur: ideo cum agit, ut a principio nullo dependet, ita nec ad finem tendit."

87 *De Libertate*, p. 69: "ejus indifferentia ad agendum & non agendum, creandum, & sit indifferentia absoluta, non autem ex conditione & pront finis ordo postulaverit."

88 *De Libertate*, p. 291: "Deus autem plane unus est, imo Unum ipsum est. . . . Unum omnem omnino vel taneum divisionis umbram eliminas, quod proinde cuiquam subjici omnino repugnat; quae est summa et perfecta libertas."

89 *De Libertate*, p. 291: "Deus non movetur ad agendum a Fine, etiam Seipso."

90 For Gibieuf's conception of God, see Ferrier, *Un Oratorien ami de Descartes* (Paris: Vrin, 1987), pp. 164–70.

91 "Altero modo potest accipi, ut opponitur necessitati, quo modo id liberum dicimus, quod positis requisitis ad agendum in potestate ipsius habet agere aut non agere, aut agere hoc aut oppositum; facultasque illa agendi et non agendi aut agendi hoc aut oppositum positis omnibus requisitis ad agendum appellatur libertas." Molina, *De Scientia Dei*, published in *Beiträge zur Geschichte der Philosophie und Theologie des Mittelalters*, vol. XXXII (Münster: Aschendorffschen, 1935), p. 207.

92 *Responses to the Sixth Set of Objection* (AT VII, 432; CSM II, 292).

wrote that indifference in our case is rather a defect than a perfection of freedom . . . and I feel confident that Father Gibieuf will defend my position well on this matter, for I wrote nothing which is not in accord with what he has said in his book *De Libertate*"[93] What was Descartes thinking about when he wrote these words? We can almost be certain that he had in mind the criticism of the freedom of indifference in *De libertate Dei.*

Jansenius, despite his reservations about Gibieuf's book on the grounds that it was "too philosophical," thought the Oratorian's criticism of the freedom of indifference was its most valuable part. "The true liberty of the *liberum arbitrium* known by the ancient authors," says Jansenius approvingly, "does not consist in this philosophical indifference to act, as is commonly proclaimed. This book demonstrates this with numerous and solid reasons, and it refutes the defenders of the contrary opinions."[94] Jansenius's *Augustinus* contains a much more severe and elaborate criticism of the freedom of indifference; there is not much on this subject in *De Libertate Dei et Creaturae* that is not in *Augustinus*. In 1630, however, Gibieuf's was the first philosophical work (for the *Augustinus* is a strictly theological work) in which an open stance was taken against the partisans of the freedom of indifference.

The significance of Gibieuf's *De Libertate Dei* in the growing conflict between the Molinists and the Augustinians might not have been apparent immediately after its publication. However, read through the prism of the *Augustinus*, Gibieuf's theses appeared much closer to the "horrible heresy" of Jansenius.[95] For example, in 1630, Isaac Habert wrote approvingly about *De Libertate*:

> I the undersigned, doctor of the Sorbonne, priest, canon, and a theologian of the Church of Paris, after reading the book by Father Gibieuf, *De Libertate Dei et Creaturae*, feel obliged to praise it, finding therein nothing which I could censure. It seemed to me full of

93 To Mersenne, 23 June 1641 (AT III, 385–86; CSMK III, 179, dates this letter for 21 April 1641).

94 The full text of the approbation reads: "Veram arbitrii Libertatem antiquis Scriptoribus notam, non esse sitam in illa Philosophica indifferentia agendi, quae vulgo praedicatur, multis praeclaris et solidis rationibus hic liber astruit et adversae opinionis defensores confutat. Et quia non modo eruditionem, sed etiam pietatem Auctoris sui testamentum fecit, et Lectoris provocat, dum animum creaturarum visco et nexibus expediendum docet, ut asseratur in libertatem gloriae filiorum Dei; merito omne tulisse punctum dici potest: quia Dei simul et hominis consuluit dignitati." Cornelius Iansenius, S., Thologiae Doctor ac Professor Ordinarius, In Universitate Louvanevsi (13 December 1629).

95 F. Ferrier, *Un Oratorien ami de Descartes*, *op. cit.*, p. 152.

> piety and erudition . . . [the author] falls short of nothing that Saint Paul thought necessary for an ecclesiastic writer. . . . If one considers the style, the manner of writing is beautiful and noble; *if one considers the depth of the doctrine and the thoughts of the author, they are sublime and edifying*. . . . Nothing of the subtleties of the School escapes him; his knowledge of its doctrine seems perfect. . . . *In a word, this is a work that deserves eternity, that will have the approbation of all and from which all will benefit.*[96]

When Habert became engaged in the anti-Jansenist campaign, he saw Gibieuf's work in a very different light. Thirteen years later, in *La Défense de la Foy de l'Eglise* . . . published in 1644, he says that *De Libertate* "contains the principal points of the doctrine of Monsieur d'Ypre [Jansenius]." A Jesuit writer, P. de Colonia, the author of *Bibliotèque janséniste*, calls Gibieuf's book *heresie propre*, apparently suggesting that Gibieuf's views are as pernicious as those of Jansenius. More recently, Jean Laporte found in *De Libertate* two propositions which the Bull *Unigenitus* of 1713 condemned as the heretical propositions of Pasquel Quesnel.[97] As late as 1666 an author appeared who apparently felt an urgent need to get engaged in a controversy which had begun more than three decades earlier, and who attacked one of Gibieuf's critics.[98] The last attack against Gibieuf's book took place in 1734 when Father Duchesne, S.J., published his *L'histoire du Baianisme*.

96 The whole text of Habert's approbation was reprinted by Batterel, *Memoires domestiques . . . , op. cit.*, vol. II, pp. 242–43. Habert's approbation never appeared in *De Libertate*, which means that he changed his mind very quickly. In *La Défense de la Foy de l'Eglise et de l'ancienne doctrine de Sorbonne, touchant les principaux points de la Grace, prêchée dans l'église de Paris par M. Isaac Habert . . . Contre le livre intituleé "Apologie de Jansenius," sans nom d'auteur [Caesaris Baronii Relatio conclii Arelatensis. Smi D. N. D. Urbani Papae VII Confirmatio Constitionum Pii Papae V et Gregorii XIII.]* (Paris, T. Blaise, 1644), 2 parts in 1 vol., p. 42, he returned to Gibieuf's book in his attack on Father Sermond: "Il [Sermond] auroi appris par cette lecture, que Iansenius declare, qu'il n'est point de l'opinion du P. Gibieuf, pour ce qui est de la liberté. Si bien qu'en approuvant le Livre du P. Gibieuf touchant la liberté, ie n'ay rien fait dont Iasenius puisse tirer avantage."

97 Jean Laporte, *Les vérités de la grâce*, pp. 418–26, 432–38. Cf. Jean Orcibal, "Néo-Platonisme et Jansénisme: Du *De Libertate* du P. Gibieuf à *L'Augustinus*," *Analecta Gregoriana* (*Nuove Ricerche Storiche sul Giansinismo*) 71 (Rome: 1954), p. 57. The propositions are the following: #10: Grace is the working of the omnipotent hand of God, which nothing can hinder and retard (*Gratia est operatio manus omipotentis Dei, quam nihil impedire potest aut retardare*); #11: (Grace is nothing else than the omnipotent Will of God, ordering and doing what He orders (*Gratia non est aliud quam voluntas omnipotens Dei iubentis et facientis, quod iubet*).

98 P. Vincent Baron, O.P. (1604–1674) published a response to Raynaud's book, *Sanctorum Augustini et Thomae vera et una mens de libertate humana et gratia divina explicatur et*

It is difficult today to reconstitute the theologico-philosophical landscape of the 1630s, and the role Gibieuf played in the battle over the freedom of indifference. The battle around the *Augustinus* in the 1640s and 1650s completely obscured this period, and relegated the people who had participated in it into near-oblivion.[99] From the perspective of the sixty years that passed between the incident at Louvain in 1587 and the condemnation of the "Five Propositions" in 1653, the publication of *De Liberatate Dei* in 1630 can be said to be merely an incident in the long battle between the Molinists and the Augustinians, whose swan song was the publication of *Augustinus*. But in 1641, when the Molinist Jesuits were busy reading the monumental *Augustinus*, the polemics around *De Libertate Dei* were fresh in the memory of French theologians, and Guillaume Gibieuf was still considered the principal critic of the freedom of indifference, the author of the idea of the simplicity of God's nature and His absolute freedom.

Descartes, insofar as his own position toward freedom of indifference overlapped with that of Gibieuf, had good reason not to proceed with the publication of his metaphysics right after the publication of *De Liberatate Dei* in 1630. "I hope to put this [doctrine of eternal truths] in writing, within the next fortnight, in my treatise on physics," he wrote to Mersenne in 1630.[100]

scholae thomistica assertitur adversus duos Theophili Raynaudi libros, aliosque hujus aetatis melioris notae theologos, where he also defends the opinions of Jansenius (pp. 18–21). See Alber de Meyer, *Les premières controverses jansénistes en France: 1640–1649* (Louvain, 1919), p. 38, footnote 3.

99 It seems that Gibieuf had bad luck not only during his life but also even after his death. Besides the works already mentioned, Gibieuf is the author of *Catéchèse de la manière de vie parfaite à laquelle les chrestiens sont appeles et en suitte les personnes consacrées à Dieu par les vœux de la religion . . .* (Paris, impr. de A. Vitré, 1653), 2 parts in 1 vol.; *La Vie et les grandeurs de la tres sainte Vierge Marie, mer de Dieu*, Part 2, (Paris, 1632). *Mémoire que le Père Gibieuf a laissé pour servir à une seconde édition de la vie de notre Bienheureux Père* (Archives nationales, M. 223 [no. 9]), *Recueil sur le jansènisme, contenant le "Sentiment du Père Gibieuf, de l'Oratoire, touchant le jansénisme"* (Arsenal, Mss. 2009). Leszek Kolakowski in his monumental classic work *Chrétiens sans église* does not mention Gibieuf even once. Bruno Neveu, in his erudite study *Érudition et religion aux XVIIe et XVIIIe siècles* (Paris: Albin Michel, 1994) mentions him in passing only two times. Henri Brémond, who devoted third volume of his *Histoire littéraire du sentiment religieux en France, op. cit.*, to the spirituality of the Oratory, mentions Gibieuf only a few times without, however, analyzing even one page from his works (see vol. III, 673–74, and vol. IV, pp. 20–35). This omission on the part of Brémond is even more curious given the fact that *De Libertate Dei* is Gibieuf's only philosophical book; all other works deal with strictly spiritual matters to which Brémond devoted his multi-volume study.

100 AT I 146; CSMK III, 23. See footnote 71 below.

This doctrine is not in any of Descartes's works. It is probable that the *Meditations* contain only a small part of what Descartes had included in the original version of the "little treatise," and that he probably withdrew the doctrine of the eternal truths.

It would not be entirely legitimate to judge Descartes's philosophy in the light of theology, either Molinist or Augustinian. However, insofar as the notion of freedom in Descartes is defined in theological terms, one is tempted to ask the question of the place of his conception of freedom in the conflict between these two parties. When Descartes's correspondence was published, Antoine Arnauld, to his great surprise, remarked that it was full of the errors of Pelagius. In the Fourth Meditation we find the following definition of freedom: "[1] This is because the [freedom of] the will simply consists in our ability to do or not do something (that is, to affirm or deny, to pursue or avoid); or rather, [2] it consists simply in the fact that when the intellect puts something forward for affirmation or denial or for pursuit or avoidance, our inclinations are such that we do not feel we are determined by any external force. In order to be free, there is no need for me to be inclined both ways; on the contrary, the more I incline in one direction – either because I clearly understand that reasons of truth and goodness point in that way, or because of a divinely produced disposition of my inmost thoughts [i.e., grace] – the freer is my choice."[101] In defining freedom as the power to choose on the one hand and as the internal disposition of man's thoughts, Descartes is trying to reconcile two things mutually exclusive. The first part of the above definition ([1]) is in conformity with Molina's definition, whereas the second ([2]) defines freedom in the Augustinian way: not as the opposite of necessity but of the *vis externa* (compulsion).[102] It seems that in saying "*rather* it consists . . ." and in calling the liberty of indifference "the lowest degree of freedom,"[103] Descartes maneuvers between the Augustinians and the Molinists.

101 Med. IV. AT VII, 57; CSM II, 40.

102 Letter to [Mesland], 2 May 1644 (AT IV, 117; CSMK III, 234).

103 Let us note that Descartes might very well have said that indifference, understood as the very possibility of choice, is the condition or the foundation of freedom. I think that the choice of words ("lowest degree of freedom") was deliberate and intended. Boyce Gibson aptly remarks that "by this deliberate and almost unnecessary allusion to 'divine grace,' and by his use of the technical term 'liberty of indifference,' which he could have easily avoided, Descartes here ranges himself with one of the parties to bitterest of the contemporary theological controversies." *Descartes* (London: Methuen and Co., 1932), p. 333. I discuss this point in my *Cartesian Theodicy*, *op. cit*., pp. 133–36, 140, 44–46.

III

The index shows how strong is the presence of Augustine's thought in the Cartesian corpus. The task now is to determine, as far as possible, whether Descartes read the works of Augustine, and if so, to what extent they were a source of inspiration in the development of his metaphysics and his doctrine of the eternal truths.

There are eleven references, explicit and implicit, to Augustine's works in the Cartesian corpus.[104] However, Descartes mentions St. Augustine by name only twice[105] (and a third time[106] only because he is referring to a passage from the *City of God*). All these references come from the period after 1641, when the *Meditations* were published. Otherwise, St. Augustine is referred to only in Descartes's exchanges with his critics, or in response to those of his correspondents who had pointed to similarities between his own thought and that of St. Augustine.

The first "Augustinian episode" took place on 25 May 1637, when Mersenne, intrigued by the appearance of "I think therefore I am" in the *Discourse on the Method*, observed that a similar argument could be found in St. Augustine. Descartes responded:

> I have received all the packets of which you made mention in your last letter, but I did not ask you to do anything about the list of printing errors because they were already printed, nor about the passage from Saint Augustine because it does not seem to me that it serves the same purpose for him that it does for me. (25 May 1637)

The following year, on 15 November 1638,[107] in response to another letter from Mersenne – who was clearly dissatisfied with Descartes's answer about the *cogito* and had therefore returned to this topic – Descartes wrote:

> I looked for the letter in which you quote the passage from St.

104 1) To Mersenne, 15 November 1638 (AT II, 439); 2) to Colvius, 14 November 1640 (AT III, 247); 3) to Mersenne, 3 December 1640 (AT III, 248); 4) to Mersenne, 3 December 1640 (AT III, 248); 5) to Mersenne, December 1640 (AT III, 261); 6) to Mersenne, 21 January 1641 (AT III, 283); 7) to Mersenne, 21 April 1641 (AT III, 360); 8) to Mersenne, March 1642 (AT III, 543–44); 9) to [Mesland], 2 May 1644 (AT IV, 232, 235); 10) *Conversation with Burman* (AT V, 169); 11) *Responses to the Fourth Set of Objections* (AT VII, 219; see also: AT VII, 197–98, 211, 216–17).

105 To Mesland, 21 April 1641 (AT III, 360; CSMK, 179. See Index: XXXIII); To Mesland, 2 May 1644 (AT IV, 113; CSMK III, 232, 235. See *Index*: XXXI).

106 To Mersenne, 21 April 1641 (AT III, 359–60; Alquié, vol. II, p. 325–26).

107 Letter to Mersenne, 15 November 1638 (AT II, 434 (435); CSMK III, 129).

> Augustine, but I have not yet been able to find it; nor have I managed to obtain the works of the Saint, so that I could look up what you told me, for which I am grateful.

In December 1640 Mersenne wrote again about the *cogito*. But again he received nothing but an abrupt and not very satisfactory answer.

> You have drawn my attention before to a passage of St. Augustine touching on my I think, therefore I am, about which, it seems to me, you have once asked me. It can be found in book eleven *De Civitate Dei*, chapt. 26. Je suis . . . , etc."

Around the same time, in November 1640, Colvius was also struck by traces of St. Augustine in Descartes's *Discourse*, and rushed to inform him that the *cogito* occurs in *De Trinitate*. Descartes gave the following answer:

> I am obliged to you for drawing my attention to the passage of St. Augustine relevant to my I am thinking, therefore I exist. I went today to the library of this town [Leiden] to read it, and I do indeed find that he does use it to prove the certainty of our existence. He goes on to show that there is a certain likeness of the Trinity in us, in that we exist, we know that we exist, and we love the existence and the knowledge we have. I, on the other hand, use the argument to show that this *I* that is thinking is *an immaterial substance* with no bodily element. These are two very different things. In itself it is such a simple and natural thing to infer that one exists from the fact that one is doubting that it could have occurred to any writer. But I am very glad to find myself in agreement with St. Augustine, if only to hush the little minds who have tried to find fault with the principle.[108]

Descartes is not being quite honest with Colvius when he says that his use of the *cogito* is very different from that of St. Augustine. Even if the consequences of his *cogito* are different, the conclusions he draws from it are not. Augustine intends, like Descartes, to demonstrate, first, the immateriality of the soul, and second, its immortality. In *On the Trinity*, X, 8, where St. Augustine analyzes the opinions of various philosophers, he states very emphatically:

> Some have thought that it [the mind] is composed of minute individual corpuscles, which they call atoms, colliding and uniting with one another. Others would make its substance to be air, or fire; others would not have it to be substantial at all, because they could

108 Letter to Colvius, 14 November, 1640 (AT III, 247–48; CSMK III, 159).

> conceive no substance that is not bodily, and found no evidence that the soul is a body. . . . *If, in face of this diversity of opinion, one can perceive that the nature of the mind is at the same time substantial an non-corporeal . . .*

If this fragment is not convincing enough, here is another from *De quantitae animae*, which Descartes knew very well.[109] On the first page, Augustine states:

> Your question about the origin of the soul brings to my mind two interpretations. It is one thing to say: Whence is man? If what we want to know is the land of his birth. It is quite another to ask: What is he composed of, that is, of what elements and realities is he made? Which of these do you expect to hear mentioned, when you ask: What is the origin of the soul? Do you want to know the district, if I may express it that way, or the country from which it came, or are you asking about its very substance? . . . I believe that God, its Creator, is, so to speak, the soul's proper habitation and its home.[110]

And he adds: as for the soul, "it has a definite substance that is neither of earth, nor of fire, nor of air, nor of water, nor their mixture." The soul, he goes on to say, "seems to me to be a certain kind of substance, sharing in reason, fitted to rule the body" (*Nam mihi videtur esse substantia quaedam rationis particeps, regendo corpori accomodata*).[111] One can call this definition functionalist. Soul is considered from the point of view of its function, but nothing is said about its substance. Although the dialogue is not conclusive, it contains an interesting detail: the soul does not have dimensions (*quantitate*). To use Cartesian idiom, the soul is not extended. Augustine does not content himself with this functionalist definition. In *On the Trinity*, X. x.14 (p. 141) – which is the subject of the correspondence between Descartes and Colvius – St. Augustine defines the soul in the following way:

> Yet who ever doubts that he himself lives, and remembers, and understands, and wills, and thinks, and knows, and judges; sees that even if he doubts, he lives; if he doubts, he remembers why he doubts; if he doubts, he understands that he doubts; if he doubts, he wishes to be certain; if he doubts, he thinks; if he doubts, he knows that he does not know; if he doubts, he judges that he ought not to assent rashly.

109 See *Index*: VI; XIII; XXVI; XXVII; XXIX.
110 *The Magnitude of the Soul*, I, 2, pp. 59–60.
111 *The Magnitude of the Soul*, XIII, 22, p. 83. For the significance of this definition, see E.

What is the soul according to Descartes?

> A thing that thinks. What is that? A thing that doubts, understands, affirms, denies, is willing, is unwilling, and also imagines and has sensory perceptions.[112]

Neither Descartes's *considerations* nor his *conclusions* seem different from St. Augustine's. Where, then, does the difference lie? "I know how much difference there is between writing a word by chance," Pascal writes, "without making a longer and more extended reflection on it, and perceiving in this word an admirable series of consequences, that prove the distinction between material and spiritual natures, and making of it a firm and sustained principle of a whole metaphysical system, as Descartes has pretended to do."[113] Pascal's phrase is often cited in support of the originality of Descartes's thought.[114] Let us note, however, that Pascal does not say that the two *cogitos* are different; he merely affirms that Descartes saw in the *cogito* the consequences that Augustine never dreamed of.

Could these similarities between Descartes and St. Augustine be no more than a series of coincidences? To answer this question let us examine Descartes's response to Arnauld, who pointed out other similarities:

> The first thing that I find remarkable is that our distinguished author has laid down as the basis for his entire philosophy exactly the same principle as that laid down by St. Augustine – a man of the sharpest intellect and a remarkable thinker, not only on theological topics but also on philosophical ones. In book II chapter 3 of *De Libero Arbitrio*, Alipius, when he is disputing with Evodius and is about to prove the existence of God, says the following: "First, if we are to take as our starting point what is most evident, I ask you to tell me whether you yourself exist. Or are you perhaps afraid of making a mistake in your answer, given that, if you did not exist, it would be quite impossible for you to make a mistake?" This is like what M. Descartes says: "But there is a deceiver of supreme power and cunning who is deliberately and constantly deceiving me. In that case I too undoubtedly exist, if he is deceiving me." But let us go from here and, more to the point, see how this principle

Gilson, *The Spirit of Mediæval Philosophy* (New York: Charles Scribner's Sons, 1936), p. 174.

112 Med. II (AT VII, 28; CSM II, 19).

113 *The Art of Persuasion*, in *Blaise Pascal, The Harvard Classics*, vol. 48, tr. by O.W. Wight (New York: P.F. Collier & Son, 1910), pp. 414–15.

114 See, for example, E. Gilson, *The Unity of Philosophical Experience* (New York: Charles Scribner's Sons, 1937), pp. 157–60.

> can be used to derive the result that our mind is separate from our body.
>
> I can doubt whether I have a body, and even whether there are any bodies at all in the world. Yet for all that, I may not doubt that I am or exist, so long as I am doubting or thinking. Therefore I who am doubting and thinking am not a body. For, in that case, in having doubts about my body I should be having doubts about myself. Indeed, even if I obstinately maintain that there are no bodies whatsoever, the proposition still stands, namely that I am something, and hence I am not a body.
>
> This is certainly very acute. But someone is going to bring up the objection that the author raises against himself: the fact that I have doubts about the body, or deny that it exists, does not bring it about that no body exists . . .
>
> I long ago learned from Augustine, in Chapter 15 of *De Animae Quantitate*, that we must completely dismiss those who believe that what we see with the intellect is less certain than what we see with these bodily eyes, which have to contend with a perpetual discharge of phlegm. This leads Augustine to say in the *Soliloquies*, Book I, Chapter 4, that when doing geometry he found the senses to be like a ship.
>
> For when they had brought me to the place I was aiming for, I sent them away, and now that I had set foot on the shore, I began to examine these matters using my thought alone. But for a long time my footsteps remained unsteady. Hence I think that a man can sooner sail on dry land than he can perceive geometrical matters through the senses, even though the senses do appear to give us some small assistance when we begin to learn.[115]

Here is Descartes's answer:

> I shall not waste time here by thanking my distinguished critic for bringing in the authority of St. Augustine to support me, and for setting out my arguments so vigorously that he seems to fear that their strength may not be sufficiently apparent to anyone else.[116]

What are we to think of Descartes's responses? First of all, it seems surprising that Descartes, convinced as he was of the originality of his thought, seems so unconcerned to learn that eleven centuries earlier, St. Augustine, the greatest authority of Latin Christendom, expressed similar ideas. And he systematically avoids a straightforward answer ("I have not yet been able to

115 *Fourth Set of Objections* (AT VII, 197–98, 205; CSM II, 139, 144).
116 *Replies to the Fourth Set of Objections* (AT VII, 219; CSM II, 154).

find it; nor have I managed to obtain the works of the Saint"; "It [the *cogito*] can be found in book eleven *De Civitate Dei*, chapt. 26"; "These are two very different things . . ."). Are we meant to conclude that he did not know the writings of St. Augustine before 1637, and saw those passages from Augustine only after his correspondents had pointed them out to him? Are we to assume that he first learned about the distinction between the soul and the body from Arnauld's *Objections*?

IV

In the letter to Mersenne of 21 of January 1641, Descartes cites a passage from Augustine's work – without, however, mentioning its title:

> I come back to your letter of 23 December, which I have not yet answered. The passage from Augustine relevant to the point at issue – namely that God is ineffable – depends merely on a small distinction which is very easy to understand. *Non possumus omnia quæ in Deo sunt verbis complecti, nec etiam mente comprehendere, ideoque Deus est Ineffabilis & Incomprehensibilis; sed multa tamen sunt revera in Deo, sive ad Deum pertinent, quæ possumus mente attingere ac verbis exprimere, imo etiam plura quam in ulla alia re, ideoque hoc sensu Deus est maxime Cognoscibilis & Effabilis* (We cannot encompass in words everything that is in God, or indeed grasp it in our minds, and hence God is ineffable and beyond our comprehension. But there are many things really in God, or that relate to God, that we are capable of reaching in our minds and expressing in words – more, indeed, than in the case of any other thing. And so in this sense God can be known and spoken of to a very great extent . . .).[117]

The passage to which he is referring comes from *The Christian Doctrine*, I, vi, 6 (Vol. II, p. 524):

> Have I spoken of God, or uttered His praise, in any worthy way? Nay, I feel that I have done nothing more than desire to speak; and if I have said anything, it is not what I desire to say. How do I know this, except from the fact that God is unspeakable? But what I have said, if it had been unspeakable, could not have been spoken. And so, God is not even to be called "unspeakable," because to say even this is to speak of Him. Thus there arises a curious contradiction of words, because if the *unspeakable* is what cannot be spoken of, it is not unspeakable if it can be called unspeakable. And this opposition of words is rather to be avoided by silence than to be explained

117 To Mersenne, 21 January 1641 (AT III, 284; CSMK III, 169).

> away by speech (*Diximusne aliquid et sonuinus aliquid dignum Deo ? Imo vero nihil me aliud quam dicere voluisse sentio: si autem dixi, non hoc est quod dicere volui. Hoc unde scio, nisi quia Deus ineffafbilis est; quod autem a me dictum est, si ineffabile esset, dictum non esset? Ac per hoc ne ineffabilis quidem dicendus est Deus, quia et hoc cum dicitur, aliquid dicitur. Et fit nescio quae pugna verborum, quoniam si illud est ineffabile, quod vel ineffabile dici potest. Quae pugna verborum silentio cavenda potius quam voce pecanda est*).

The above passage is part of a paragraph whose second half reads:

> And yet God, although nothing worthy of His greatness can be said of Him, has condescended to accept the worship of men's mouths, and has desired us through the medium of our own words to rejoice in His praise. For on this principle it is that He is called *Deus*. For the sound of those two syllables in itself conveys no true knowledge of His nature; but yet all those who know the Latin tongue are led, when that sound reaches their ears, to think of a nature supreme in excellence and eternal in existence.

This passage leads to the well-known letter to Mersenne of May 6, 1630:

> It is easy to be mistaken about this because most people do not regard God as a being who is infinite and beyond our grasp, the sole author on whom all things depend; they stick to the syllables of his name and think it sufficient knowledge of him to know that "God" means what is meant by *Deus* in Latin and what is adored by men.[118]

We may conclude that Descartes knew *The Christian Doctrine* before 1630: a fact he did not mention to Mersenne in 1630, or to anyone else for eleven years.

In reading Descartes through the "metaphysical prism" of Augustine (for example on the idea of God's incomprehensibility), one can see that the question of borrowings cannot be reduced to looking for a precise correspondence of certain ideas in the two authors. From the statement: "the sound of those two syllables in itself conveys no true knowledge of His nature," Augustine did not reach Descartes's conclusion that those who stop at the syllables of God's name can become atheists. Most likely certain passages in Augustine inspired Descartes to formulate an idea which subsequently developed a life of its own in his philosophy, independent of its source. There is no doubt that the passages from the *Christian Doctrine* served Descartes as

118 To Mersenne, 6 May 1630 (AT I, 150; CSMK III, 24–25).

the basis for two ideas: God's incomprehensibility (*God is ineffable*[119] *depends merely on a small distinction*), and the statement that the word *deus* is not confined to a purely religious function ("who is adored by men"), but is a guarantee of the existence of Truth itself.

V

The second text with reference to which Descartes mentions St. Augustine by name is the *Confessions*. In a letter to Denis Mesland, S.J., in 1644, fourteen years after formulating the doctrine of the eternal truths, Descartes refers to a passage from the *Confessions* in an attempt to lend official authority to his doctrine of divine simplicity:

> But if we would know the immensity of his power we should not put these thoughts before our minds, nor should we conceive any precedence or priority between his intellect and his will; for the idea that we have of God teaches us that there is in him only a single activity, entirely simple and entirely pure. This is well expressed by the words of St. Augustine: *Quia vides ea, sunt, etc. [They are so because thou see'est them to be so']*; because in God *seeing [videre]* and *willing [velle]* are one and the same thing.[120]

According to Descartes, St. Augustine believed that eternal truths owe their existence to the act of divine knowledge. The following passage, from a letter of May 6, 1630, corresponds to the idea that "*Quia vides eas, sunt*": "If men really understood the sense of their words, they could never say without blasphemy that the truth of anything is prior to the knowledge God has of it. In God willing and knowing are a single thing."[121] Although the letter was written in 1644, there are indications that Descartes was familiar with the

119 In the *Second Set of the Responses to the Meditations* (AT VII, 140; CSM, II 100), Descartes says: "Finally, when it is said that God 'cannot be thought of' (*Deus esse incogitabilis*), this refers to the kind of thought that has an adequate grasp of God, not to the inadequate thought which we possess, and that is sufficient for knowledge of the existence of God." It is likely that in using the expression *Deus esse incogitabilis*, Descartes had in mind the *Christian Doctrine* of St. Augustine to which he referred in his letter to Mersenne.

120 To Mesland, 2 May 1644 (AT IV, 119; CSMK III, 235). In the *Confessions*, XIII, xxxviii. 53, we read: "We see things You have made, because they are; and they are, because You see them. Looking outside ourselves we see that they are, and looking into our own mind we see that they are good; but You saw them as made when You saw that they were to be made." Augustine, *Confessions*, translated by F.J. Sheed (Indianapolis: Hackett Publishing Company, Inc., 1992), p. 287.

121 To Mersenne, 6 May 1630 (AT I, 149; CSMK III, p. 24).

Confessions before 1641 or even before 1637.[122] It is even probable that he read them before 1630.

But are the *Confessions* the only work that could have inspired Descartes? In *On the Trinity*, XV, xiii, 22, St. Augustine says: "And with respect to all His creatures, both spiritual and corporeal, *He does not know them because they are*, but they are *because He knows them*" (*non quia sunt ideo novit; sed ideo sunt quia novit. Non enim nescavit quae fuerat creaturus. Quia ergo scivit, creavit; non quia creavit, scivit*). In the letter to Mersenne of 15 April 1630, Descartes explains that the eternal truths "are true or possible only because God *knows them as true or possible*." Although the passage in *On the Trinity* is not about mathematical beings or essences of things, with which Descartes's doctrine is concerned, the idea that God creates by an act of *understanding* is common to both authors. We therefore cannot exclude the possibility that Descartes knew this passage before he formulated the doctrine of eternal truths.

In his third letter to Mersenne of May 27, 1630, Descartes gives the following definition of eternal truth: "For it is certain that he is the author of the essence of created things no less than of their existence; and this essence is nothing other than the eternal truths."[123] In the *City of God*, XXI, viii, 2[124] Augustine states that "the will of the great Creator assuredly is the nature of every created thing" (*cum voluntas tanti utique conditioris conditae rei cuiusque natura sit*[125]), and he adds:

> But because God is the author of all natures, why do they object to our supplying a stronger reason? For when they refuse to believe something, alleging its impossibility, and demand that we supply a rational explanation, we reply that the explanation is the will of Almighty God. For God is certainly called "Almighty" for one reason only; that he has the power to do whatever he wills.[126]

Did Descartes know the *City of God*? He did not admit it either in 1637 or in 1638, in his letters to Mersenne. He also avoided any direct comment on the matter in 1640, when Mersenne wrote him about the *cogito* for the third time. There are, however, indications that he had a very thorough knowledge of

122 In the *Discourse on Method*, IV (AT VI, 38; CSM I, 130), Descartes uses the expression "to participate in nothingness" (*participer du néant*), which corresponds to Augustine's idea in the *Confessions* XII, vi, 6 (*Index*: XIX). See also St. Thomas, *Summa Theologiae*, Ia, Q. 22, Art. 2.

123 To Mersenne, 27 May 1630 (AT I, 151; CSMK III, p. 25).

124 Cf. St. Augustine, letter 205 (*Patrologia Latina*, vol. XXXIII, p. 943), and supplementary note no. 40 in *Oeuvres de saint Augustin*, vol. 37, p. 800.

125 St. Augustine, *The City of God*, tr. by Henry Bettenson (London: Penguin Books, 1984), p. 980.

126 *Ibid.*, p. 977.

this work. In responding to the question posed by the authors of the *Sixth Set of Objections*, Descartes says:

> On this point all theologians are agreed, and the entire certainty of the Christian faith depends on it. For why should we believe what God has revealed to us if we thought that we were from time to time deceived by Him? And although the theologians commonly say that the damned are tormented by the fires of hell, they do not therefore believe that they are deceived by the fires of hell.[127]

And referring to this in his letter to Mersenne, he adds:

> Those who say that God continually deceives the damned, and that he might similarly be continually deceiving us, contradict the foundation of faith and all our belief, which is that *Deus mentiri non potest*[128] *[God cannot lie]*. This is stated over and over again in so many places in St. Augustine, St. Thomas, and others that I am surprised that any theologian denies that.[129]

127 *Replies to the Sixth Set of Objections* (AT VII, 428; CSM II, 289).

128 "Fourth, you say that God cannot lie or deceive," wrote the authors of the *Second Set of Objection to the Meditations*. "Yet there are some schoolmen who say he can. Gabriel [Biel], for example, and Ariminensis [Gregory of Rimini], among others, think that in the absolute sense God deceives that is communicates to men things that are opposed to His intensions and decrees" (AT VII, 125–26; CSM II, 89–90). For the texts the theologians probably had in mind, see: *Gregorii Arimienensis Oesa Lectura Super Primum Et Secundum Sententiarum* (Berlin/New York: Walter De Gruyter, 1987), vol. VII (*Index Rerum*): entries: *decipere* (p. 50), *fallacia* (p. 70), *mentiri* (p. 118). See also Gordon Leff, *Gregory of Rimini* (Manchester: Manchester University Press, 1961), esp. chap. III ("God and His Attributes").

For the citations from Gabriel Biel, see: *Collectiorum circa quattor libros Sententiarum: Prologus et Liber primus*, Gabriel Biel (*Collectiorum circa quattor libros Sententiarum: Prologus et Liber primus*, ed. Wilfridus Werbeck and Udo Hofmann (Tübingen: J.C.B. Mohr et Paul Siebeck, 1973), "Distinctio Quadragesima Septima, Questio Unica," "Utrum Deus potest facere malum fieri" (A, B, C), pp. 765–66. In section "C" Gabriel Biel states:

"Conclusio responsalis: Deus non potest facere malum nec praecipere malum secundum intentionem sanctorum, quia non potest facere male nec male praecipere. Ita si ex usu loquendi idem valet: *Deus malum facit* et *Deus facit male*, omnes sunt negandae, quia usus teneudus est, ne detur occasio erroris simplicibus.

"Sed diceres: Deus posset praecipere quod contra praeceptum ageretur, sicut dixit Osee: Accipe fornicariam. E ita praeciperet male agere.

"Solutio : In casu tollit praeceptum quantum ad illum; sed manente praecepto, non potest oppositum praecipere, quia hoc implicat : *praecipere* et *non praecipere*."

The problem of deception by God in the Middle Ages is discussed by Robert Pasnau, *Theorires of Cognition in the Later Middle Ages* (Cambridge: Cambridge University Press, 1997), pp. 229–36.

129 To Mersenne, 21 April 1641 (AT III, 359–60; CSMK III, p. 179).

Which works did Descartes have in mind? In St. Anselm's *Proslogion*, VII, we read: "Or, if Thou canst not be corrupted, and canst not lie, nor make what is true, false . . ."[130] A major part of the Fourth Book of Aquinas's *Summa Contra Gentiles* is devoted to the Last Judgment.[131] In chapter XC, Aquinas concerns himself with the following problem: "How can immaterial substances be tormented by material fire?" As for St. Augustine, he writes about lying only in the *City of God*:

> As for God's omnipotence, I have said a great deal about this already. But if our friends want to discover something that the Almighty cannot do, here they have it: God cannot lie! (Sed de omnipotentia eius, qua tot et tanta facit incredibilia, iam multa diximus. Si volunt invenire quod omnipotens non potest, habent prorsus, ego dicam: mentiri non potest).[132]

> . . . we cannot believe that God is impotent or that God is a liar (eique nos credere praedicenti, quem neque inpotentem neque mentientem possumus credere).[133]

Descartes repeats verbatim St. Augustine's phrase "God cannot lie" (*Deus mentiri non potest*). As for the deception of the damned, the whole of book XX of the *City of God* is devoted to the Last Judgment.

> In the punishment of the wicked, on the other hand, the unquenchable fire and the undying worm are explained by different authorities. Some people, in fact, refer both to the body in the literal sense, and the worm of the soul in the metaphorical sense, and this interpretation seems more credible (*In poenis autem malorum et inextinquibilis ignis et vivacissimus vernis ab allis atque aliis aliter atque aliter est expositus. Alii quippe utrumque ad corpus, alii utrumque ad animum retulerunt; alii proprie ad corpus ignem, tropice ad animum vermem, quod esse credibilius videtur*).[134] (*The City of God*, XX, xxii, p. 944).

In 1648, in the *Conversation with Burman*, Descartes makes the following remark:

130 In a letter to Mersenne, December 1640 (AT III, 261; CSMK III, 161), Descartes writes: "I shall look at St. Anselm at the first opportunity."

131 See also Book III. Cf. *Summa Theologiae*, 3a, LXXXVI (*De conditionibus corporum damnatorum resurgentum*), and XCVII, art. VI (*Utrum ignis inferni sit ejusdem speciei cum igne nostro*).

132 *The City of God*, XXII, xxv, p. 1077. Cf. Ibid. XXII, xxx.

133 *Ibid.*, XXI, v, 2, p. 973. Cf. *Ibid.* II, 26; II, 14; III, 7.

134 *Ibid.*, XX, xxii, p. 944.

> As far as *Genesis* is concerned, however, the story of the creation to be found there is perhaps metaphorical, and so ought to be taken as divided into six days, but the division into days should be taken as intended purely for the sake of our way of conceiving of things; this was the way Augustine proceeded when he made the divisions by means of the thoughts of angels (*Quantum autem ad Genesin attinet, forsan illa creations narratio, quae ibi habetur, est metaphorica, ideoque Theologis relinquenda; nec tum sumi debet creatio tanquam sex diebus distincta, sed tantum hoc ob nostrum concipiendi modum ita distingui dicidebet, quemadmodum Augustinus per cogitationes Angelicas illa distinxit*).[135]

Two works of St. Augustine could have inspired Descartes's response: *The Literal Meaning of Genesis* and the *City of God.* In the first, St. Augustine explains:

> . . . can we say that these three moments were simultaneous? They were not subject to the slow passage of time, as in the case of our days with the rising and setting of the sun and the return of the sun to the place of its rising. Day, evening, and morning at creation took place in the spiritual power of the minds of angels, who without any effort grasped at one and the same time all that they wished. . . . But the minds of angels, united to the Word of God in pure charity, created before the other works of creation, first saw in the Word of God those works to be made before they were actually made; and thus those works were first made in the angels' knowledge when God decreed that they should come into being, before they were made in their own proper natures.[136]

And in a passage in Book XI of the *City of God* (which also contains the *cogito*) he elaborates on this at much greater length:

> I have undertaken to treat of the origin of the Holy City, and I have decided that I must first deal with the subject of the holy angels. They form the greater part of that City, and the more blessed part, in that they have never been on pilgrimage in a strange land; and I shall be at pains to explain, with God's aid, the information given on this subject in the inspired testimonies of Scripture, as far as shall seem sufficient. When the sacred writings tell of the making of the world, there is no explicit statement about whether the angels were created, or in what order they were created. But if they

135 *Conversation with Burman* (AT V, 168; CSMK III, 349).
136 *The Literal Meaning of Genesis*, IV, 49, vol. I, p. 139.

> were not passed over in the narrative, they were referred to either under the name of "heaven," when it is said that "in the beginning God created heaven and earth," or, more probably, under the name of the "light," about which I have been speaking.
>
> I do not think that the angels were passed over, for this reason: that the Scripture says that God rested on the seventh day from all the works that he had done, while the whole book starts with the statement: "In the beginning God made heaven and the earth itself," which he made first, was, according to the next statement in Scripture, "invisible and disordered" and, because light had not yet been created, "darkness was over the abyss," that is, over a kind of confused and indistinct mass of land and water – because there must needs be darkness where light does not exist; then all things were set in order by God's creative act, all the things that, in the narrative, were completed in the course of the six days. How, then, could the angels have been passed over, as though they were not among those works from which God rested on the seventh day? . . . Although this is true, I do not think it would be out of harmony with the ways of God's working to suggest that, assuming the creation of the first light to refer to the creation of the angels, the distinction between holy and the unclean angels is described in the passage, "And God divided the light from darkness: and God called the light 'Day'; and he called the darkness 'Night.' . . . I am assuming that we are right in taking "first created light" a referring to them, or, more probably, in so interpreting "heaven" in the statement, "In the beginning God created heaven and earth." For the angels did not exist before they were made; otherwise these eternal beings would be thought to be co-eternal with God, if they are said to have existed always (*angeli creati sunt, si eos recte lux illa primum facta sunt significat*).[137]

Descartes's answer to the authors of the *Sixth Set of Objections* and the letter to Mersenne of late 1640 show that he almost certainly knew the *City of God* before he finished his *Meditations* in 1641. This in turn shows that he knew the Augustinian *cogito* before formulating his own in 1641.

We can go yet further and ask: did Descartes know the *City of God* before writing the *Discourse* in 1637? Let us recall that the *City of God* contains the *cogito* (which is also in the *Discourse*), as well as the phrase: "the will of the great Creator assuredly is the nature of every created thing" (*cum voluntas*

137 *The City of God*, XI, ix–xi, xix, pp. 438, 450; XII, xvi, 1, pp. 490–91 Cf. *The City of God*, XII, xvi, 1–3.

tanti utique conditioris conditae rei cuiusque natura sit), a formulation similar to Descartes's definition of the eternal truths in the 1630 letter to Mersenne.

On May 27, 1630, in responding to a series of questions posed by Mersenne, Descartes says: "As for the question whether *an Dei bonitati sit convieniens homines in æternum damnare [it is in accord with the goodness of God to damn men for eternity]*, this is a theological question: so if you please you will allow me to say nothing about it."[138] This speaks against the hypothesis that Descartes had read the *City of God* before 1630. However, his refusal might, of course, have been due to his unwillingness to get involved in theology (to "mix theology and philosophy"), rather than a case against the hypothesis that he knew the *City of God* in 1630.

There are a few indications that Descartes did know the *City of God* before 1630. First, the formulation of the *cogito* (at least the formulation as we know it in the *Meditations*)[139] is based on the hypothesis of the deceiving God and that of the evil genius. The hypothesis of the deceiver is refuted because God cannot lie, i.e., be a deceiver. If the "little treatise" did indeed contain the *cogito*, it must have also contained, in implicit or explicit form, the deceiver hypothesis. As far as I was able to verify, the only text in which St. Augustine says that God cannot deceive or lie, and to which Descartes refers, is the *City of God*. In other words, when Descartes formulated his *cogito*, he probably knew the *City of God*.

In the letter of 17 February 1645 to Clerselier, Descartes says:

> I am greatly obliged to you for the victories you are winning on my behalf. Your answer to the argument that *Pagani habuerunt ideam plurium Deorum [the pagans had the idea of many gods]*, etc., is very sound. For although the idea of God is imprinted on the human mind in such a way that everyone has within himself the power to know him, this does not prevent many people passing through their whole lives without ever having a distinct representation of this idea. Indeed those who think they have an idea of many gods have no idea of God at all. For, as you have so well noted, to conceive of many supremely perfect gods implies a contradiction.

And:

> When the Ancients referred to many powerful gods, they did not

138 To Mersenne, 27 May 1630 (AT I, 151–52; CSMK III, 26).

139 For differences between the two formulations of the *cogito*, see Jean-Luc Marion, *Questions cartésiennes II* (Paris: PUF, 1997), pp. 3–47; Ferdinand Alquié, *Descartes Œuvres philosophiques* (Paris: Classiques Gernier, 1989), vol. II, p. 604, note 4; and Etienne Gilson, *Discours de la méthode. Textes et Commentaire* (Paris: Vrin, 1987), p. 309.

> mean all-powerful gods but only many very powerful gods above whom they imagined a single Jupiter as sovereign; and consequently, to this Jupiter alone they applied the idea of the true God, this idea being presented to them in a confused manner.[140]

Cartesian commentators have tried to find the source of the famous Jupiter metaphor: "It is to talk of Him as if he were Jupiter or Saturn and subject him to the Styx and the Fates."[141] Is it an invention of Descartes's, or did Descartes take it from someone? We can be almost certain that the metaphor comes from Francis Bacon's *De sapientia veterum* (see Appendix III, ix below), but there a few small details in the above quotation from *The City of God* which one does not find in Bacon and which are present in the letter to Mersenne of 1630. The greater part of Book VII of *The City of God* is devoted to the issue of the plurality of heathen gods:

> There are those who use the name "destiny" to refer not to the conjunction of stars at the moment of conception, or birth, or beginning, but to the connected series of causes which is responsible for anything that happens. . . . For in fact they ascribe this orderly series, this chain of causes, to the will and power of the supreme God, who is believed, most rightly and truly, to know all things before they happen and who leaves nothing unordered. From him come all powers, but not all wills. What they mean by "destiny" is principally the will of the supreme God, whose power extends invincibly through all things . . .
>
> At all events, here are the gods to whom Varro, in the course of one book, gives the testimonial of "select": Janus, Jupiter, Saturn, Genius, Mercury, Apollo, Mars, Vulcan, Neptune, the Sun, Orcus, Father Liber, Earth, Ceres, Juno, the Moon, Diana, Minerva, Venus, Vesta – twenty in all, twelve males, eight females. . . . And now I should like our friends to explain what interpretation they want to be put on Jove, who is also called Jupiter. "He is the god," they say, "who has power over causes that effect all that happens in the world." There is a famous line of Virgil that attests the importance of this responsibility: "I call him happy Who could discern the causes of all things." . . . The reason is that the start of things rests with Janus, but the fulfillment with Jupiter, who is therefore rightly held to be the king of all (*rex omnium*), for the fulfillment sur-

140 To Clerselier, 17 February 1645 (AT IV, 187–88; CSMK III, 248).

141 For an extensive discussion of ancient sources, see Jean-Luc Marion, *Questions cartésiennes II* (Paris: PUF, 1997), pp. 119–41.

> passes the beginning. . . . But the causes which are assigned to Jupiter are efficient causes, not effects (*causae autem, quae dantur Iovi, efficientia sunt, non effecta*). . . . Is it then suggested that, if a man has two different powers and accomplishments in two different spheres, it follows from the diversity of the particular abilities that we should speak of two judges or two craftsmen. Similarly, the one God has the power over origins and causes; but are we therefore bound to suppose the existence of two gods, because origins and causes are two different things. . . . There is also a star called Saturn . . . they call Jupiter the king of all things. . . . Jupiter's star ought to be as much more brilliant than the others as Jupiter himself is more powerful than other gods.[142]

In this passage, St. Augustine addresses *all* the questions Descartes mentions in his letter to Clerselier: the plurality of gods; whether Jupiter and Saturn are one and the same god; whether Jupiter is the absolute sovereign. We can safely assume that Descartes knew the *City of God* before 1641. It is probable that in writing to Clerselier in 1644, he had in mind book VII of this work. Jupiter, in the terms used by St. Augustine, operates through efficient causes (*causa efficientia, non effecta*); and Descartes explains to Mersenne that God creates as the efficient and total cause (*ut efficiens & totalis causa*).[143] In the *City of God*, St. Augustine on several occasions defines Jupiter as a king; in the letter of 15 April 1630, Descartes, after explaining that God, unlike Jupiter or Saturn, is not subject to any force, compares God to a king who lays down eternal truths as a king might lay down laws. In 1641, when he returns to the subject of the creation of eternal truths, the metaphor of the king is absent: God, Descartes says, is like a "supreme legislator" (*summus legislator*[144]). Although it might be far-fetched to consider the use and change of the royal metaphor as proof that Descartes had read the *City of God* before 1630, it is possible that he was under its influence when writing the letter to Mersenne in 1630, and used the royal metaphor that he found there.

Furthermore, it is probable that the passage "the will of the great Creator is assuredly of the nature of every created thing" from the *City of God* served as the model for his definition of eternal truths in the letter of 27 May 1630 (*[God] is the author of created things no less than of their existence*). However, even if Descartes knew the *City of God* in 1630, this does not imply that he formulated the entire doctrine of eternal truths on the basis of the above phrase.

142 *The City of God*, V, 8 (pp. 188–89); VII, ii (p. 255), ix (pp. 265–66), x (pp. 267–68), xv (pp. 272–73

143 To Mersenne, 27 May 1630 (AT I, 152; CSMK III, 25).

144 *Réponses to the Sixth Set of Objections* (AT VII, 436; CSM II, 294).

His idea that the nature of things depends on God is not the cause but the consequence of his blurring the distinction between divine will and intellect. In other words, there is no logical passage from the statement: "the will of the great Creator assuredly is the nature of every created thing" (*The City of God*) to Descartes's thesis about the simplicity of divine nature (in God *velle* [to will] and *videre* [to see] are one and the same thing); nor to the conclusion that the nature of things depends on (the "will" of) God. The idea that "God is the author of both the essence and the existence of things" is a consequence of Descartes's conception of God. The conception of God according to which He creates things through an act of His cognition is a reply to the question: What is the *modus operandi* of God, whose nature is absolutely simple? Descartes could formulate this doctrine exclusively on the basis of the passage from *On the Trinity* (which would imply that he knew it before 1630), and not on the basis of any passage from the *City of God*.

VI

The doctrine of eternal truths is also based on another element: inneism.[145] The eternal truths are "*mentibus nostris ingenitæ* [innate in our minds], just as a king would imprint his laws on the hearts of all his subjects if he had enough power to do so." Two works by St. Augustine contain this idea: *On Free Will* and *The Literal Meaning of Genesis*, I, ix, 17. In *The Literal Meaning of Genesis*, St. Augustine says: "the forms (*rationes*) . . . are, so to speak, intelligible utterances impressed upon the intellect by the unchangeable Wisdom of God" (Vol. I, p. 29). In *On Free Will*, II, viii, 21 (p. 54), on the occasion of the discussion concerning the status of numbers, Augustine states:

> —A. If someone were to say to you that numbers were impressed upon our spirit not as a result of their own nature, but as a result of those objects we experience with bodily senses, what answer would you make? Or do you agree with this?
> —E. No, I do not. Even if I did not perceive numbers with the bodily senses, I would not be able to perceive with the bodily senses the meaning of division and addition. It is with the light of the mind that I would prove wrong the man who makes an error in addition or subtraction.

The numbers, like virtues, are "imprinted" in our minds.[146] As far as *The*

145 The sources of Descartes's "inneism" are discussed by E. Gilson in his "L'Innéism Cartésien et la théologie," in *Revue de Métaphysique et de Morale* 22 (1914).

146 In the *Immortality of the Soul*, St. Augustine defines as "rational" the relationship between numbers. In *Against the Academics*, the relationship called "rational" in the

Literal Meaning of Genesis is concerned, a passage from the *Discourse* suggests that Descartes read it before 1637.[147] As for *On Free Will*, there are three possible dates when Descartes could have read it: before 1630; after 1630[148] but before the publication of the *Discourse*; or after 1637 but before the publication of the *Meditations* in 1641. E. Gilson notices that the theme of free will, which occupies a large part of the Fourth Meditation, is completely absent from the *Discourse*, which seems to imply that at the time of the *Discourse* Descartes had not yet elaborated his conception of human liberty. This argument is not, however, very convincing. First, there are many themes in the *Meditations* which are absent from the *Discourse*. The absence of a discussion of human freedom in 1637 may be due either to formal reasons or, as I suggest above, to the "political" situation within the Church. Second, even if the reasons for supposing that Descartes was acquainted with this text before 1630 are purely conjectural, it is highly unlikely that Descartes formulated the conception of divine liberty (i.e., the doctrine of eternal truths) in 1630 without formulating its counterpart. In other words, if he formulated the conception of divine liberty in 1630, he probably also formulated the conception of human freedom.

> Thus the supreme indifference to be found in God is the supreme indication of His omnipotence. But as for man, because he finds that the nature of all goodness and truth is already determined by God, and his will cannot tend towards anything else, it is evident that he will embrace what is good and true all the more willingly, and hence more freely, in proportion as he sees it more clearly.[149]

The conception of human and divine freedom are two aspects of the same problem – the relation between man and God, creation and the Creator, the

Immortality of the Soul (in contradistinction to corporeal senses, which can be rendered doubtful as a result of sleep or of dementia) is called "certain." The examples that Augustine invokes (dreams and dementia on the one hand, and that three times three makes nine) are almost identical to those that Descartes uses in the First Meditation (AT VII, 20; CSMK, 14). It is almost certain that Descartes knew the *Against the Skeptics*. In the *Responses to the Second Set of Objections* (AT VII, 130; CSM II, CSM II, 94) he says: "Although I had seen many ancient writings by the Academics and Sceptics on this subject, and was reluctant to reheat and serve this precooked material, I could not avoid devote one whole Meditation to it." Did Descartes have in mind Augustine's *Contra Academicos*?

147 See *Index*: XXXV.

148 "I did not know that he [Father Gibieuf] published anything, but I will try to have his treatise sent from Paris as soon as possible so that I can see it." To Mersenne, 27 May 1630 (AT I, 153; CSMK III, 26).

149 *Responses to Sixth Set of Objections* (AT VII, 432; CSM II, 292).

Infinite and the finite. While God, insofar as He is the supreme Being, is "condemned" to be indifferent (and is by the same token free, in the sense of enjoying the liberty of indifference), man, insofar as he is a finite being, suffers from "ontological impotence"; he is condemned to follow the rules of the good and the true created by God. To be sure, nothing in Descartes's conception of human liberty compels us to accept the thesis that his reading of *On Free Will* was indispensable to his formulating the doctrine of human freedom: the conception of human liberty is a logical consequence of the conception of divine liberty. Descartes's conception of human liberty, however, requires an explanation of the cause of error, and this he certainly took from St. Augustine. When the will becomes indifferent, Descartes says in the Fourth Meditation, "it easily turns aside from what is true and good, and this is the source of my error and sin."[150] This explanation is almost certainly taken from *On Free Will*, II, xix, 53–xx,–54 (p. 162): "when it turns away from immutable and common goods, toward its private good, then the will sins . . . evil is turning away from immutable goods and a turning toward changeable goods. This turning of the will from the Lord God, is without doubt a sin." In the *Confessions*, in turn (VII, xvi, 22, vol. I, p. 111), St. Augustine says: "And I inquired what iniquity was, and ascertained it not to be a substance, but a swerving of the will that is turned toward lower things and away from Thee, O God, who are the Supreme Substance, toward these lower things, and casting out its bowels, and swelling outwardly."[151] It is improbable that Descartes formulated his conception of human freedom without having an answer to the question of the cause of error (why does the will turn from the good and the true?). The explanation that he gives in the *Meditations* comes either from *On Free Will* or from the *Confessions* or from both.

We will probably never know with absolute certainty that Descartes read *On Free Will* and the *Confessions* before 1630. However, he could have found the idea of inneism, the explanation of the cause of error, as well as the *cogito*, in *On Free Will*. In the *Confessions*, he could have found the explanation of the cause of error and, above all, the idea that *velle et videre* – the conception of the simplicity of divine nature which he formulated in 1630.

150 Med. IV (AT VII, 58; CSM II, 40–41).

151 This is how St. Augustine explains why the will turns away from the good: "Thus, according to the ancients [cf. Cicero, *Tusculan Disputations*, III, viii, 16–18], the very word *nequita* (worthlessness) – the mother of all vices – springs from *nequicquam*, that is, from that which is a nothing. The virtue which is opposite to this vice is called *frugalitas* (frugality), for, as this latter is called after the word *frux* (fruit), i.e., after *fructus* (enjoyment), because of a certain fecundity of the souls, so is *nequita* named after this sterility, i.e., after *nihil* (nothing); nihil is all that flows, that is dissolved, that melts and

VII

As I suggested above, the origin of the title of Descartes's *Meditations* should be sought in the tradition of Christian spiritualism. But which tradition? That of St. Ignatius of Loyola? Or that of Cardinal de Bérulle and the Augustinian-Oratorian Movement?

Let us again quote the sentence from the *Responses to the Second Set of Objections*:

> Many people had previously said (*jam ante dictum sit a multis*) that in order to understand metaphysical matters the mind must be drawn away from the senses (*mentem a sensibus esse abducendam*); but no one, so far as I know, had shown how this could be done. The correct, and in my view unique method of achieving this is contained in my Second Meditation.[152]

Who are these "many people"[153]? St. Augustine? And if so, which work(s) is Descartes thinking of? There are several possibilities. In *The Literal Meaning of Genesis*, the *Immortality of the Soul*, and *On the Trinity* Augustine frequently talks about the detachment of the spirit from the body. Here is a passage from *The Literal Meaning of Genesis*:

> But the soul itself is of a different nature, so that when it wishes to understand the divine or God, or simply to understand itself and consider its own virtues, it turns away from this light of the eyes in

steadily perishes. Because of this, we consider such men lost." *The Happy Life* (*De beata vita*); II, 8, p. 54.

152 *Responses to the Second Set of Objections* (AT VII, 131; CSM II, 94).

153 In Cicero's *Tusculan Disputations* (which Descartes certainly knew) and in Thomas's *Summa Contra Gentiles* is the following: "To withdraw the mind from sensual object, and abstract our thoughts from what we are accustomed to, is an attribute of a great genius (*Magni autem est ingenii, sevocare mentem a sensibus et cogitatinem ab consuetudine abducere*). . . . For the whole life of a philosopher is, as the same philosopher [Socrates] says, a meditation on death. For what else do we do, when we call off our minds from pleasure, that is to say our attention to the body. . . . What else is it, I say, that we do, but invite the soul to reflect on itself? oblige it to converse with itself, and, as far as possible, break off its acquaintance with the body? Now to separate the soul from the body, is to learn to die, and nothing else whatever." *The Tusculan Disputations,* I, xvi, I, xxx–xxxi, tr. by C.D. Yonge (London: George Bell and Sons, 1880), pp. 300, 316–17. "And this is all the more true of those in a fainting condition or in ecstasy, because such states involve an even greater withdrawal from the bodily senses. Nor does this come to pass undeservedly. For, because the human soul, as we have shown already, is situated on the boundary line between corporeal and incorporeal substances, as though it existed on the horizon of eternity and time, it approaches to the highest by withdrawing from the lowest." St. Thomas, *Summa Contra Gentiles*, II, 81.

> order to have true and certain knowledge, and recognizing that this light is no help for its purpose, in fact is even something of an obstacle, it raises itself up to the vision of the mind[154] (*cum vult intellegere vel divina vel Deum vel omnio etiam se ipsam suasque considerare virtutes, ut aliquid veri certique conprehendat, ab hac ipsorum quoque oculorum luce se avertat eamque ad hoc negotium non tantum nullo adivmento, verum etiam nonnullo inpedimento esse sentiens se in obtutum mentis adollat* . . . ; VII, xiv, 20. Vol. II, 16).
>
> We must distinguish the soul itself from its corporeal agents, whether vessels or organs or whatever else they may be called. The difference is evident from the fact that the soul is frequently concentrated in thought and turns itself away from everything, so that it is ignorant of many things which are present before the eyes when they are wide open and able to see (*Namque aliud esse ipsam, aliud haec eius corporalia ministeria, vel vasa vel organa vel si quid aptius dici possunt, hinc evidenter elucet, quod plerumque se vehementi cogitationis intentione avertit ab omnibus, ut prae oculis patentibus recteque valentibus multa posita nesciat* . . . ; VII, xix, 26. Vol. II, p. 20).
>
> But when the attention of the mind is completely carried off and turned away from the senses of the body, then there is rather the state called ecstasy (*Sed cum spiritalis visio penitus alienato a sensibus corporis animo imaginibis corporalium detinetur sive in somnis sive in extasi*. . . ; XII, xii, 26. Vol. II, p. 194).

Augustine's discussions in the *Literal Meaning of Genesis* are long and often vague; they certainly lack Cartesian precision. But the idea of detachment is essentially the same. If the passages cited above are not sufficiently convincing, here is a passage from *On Order*:

> The chief cause of this error is that man does not know himself. Now, for acquiring this self-knowledge, he needs a constant habit of withdrawing from things of the senses (*recedendi a sensibus*)[155] and of concentrating his thought within himself, and holding it there. This they alone succeed in doing who definitely mark out in solitude the impressions of opinion which the course of daily life has made, or correct them by means of the liberal branches of learning.
>
> When the soul has returned to itself in this manner, it understands what is the beauty of the universe; this term is evidently

154 See note 32 in *Oeuvres de saint Augustin*, vol. 48, pp. 701–4.
155 Cf. *Retractiones*, I. 3, 2.

> derived from the *unum* (one). Wherefore, the beholding of oneness is not granted to that soul which wanders toward many objects and eagerly pursues mental beggary, which, though it does not know it, can only be avoided by keeping aloof from the multitude; and I mean, not just the multitude of men, but of all things that the senses reach.[156]

The case being considered here is similar to that of the *cogito*. The conclusions Descartes draws from the idea of detachment are, to be sure, more extreme than St. Augustine's, but Descartes does not hesitate to exaggerate: "no one, so far as I know, had shown how this could be done." The Bishop of Hippo had traveled the same path before Descartes and showed him the way to the treasures in the Second Meditation: the *cogito* and the distinction between the thinking and extended substances.

Before considering the Second Meditation, let us turn to *On Order*. The structure of this work is strikingly similar to that of the *Discourse*. The language is very personal; like Descartes in the *Discourse*, St. Augustine tells how he was brought to study philosophy; like Descartes, he was tormented by the feeling of uncertainty, and to overcome it he decided to search for truth in solitude by acquiring the habit of detachment from the senses. It is likely that the structure of *On Order* served Descartes as a model for writing the *Discourse*. But the influence of *On Order* does not limit itself to the *Discourse*. Here is one of the most famous passages from the very beginning of the *Meditations*:

> I have always thought that two topics – namely God and the soul – are prime examples of subjects where demonstrative proofs ought to be given with the aid of philosophy rather than theology . . .[157]

In *On Order* II, xviii, 47 (p. 324) Augustine says:

> To philosophy pertains a twofold question: the first treats of the soul; the second, of God.[158] The first makes us know ourselves; the second, our origin. The former is the more delightful to us; the latter, more precious. The former makes us fit for a happy life; the latter renders us happy. The first is for beginners; the latter, for the will instructed. This is the order of wisdom's branches of study by which one becomes competent to grasp the order of things and to

156 *On Order*, I, i–ii, p. 241. See also *Index*: XII.

157 *Meditations*, AT VII, 1; CSM II, 3.

158 In *Soliloquies* I, ii, 7, St. Augustine says: "I long to know God and the soul. Nothing more? Absolutely nothing!" Cf. *Ibid*. II, i, 1.

> discern two worlds and the very Author of the universe, of whom the soul has no knowledge save to know how it knows Him not.

It is almost certain that Descartes read *On Order* before 1637[159]; whether he read it before discovering his "fine method," around 1628–29, will probably forever remain a mystery.

VIII

In the Second Meditation, Descartes shows us the fruits of the "method" of detachment. All the Augustinian citations gathered in the *Index* that correspond to passages in the Second Meditation come from five (four if we leave aside the *City of God*) works: *On the Trinity, The Literal Meaning of Genesis, The Immortality of the Soul*, and the *Magnitude of the Soul*. The Second Meditation contains two elements from *The Immortality of the Soul*: (1) *adspectus animi* (called by Descartes *mentis inspectio*), and (2) the famous example of the piece of wax. In *The Literal Meaning of Genesis* there are passages corresponding to (1) the (Cartesian) definition of the soul as something that is neither rarified air, nor wind, nor breath; (2) the idea that the soul is a substance radically different from the body, (3) the hypothesis of the evil genius, and (4) the idea that the soul, to know itself, must detach itself from the body. *The Magnitude of the Soul*, like *The Literal Meaning of Genesis*, contains a definition of the soul, and from this work Descartes almost certainly took the term "extension."[160] In *On the Trinity* there are several Cartesian themes: (1) the *cogito*, (2) the idea that the soul knows itself directly, (3) the idea that to know oneself one does not need the senses, (4) the idea that I am a thinking thing, and (5) the idea that the soul is a substance which does not occupy space. We know that Descartes knew these works. But when did he come to know them? As far as *The Literal Meaning of Genesis* is concerned, it is certain that Descartes had read it before writing the *Discourse*.[161] As for *On the Trinity* and *The Immortality of the Soul*, we have no additional information that might help us to establish the exact dates when he read them. We can only speculate.

Let us recall a few facts. In 1628, during the meeting at the nuncio's, Descartes talked about his "fine rule or method" which allowed him to determine the status of eternal truths. Around July 1629, he started editing his "lit-

159 In the *Discourse on the Method* (AT IX, 39; CSM I, 130) we read: "But once *the knowledge of God and the soul* has made us certain of this rule, it is easy to recognize that the things we imagine in dreams should in no way make us doubt the truth of the thoughts we have when awake."

160 See *Index*: XVI, XVIII.

161 See *Index*: XXXV.

tle treatise" on Divinity. At the same time, the *cogito* and the argument for the distinction between the soul and the body were elaborated. In 1630, Descartes explained to Mersenne that his conception of divine liberty, i.e., his doctrine of eternal truths, is inseparable from the method, which in turn depends on the method of detaching the mind from the body. I now juxtapose these facts in a very schematic way with the arguments in the *Meditations*.

Let us start with Descartes's proof for the existence of God. The proof depends on the distinction between soul and body; this distinction is preceded by the demonstration of the *cogito*; the *cogito* is preceded by the hypothesis of the *deus deceptor*, which presupposes the conception of science as knowledge that cannot be rendered dubitable. All these arguments are part of the way to attain "detachment" of the soul from the body through meditation; the goal of this detachment is the acquisition of "very clear and intuitive" knowledge of God and the soul. In which of Augustine's works do these elements occur?

1. The idea of detachment: *The Literal Meaning of Genesis, On Order, Immortality of the Soul, The Magnitude of the Soul* (*Index*: XL).
2. The distinction between science (*scientia*) and conviction (*persvasio*): *The Magnitude of the Soul* (*Index*: VI).
3. The deceiving god: *The Literal Meaning of Genesis* (*Index*: VI).
4. The *cogito* : *On the Trinity, On Free Will, City of God* (*Index*: IX).
5. The distinction between the soul and the body: *On the Trinity, The Immortality of the Soul, The Magnitude of the Soul,* and *The Literal Meaning of Genesis* (*Index*: XI–XIV).

A careful study of the above works leads to several conclusions. First, because the demonstration of the eternal truths depends on the detachment of the soul from the body, Descartes probably read *The Literal Meaning of Genesis* or *On Order*, or both, before 1630. Second, the proof for the existence of God precedes the demonstration of the *cogito*, and this implies that Descartes took it from *On the Trinity*, or *City of God*, or *On Free Will*. Moreover, because the *cogito* follows the hypothesis of the evil genius, which occurs only in *The Literal Meaning of Genesis*, Descartes must have read this work before 1630. Third, it is possible that Descartes read the *City of God* and *On Free Will* before 1630; but since there is no compelling argument to support this thesis, only one hypothesis remains: that Descartes probably read *On the Trinity* before 1630. If we do not accept this thesis, we must accept its opposite: that Descartes read either *City of God* or *On Free Will,* or both, before 1630.

The first alternative is supported by the phrase from the letter to Mersenne: "If men really understood the sense of their words they could never say without blasphemy that the truth of anything is prior to the knowledge that God has of it, because *in God willing and knowing are a single thing*."[162] Descartes could have found this phrase in the *Confessions*. But in the *Confessions*, this phrase – which Descartes cites in the letter to Mesland of 1641 – fails to take into account the *modus operandi* of God: in other words, it does not explain *how* God creates. On the other hand, the formulation in Descartes's letter to Mersenne repeats almost verbatim St. Augustine's phrasing in *On the Trinity*: "And with respect to all His creatures, both spiritual and corporeal, *He does not know them because they are*, but they are *because He knows them*." Descartes had only to modify the first part of the phrase (*all His creatures, both spiritual and corporeal*) by substituting "eternal truths" for "creatures" to arrive at the doctrine of the eternal truths. The sentence from the *Confessions* that in God *velle* et *videre* are one and the same could only strengthen Descartes's conviction that St. Augustine shared his view about the status of eternal truths.

IX

In the eyes of his contemporaries, Descartes's *Meditations* contained a completely new philosophy. After centuries of Scholasticism, Descartes created a philosophy that was written in a new language. With the exception of a few traditional terms *la nouvelle philosophie* was free of Scholastic terminology. Almost all the building blocks of this new philosophical edifice appeared to be different from the previous systems. What are these building blocks of Cartesianism?

1. The goal of philosophy: knowledge of God and the soul.
2. The distinction between science (*scientia*) and conviction (*persvasio*).
3. Mathematics is certain regardless of whether I am awake or asleep.
4. The evil genius.
5. The *cogito*.
6. The definition of the soul.
7. The notion of extension (*extensio*).
8. The example of a piece of wax.
9. *Inspectio mentis*.
10. I am a something mid-way between being and non-being.
11. The explanation of the source of error.

162 To Mersenne, 6 May 1630 (AT I, 149; CSMK III, 24).

12. In intellectual vision there is no error.
13. The intellect arbitrates among the data of the senses.
14. The soul is not like a pilot on a ship.
15. The "voluntarist" definition of eternal truths.
16. God creates by the act of his understanding.
17. Inneism.

This list is neither exhaustive nor definitive.[163] We should note, however, that all these elements can be found in the works of St. Augustine:

163 "Note, for example," Alfred Espinas writes, "certain common points between Descartes and St. Augustine that appear to me significant: the affirmation of absolute agreement between reason and faith, the possibility for all men to avoid error by suspending judgment, the constant reminder that the principle of the method is to detach the spirit from the body and from corporeal sensations that allow us to seize the truth, the certainty attributed to spiritual intuition and the life differentiated by the interior light that spreads over different phases of reasoning; the superiority of that which comes from the soul over that which is alien to it; the absorption of memory by intuition for all rational truths; the existence in us of an intellectual memory and of the intellectual cognition of the matter itself; the possibility of demonstrating metaphysical truths with the same certainty as in mathematics; definition of matter as something that is three dimensional and subject to changes; the incompatibility of the nature of matter defined in opposition to spirit that is indivisible and non-spatial; the soul is better known and is richer in its determinations than the body, but is inferior to God, and is kept on the level of creatures and placed in the center of things in an equal distance between God and matter, ruled by God who rules bodies; the idea that the soul is always the same, in infancy, in sleep, even in [man's] death; God is said to be good, exonerated from the existence of evil for this reason alone, that evil is privation and that error results from human freedom; God's goodness is invoked eleven times in the *Meditations*, the same number of times as it is invoked in Augustine to alleviate the inconvenience of the relationship between the body and the soul, but above all to demonstrate that God is not a deceiver, and to show that we can trust our cognitive faculties; Providence is praised for the mere fact that it created beings that float between nothingness and being (such as matter), because lower existences and created things lack the order and beauty of the universe; the establishment of the first principles by the act of divine arbitrary will; the direct action of God on matter; finally, a peculiar hesitation in acting on account of the soul's intimacy with the body; the clearness results from the sensible perception of figures and lesser or minor clarity results from the intuition of the intelligibles. Here we have the fundamental doctrines where Descartes and St. Augustine meet. They concern the most essential problems of philosophy and theology: namely, that of method, of the relationship between the soul and the body, and of the relationship between God and the world." *Descartes et la morale* (Paris: Éditions Bossard, 1925), vol. I, pp. 185–87. E. Gilson (*Discours de la méthode* [Paris: Vrin, 1987], p. 327) adds Augustinian theory of sensation.

1. The goal of philosophy: knowledge of God and the soul: *De Ordine*, II, xviii, 47 (*Index*: I).
2. The distinction between science (*scientia*) and conviction (*persvasio*): *De quantitate animae*, XXX, 58 (*Index*: VI)
3. Mathematics is certain regardless of whether I am awake or asleep: *De immortalitate animae*, XIV, 23 (*Index*: VIII); *Contra academicos*, III, xi, 25 (*Index*: IV); *De libero arbitrio*, II, viii, 21 (*Index*: IV).
4. The evil genius: *De Genesi ad litteram*, XII, xiii, 27–28–xiv, 30 (*Index*: VI).
5. The *cogito*: *De Civitate Dei*, XI, 26 (*Index*: XIX); *De Trinitate*, XV, xii, 21 (*Index*: XIX); *De libero arbitrio*,
6. The definition of the soul: *De Genesi ad litteram*, VII, xxi, 27; VII, xv, 21 (*Index*: X, XIII); *De quantitate animae*, I, 2 (*Index*: XIII).
7. The notion of extension (*extensio*): *De immortalitate animae*, V, 8; VI, 10 (*Index*: XVI, XVIII).
8. The example of a piece of wax: *De immortalitate animae*, V, 8 (*Index*: XVI).
9. *Inspectio mentis*: *De immortalite animae*, I, i, 1 (*Index*: XII); *De Trinitate*, X, x, 14 (*Index*: XIV).
10. I am something mid-way between being and non-being: *Confessiones*, XII, vi, 6 (*Index*: XIX).
11. The explanation of the source of error: *De libero arbitrio*, II, xix, 53–xx, 54; I, xvi, 35 (*Index*: XX); *Confessiones*, VII, xvi, 22 (*Index*: XX).
12. In intellectual vision there is no error: *De Genesi ad litteram*, XII, xxv, 52; XII, xxiv, 51 (*Index*: XXIV).
13. The intellect arbitrates among the data of the senses: *De vera religione*, XXIX, 53.
14. The soul is not like a pilot on a ship: *De quantitate animae*, XIV, 23 (*Index*: XXIX).
15. The definition of an eternal truth: *De Civitate Dei*, XXI, vii, 2 (*Index*: XXXIV).
16. God creates by the act of his understanding: *De Trinitate*, XV, xiii, 22; *Confessiones*, XIII, xxxviii. 53 (*Index*: XXXIV).
17. Inneism: *De libero arbitrio*, II, viii, 21 (*Index*: XXXVI).

Second, all these elements appear in the First, Second, Fourth, and Sixth Meditations, and in some of the letters to Mersenne where Descartes sets out the doctrine of the eternal truths. Why these four Meditations? Why are there no traces of St. Augustine in the Third[164] and Fifth? Unlike the First, Second,

164 In *Tractatus in Iohannis Evangelium*, XXIII, 10, there is a passage that sounds like the beginning of the Third Meditation: "Recognize in thyself something which I wish to

Fourth, and Sixth Meditations, the Third and Fifth Meditations deal with the proof for the existence of God – the Scholastic theme *par excellence.*[165] So it is not surprising that Descartes should use Scholastic terminology *only* in these two Meditations. But even here he uses only a handful of such terms. Compared to any text from the beginning of the seventeenth century,[166] the *Meditations* is free of Scholastic terminology. Here is a random and by no means exhaustive list of Scholastic terms:

> *esse seperatum, esse actu, esse non-actu, esse simpliciter, esse specificum, esse individuale, esse corporeum, esse ut quod, esse ut quo, propria existentia, actus purus, actus formalis essendi, ens actu, ens in potentia, ens in actu, entia actu, potentia intellectiva, potentia objectiva sive logica, potentia Dei ordinata, principium operandi, materia (prima) spiritualis, materia secunda, materia concretarationes seminales, inchoationes formarum, potentia activa, potentia passiva, forma corporeitatis, forma corporea, ultima forma, forma substantialis, forma corporeitatis, forma cadaverica, materia prima, materia absoluta, unitas specifica, unitas specifica positiva, compositio substantialis, ordo existendi, ordo essendi, intellectus agens, intellectus possibilis, principium factionis, principium cognitionis, causa prima, causa secunda, causa efficiens, propria existentia, distinctio realis, distinctio virtualis intrinseca, distinctio rationis rationitatae, appetitus rationalis, appetitus metamorphicus, appetitus elicitus, unitas ordonis.*

The *Meditations* is written in a new language. Neither doubt, nor the *cogito*, nor dualism, nor the distinction between extended and unextended substances – the subject-matter of the four "Augustinian" Meditations – belong to the Scholastic intellectual armory. With, on top of this, the conception of

say within, in thyself; not within as if in thy body, for in a sense one may say, 'in thyself'. . . Leave outside thy garment and thyself, descend into thyself, go to thy secret place, thy mind, and there see, if thou canst, what I wish to say. For if thou art far from thyself, how canst thou come near to God?" (*Agnosce in te aliquid, quod volo dicere, intus, intus in te, non in te quasi in corpore tuo, na, et ibi potest dici in te. . . . Sed relinque foris et vestem tuam et carnem tuam, descende in te, adi secretarium tuum, mentem tuam, et ibi vide quod volo dicere, si potueris*). Descartes: "I will now shut my eyes, stop my ears, and withdraw all my senses. I will eliminate from my thoughts all images of bodily things" (AT VII, 34; CSM II, 24). Cf. St. Anselm's *Proslogion*, I.

165 For Augustine's proofs for the existence of God, see A. De Mendonica, "To God through Self (or St. Augustine's Proof for the Existence of God)," *Philosophical Quarterly*, Amalner (India), 26, 1953, 1–17; Charles Boyer, "La preuve de Dieu augustinienne," in *Archives de Philosophie*, vol. VII, 2, 1929.

166 See for example Scipion Dupleix's *La métaphysique ou science surnaturelle*, Rouen: Louys du Mesnil, 1610.

Divine liberty, in 1641 Cartesian metaphysics must have appeared completely new. So it is not surprising that it soon came to be known as *la philosophie nouvelle*. What was not immediately apparent, however, at least to the Scholastically minded Jesuits, was the Augustinian provenance of this philosophy.

In the *Index* I cite eleven works by St. Augustine. Here I present a chart constructed according to the following criteria: the degree of probability of their reading (C=certain; VP=very probable; P=probable), and the probable dates when Descartes read them. I retain three principal dates: 1630 (the doctrine of eternal truths), 1637 (the publication of the *Discourse on the Method*), and 1641 (the publication of the *Meditations*).

	Before 1630	Before 1637	Before 1641
1. *The Christian Doctrine*	C		
2. *On Order*	P	C	
3. *The Immortality of the Soul*	VP		C
4. *The Magnitude of the Soul*	VP		C
5. *On Free Will*	VP		C
6. *On the Trinity*	(V)P		C
7. *The Confessions*	(V)P		C
8. *The Literal Meaning of Genesis*	VP		C
9. *The City of God*	P		C
10. *Against the Skeptics*			C
11. *True Religion*			VP

X

How did Descartes come to know the writings of St. Augustine? Like most of his contemporaries, Descartes received a Scholastic education; yet his sys-

tem has nothing or very little in common with that of his Jesuit masters in La Flèche. One of the teachers of theology there was Philippe Moncée, S.J., (1570–1619), the author of the *Disputationes theologicae in aliquot selectas D. Thomae quaestiones* (Lyon, 1621). Moncée's *Disputationes* was one of the most important Jesuit works in the early stage in their anti-Augustinian war. His theses were later accepted by all Jesuits in France which set the vectors for the subsequent theological discussions that culminated in the condemnation of Jansenius's teaching in 1653.[167] Besides, François Annat, an adversary of Gibieuf and an enemy of the Jansenists, agreed wholeheartedly with Moncée's anti-Augustinian position. We do not know whether Descartes knew Moncée while he was a student at La Flèche (1606–14), or whether he read his book; but the semi-Pelagian and anti-Augustinian position of Moncée was probably held by other theology teachers at the Jesuit colleges. The only plausible explanation of how Descartes came to know the writings of St. Augustine is the old thesis about his acquaintance with the charismatic Cardinal Pierre de Bérulle who spread his own Augustinianism among those who fell under his spell.[168]

Be that as it may, the question arises of why Descartes never admitted to having read the works of St. Augustine. There are several explanations. The first belongs to the domain of psychology and the nature of his project. Descartes knew very well that he was revolutionizing philosophy,[169] and like all revolutionaries he knew that no one could be trusted – even his closest friends. Second, it seems to have been part of Descartes's general attitude never to respond directly to questions concerning the relationship between his thought and that of St. Augustine. Third, Descartes may simply have wanted to preserve the originality of his thought. Perhaps. But he must have known that he was not the first to use the *cogito*: it occurs in the writings of

167 See Albert de Meyer, *Les premières controverses jansénistes en France: 1640–1649* (Louvain, 1919), p. 39.

168 See my *Cartesian Theodicy. Descartes' Quest for Certitude* (Dordrecht: Kluwer Academic Publishers, 2000), pp. 30–31.

169 "I may tell you, between ourselves, that these six Meditations contain all the foundations of my physics. But please do not tell people, for that might make it harder for supporters of Aristotle to approve them. I hope that readers will gradually get used to my principles, and recognize their truth, before they notice that they destroy the principles of Aristotle." (To Mersenne, 28 February 1641, AT III, 297–98; CSMK III, 173), and: "I have decided not to keep silent on this matter, and fight with their own weapons the people who confound Aristotle with the Bible and abuse the authority of the Church in order to vent their passions – I mean the people who had Galileo condemned. They would have my views condemned likewise if they had the power" (To Mersenne, 31 March 1641, AT III, 349–50; CSMK III, 177).

Eriugena, Antoine Sirmond, Jean de Silhon (Descartes's friend), and Campanella,[170] whose works he knew.[171] I believe that the reasons for his silence derive from the growing conflict in the Church after the publication in 1630 of *De Libertate Dei et creaturae* by Guillaume Gibieuf.

The question remains as to why Descartes was not more sincere with the Augustinians. Or, to put it another way, did he conceal his knowledge of the works of the spiritual patron of the seventeenth-century Augustinians? The question is by no means rhetorical. Consider again the reaction of Arnauld and Descartes's response.

> The first thing that I find remarkable is that our distinguished author has laid down as the basis for his entire philosophy exactly the same principle as that laid down by Saint Augustine – a man of sharpest intellect and a remarkable thinker, not only on theological topics but also on philosophical ones . . . I long ago learned from Augustine, in Chapter 15 of *De Quantitate animae* . . . (CSMK, II, 139–44).

What did Descartes answer?

> I shall not waste my time here by thanking my distinguished critic for bringing in the authority of divine Augustine to support me, and for setting out my arguments in a way betokening a fear that others might not deem them strong enough. (CSMK II, 154)

Etienne Gilson explains the encounter of the two thinkers in the following way: "quoting an authority against Descartes's clear and distinct ideas would have been a foolish thing to do, but quoting an authority in their favor was worse: it was an insult."[172] Gilson seems not to have fully appreciated the subtlety of Arnauld's remark, nor that of Descartes's response. Consider carefully Descartes's tactic. On the one hand, he goes to great lengths to avoid any association between his philosophy and the name of St. Augustine; on the other, he quotes almost verbatim from the writings of St. Augustine in his *Meditations*. And he does not even take the trouble to change the examples used by St. Augustine. Here are some comparisons:

170 See Léon Blanchet, *Les précédents historiques "je pense, je suis"* (Paris: Félix Alcan, 1920); Etienne Gilson, *Introduction à l'étude de saint Augustin* (Paris: Vrin, 1968), pp. 49–51.

171 To Mersenne, 9 March 1638 (AT II, 659). Cf. letter to Beeckman, 17 October 1630 (AT I, 158; CSMK III, 27).

172 E. Gilson, *The Unity of Philosophical Experience* (New York: Charles Scribner's Sons, 1937), p. 157.

1) St. Augustine:

> If, for example, wax somehow changes from a white to a black color, it remains, none the less, wax. It is also the same if it changes to a round from a square, or from soft to hard, or from warm to cold. All these changes are within the subject, and wax is the subject. And wax remains no more and no less wax, even though these qualities are changed (*The Immortality of the Soul*, V. 8, p. 25).

1) Descartes:

> Let us take, for example, this piece of wax . . . it is hard, cold and can be handled without difficulty; if you rap it with your knuckle it makes a sound. In short, it has everything that appears necessary to enable a body to be known as distinctly as possible. But even as I speak, I put the wax by the fire, and look: the residual taste is eliminated, the smell goes away, the color changes, the shape is lost, the size increases; it becomes liquid and hot; you can hardly touch it, and if you strike it, it no longer makes sound. But does the same wax remain? (Med. II. AT VII, 30–31; CSM II, 20).

2) St. Augustine:

> For it is the entire soul that feels the pain of a part of the body, yet it does not feel it in the entire body. When, for example, there is an ache in the foot, the eye looks at it, the mouth speaks of it, and the hand reaches for it. This, of course, would be impossible if what the soul is in these parts did not also experience a sensation in the foot; if the soul were not present, it would be unable to feel what has happened then. First, it would be incredible for a messenger to announce a fact, the occurrence of which he had not experienced (*The Immortality of the Soul*, XVI. 25, pp. 46–47).

2) Descartes:

> [W]hen I feel pain in my foot, physics tells me that this happens by means of nerves distributed throughout the foot, and that these nerves are like cords that go from the foot right up to the brain. When the nerves are pulled in the foot, they in turn pull on inner parts of the brain to which they are attached, and produce a certain motion in them; and nature has laid it down that this motion should produce in the mind a sensation of pain, as occurring in the foot (Med. VI. AT VII, 86–87; CSM II, 60).

3) St. Augustine:

> Hence, the human soul is not made of earth or of water or of air, or of fire (*The Literal Meaning of Genesis*, VII, xv, 21, vol. II, p. 16).

3) Descartes:

> I am not even some thin vapor which permeates the limbs – a wind, fire, air, breath, or whatever I depict in my imagination (Med. II. AT VII, 27; CSM II, 18).

4) St. Augustine:

> Yet whoever doubts that he himself lives, and remembers, and understands, and wills, and thinks, and knows, and judges. Seeing that even if he doubts, he lives; if he doubts, he remembers why he doubts; if he doubts, he understands that he doubts; if he doubts, he wishes to be certain; if he doubts, he thinks; if he doubts, he knows that he does not know; if he doubts, he judges that he ought not to assent rashly (*On the Trinity*, X, x, 14, p. 141).

4) Descartes:

> But what then am I? A thing that thinks. What is that? A thing that doubts, understands, affirms, denies, is willing, is unwilling, and also imagines and has sensory perceptions (Med. II. AT VII, 28; CSM II, 19).

5) St. Augustine:

> And in all these it [the soul] comes to know and seek what suits the nature of its body; it rejects and shuns what is unsuited (*The Magnitude of the Soul*, XXXIII, 71, p. 138).

5) Descartes :

> But a further problem now comes to mind regarding those very things which nature presents to me as objects that I should seek out or avoid (Med. VI. AT VII, 83; CSM II, 58).

6) St. Augustine:

> The will, however, commits sin when it turns away from immutable and common goods, toward its private good . . . evil is turning away from immutable goods and a turning toward

> changeable goods. This turning of the will from the Lord God, is wihout doubt a sin (*On Free Will,* II, xix, 53–xx–54, pp. 82–83).

6) Descartes:

> Because the will is indifferent in such cases, it easily turns aside from what is true and good, and this is the source of my error and sin (Med. IV. AT VII, 58; CSM II, 40–41).

7) St. Augustine:

> But what is this? Is it soul? Is it body? Is it any species of soul or body? If it were allowable to say that it is a nothing that is in some way something, or that it is and yet is not, that is what I should say (*Confessions*, XII, vi, 6, p. 237).

7) Descartes:

> I am, as it were, something intermediate between God and nothingness, or between supreme being and non-being (Med. IV. AT VII, 54; CSM II, 38).

Descartes does not give the impression of wanting to conceal anything; on the contrary, he behaves as though he wanted some of his readers to recognize the origin of his metaphysics. If he really did not want to be recognized as a reader of St. Augustine, he would not have left such explicit traces of his reading of St. Augustine's works. And there is nothing singular in St. Augustine's examples of a piece of wax or a foot. Descartes could perfectly well have changed the foot to a finger, or a hand, and the piece of wax to, say, a piece of iron.[173] Why didn't he? There seems to be only one answer: he sincerely wanted some of his readers – the Augustinians – to recognize them.

The exchange between Arnauld and Descartes is like a conversation between two English gentlemen. Once they realized that they went to the same college, they tacitly concluded that further questions are unnecessary.

173 "For when iron is melted in fire and reduced to a liquid, nothing of its nature appears to the senses to remain, but all is changed into the quality of fire, and it is by the reason alone that it is known to preserve its own nature, although reduced to a liquid state. So, just as the air appears wholly as light, and iron when melted appears to take on wholly the quality of fire, as we have said, and in fact to be fire, although their substances persist: so the sound intellect must hold that after the end of this world every nature, whether corporeal or incorporeal." *Iohannis Scotti Eriugenae Periphyseon* (*De Divisione Naturae*), Bk. I, 451, I.P. Sheldon-Williams ed. (Dublin: The Dublin Institute for Advanced Studies, 1968), pp. 57–59.

After exchanging a few courtesies, they plunge straight into the arguments. Arnauld had no need to cite other passages from the works of St. Augustine, nor to remind Descartes of the examples of a piece of wax or a foot and others, to let him know that he had recognized the source of the *nouvelle philosophie.*[174] To do so would have been an affront. Let us not forget that in 1641 the four great Augustinians – Bérulle, Gamasches (the professor of Charles de Condren, who was the second general of the Oratory), Saint-Cyran, and Jansenius – were dead,[175] and Arnauld was working on *La fréquente communion*, which was to appear in 1643. No one at that time knew the works of St. Augustine as well as Gibieuf and Arnauld. Allowing the Molinist-Scholastic Jesuits to realize that this author, too, a year after the publication of *Augustinus* by Jansenius and two years before the publication of Arnauld's "Jansenist manifesto,"[176] was making use of St. Augustine, would have been – to paraphrase Gilson – not only a stupid but, above all, a dangerous thing to do. Arnauld seems to have given Descartes a kind of sign, which the latter appreciated, and for which he politely thanked him (*I shall not waste my time here by thanking my distinguished critic for bringing in the authority of divine Augustine to support me*). The history of Cartesian philosophy, and by the same token the history of European philosophy, would almost certainly be very different if Arnauld had composed a list of passages in Augustine's writings corresponding to those in the *Meditations* to reveal Descartes's debt to St. Augustine.

One more question remains: what did Descartes expect from the Jesuits? If he was counting on their ignorance, he had good reason. The case (reported by Lancelot) of a certain doctor of the Sorbonne who in 1635 admitted that

174 Vincent Carraud proposes a different explanation: "[O]n peut s'étonner de l'absence de certains rapprochements – pour nous évidents –, qui apparaîtront peu à peu chez les cartésiens de la seconde moitié du siècle. Cette absence nous oblige à formuler l'hypothèse d'une connaissance assez réduite d'Augustin par Arnauld. Si par exemple, en 1641, Arnauld rapproche le cogito cartésien du *De libero arbitrio*, liv. II, c. III, on peut s'étonner qu'il faille attendre 1648 pour le voir mentionner avec enthousiasme le livre X du *De Trinitate*, pourtant beaucoup plus proche de l'ensemble de l'argumentation cartésienne (passage du doute à la pensée, distinction de l'esprit et du corps, fonction de l'imagination, etc.); le même *De Trinitate* pouvait être cité avec profit concernant les définitions de la substance, ce qu'Arnauld ne fait pas." "Arnauld: De l'occamisme au cartésianisme," *Chroniques de Port-Royal: Antoine Arnauld (1612–1694). Philosophe, écrivain, théologien* 44 (1995), pp. 261–62.

175 There was also a lay Augustinian, Nicolas Ysambert (1565–1642), professor at the Sorbonne, author of a commentary to Augustine's *De libero arbitrio*. Very little is known about him.

176 Leszek Kolakowski, *God Owes Us Nothing. A Brief Remark on Pascal's Religion and on the Spirit of Jansenism* (Chicago: The University of Chicago Press, 1995), pp. 67–68.

he had never read St. Augustine might be considered extreme,[177] but the correspondence between Saint-Cyran and Jansenius also leaves a strong impression that knowledge of the works of St. Augustine in the first half of the seventeenth century was rather rare. This explains why Descartes was never accused of "Augustinianism": in 1641 the authors of the *Objections to the Meditations*, with the exception of Arnauld (and probably Gibieuf and Mersenne[178]), were simply not aware of the "Augustinianism" of the *nouvelle philosophie*. The epoch of Augustinianism Cartesianized, or Cartesian Augustinianism, belongs to the second half of the seventeenth century, the second generation of the Oratorians – Ambrosius Victor, de Louis de La Forge, Bernard Lamy, and others. Had it not been for the labour of Saint-Cyran and Jansenius on the one hand, and that of Cardinal de Bérulle and the Oratorians of the first generation on the other, who reanimated interest in "positive theology,"[179] St. Augustine would have remained the greatest authority of the Latin Church known only through the intermediary of the Scholastics.

The success of Descartes's philosophy was somewhat accidental. Let us recall a few facts. The Oratory was founded in 1619, and in 1641 when Descartes published his *Meditations* it was entering only its third decade of existence. In terms of its educational infrastructure, it obviously could not compete with a hundred-year old Society of Jesus, which explains why Descartes thought it necessary to approach what was then the most powerful *international* educational institution. However, the idea of publishing *The Principles of Philosophy* (1644) that Jesuit philosophy professors could use in their courses as a textbook was as cunning as it was naïve. It was cunning because Descartes realized that to succeed in replacing "the philosophy of Aristotle," one has to seize the minds of young philosophy students; it was naïve because as an *educational* order, the Society of Jesus was by definition suspicious of novelties in education. Besides, when in 1543 Ignatius of Loyola founded the Society of Jesus, the order obligated itself to accept the

177 *Mémoires touchant la vie de Saint-Cyran* (Cologne, 1738), vol. I, p. 9.

178 The question arises as to what extent Mersenne was aware of Augustianism of his friend's philosophy. In a letter to Voetius, 13 December 1642 (AT III, 603), Mersenne says "the more one is acquainted with the doctrine of St. Augustine, the more one will be disposed to embrace the philosophy of Descartes." For a discussion of this question, see Henri Gouhier, *Cartésianisme et Augustinisme au XVIIe siècle* (Paris: Vrin, 1978), pp. 15–31.

179 See Joseph Turmel, *Histoire de théologie positive depuis l'origine jusqu'au Concile de Trente*, 2nd ed., Beauchesne, 1904; Henri Gouhier, "La crise de la théologie au temps de Descartes," *Revue de Théologie et de Philosophie* 4 (1954); Jean Dagens, *Bérulle et les origines de la restauration catholique: 1575–1611* (Paris: Desclée de Bouwer & Co., 1952).

theology of St. Thomas as its official doctrine: "In theologia legetur vetus et Novum testamentum et doctrina scholastica D. Thomae." This rule was confirmed by its General Claude Aquaviva in a memorandum of June 18, 1613.[180] The Society was then joined to the Holy See. Unlike the Jesuit Order, the Oratory was joined to the prelates. The Oratorians were united by the love of piety and sciences, following the constitution of the primitive Church. "Only the rule of charity binds us," Bernard Lamy says in his *Entretiens sur les sciences* (1768, p. 178). "If this bond is broken, we are no more." All those points are stressed by Bossuet in his funeral oration in memory of Father Bourgoing, the third general of the Oratory (and the editor of Gibieuf's writings). "It seems that the eulogy is a satirical tract against the Jesuits. What Bossuet praises in the Oratory stands in direct opposition to the constitution of the Jesuit Order. The two orders are no less opposed to each other in their respective constitutions, as in their spirit and their philosophical tendencies as well."[181]

If Descartes ever really succeeded in convincing the Jesuits, it was only when the Order almost completely lost its influence. When the Society was suppressed in Europe in 1762, one cannot find among its ranks one well-known, let alone outstanding writer. One should also note that around the middle of the eighteenth century all the famous enemies of Descartes's philosophy are dead: Daniel (†1728), Hardouin (†1729), Bouffier (†1737), Tournemine (†1739), Baltus (†1743).[182] If one wishes to establish a symbolic temporal caesura for the success of Descartes's philosophy among the Jesuits, there are two dates: 1741, the hundredth anniversary of the publication of the *Meditations*, when Father André, the celebrated convert into Cartesianism, publishes the *Essais sur le Beau*; or, 1755, when the twenty-nine year old Jesuit Father Antoine Guénard is awarded first prize by the French Academy in the essay-contest on the subject *L'Esprit philosophique*. Father Guénard's essay is a eulogy for Descartes for liberating philosophy from the yoke of the spirit of Aristotle and reintroducing the Christian spirit into philosophy.[183]

180 For the text, see Antoine Touron, *La Philosophie de St. Thomas d'Aquin* (Paris: Gissey et Boudelet, 1737), pp. 657–59.

181 Francisque Bouiller, *Histoire de la philosophie cartésienne* (Paris: Delgrave, 1868), vol. II, 6. See Bossuet, *Oraison funèbre du Père Bourgoing*, in Bossuet, *Oraisons funèbres de Bossuet*,, J. Truchet ed. (Paris: Éditions Garnier Frères, 1961), pp. 43–63. For the project of the Oratory designed by Bérulle and presented to the Archbishop of Paris, see Germain Habert, *Vie du Cardinal de Bérulle* (Paris, 1866), p. 333.

182 For a detailed account of their anti-Cartesianism, see Gaston Sortais, "Le Cartésianisme chez les Jésuites Français au XVIIème et au XVIIIème siècles," in *Archives de Philosophie* 6 (1929).

183 For the text of Father Antoine Guénard's eulogy, see Victor Cousin, *Fragments de*

All four commentators I cite in the Introduction – Bouiller, Rodis-Lewis, Gilson, and Carraud – stress the same point: before 1641, no one had been aware of the philosophical significance of the works of St. Augustine. Descartes was the first to recognize it. Not only did he create a new philosophy, but it was the first philosophy written in the language of Augustinian categories. Whether there is a logical or a causal link between the two systems of thought is not the issue here. The crucial fact is that the Cartesian idiom is that of St. Augustine. And this explains why the Augustinians embraced the *nouvelle philosophie* as their own. The Calvinist Pierre Jurieu was right to remark that there was something strange in the attachment of the Port-Royalists to Cartesianism. André Martin, in his Cartesian zeal, edited the writings of St. Augustine in light of the essential points of Descartes's philosophy. His veneration for St. Augustine equaled that of the French philosopher: "St. Augustine had more beauty and genius than Descartes; but Descartes had it more in other respects. Saint Jerome did not reason equally well."[184] Nicholas Poisson, another Oratorian admirer of Descartes, stated the issue of the relationship between the two thinkers even more emphatically: "St. Augustine sometimes speaks in language that he seems to have borrowed from Monsieur Descartes, or as if he were Descartes himself. For example, a passage from his letter to the Bishop Evodius is a *Discourse on Method*, which St. Augustine composed in the fourth century and which was published in the seventeenth century under the name of Monsieur Descartes."[185] A later disciple of Descartes went further than anyone else: there is no salvation in philosophy outside the philosophy of Descartes.[186]

"If one thinks about [the relationship between Augustine and Descartes]," writes Etienne Gilson, "it follows that despite the fact that they use the same concepts and put them in the same order, the two philosophies do not say the same thing."[187] Whatever our final judgment about the rela-

philosophie cartésienne pour faire suite aux fragments philosophiques (Paris: Didier, 1852), ccxxiv–ccxxxvj.

184 *Revue de Fribourg*, 1908, pp. 77–78.

185 *Commentaire ou Rémarques sur la Méthode de René Descartes, où on établit plusieurs Principes generaux, necessaires pour entendre toutes ses Oeuvres* (A Vandosme, chez Sebastien Hip, MDCLXX) p. 165. I was unable to find the fragment from the letter quoted by Poisson in Augustine's letters to Evodius.

186 These words are held in Charles de Quens's papers ("Notes on the Jesuits") held in Bibliothèque de Caen, MS. 267. Cited by Gaston Sortais, "Le Cartésianisme chez les Jésuites Français au XVIIème et au XVIIIème siècles," in *Archives de Philosophie* 6 (1929), p. 22.

187 E. Gilson, "L'Avenir de la métaphysique augustinienne," *Revue de Philosophie* 1 (1930), p. 701. Cf. *Discours de la méthode. Textes et Commentaire, op. cit.*, pp. 297–98. See also M.

tionship between Augustinianism and Cartesianism, we may safely conclude that even if Cartesianism is not the most faithful interpretation of the thought of St. Augustine, it is certainly a legitimate one. The metaphysics of Descartes cannot be reduced to the theology of St. Augustine. By the same token, we can be almost certain that the opposition of Descartes to the Scholastics is not limited to Aquinas or Suarez. However, as Etienne Gilson and Jean-Luc Marion have demonstrated, there is no question that Aquinas and Suarez were Descartes's greatest intellectual adversaries. Thus, in order to understand Descartes's metaphysics properly, one must read it in the light of the writings of Aquinas, Suarez, and St. Augustine.[188]

The dependence of Cartesian metaphysics on Augustinian theology does not diminish the genius and originality of Descartes's thought. Nor does the fact that his metaphysics owes a great deal to St. Augustine detract from its novelty. But it must be said that without the the Bishop of Hippo the French Philosopher would never have created his philosophy, at least in the form in which we know it. And without Cartesianism, European philosophy would not be what it is.[189]

E. Bandin, "Les rapportes de la raison de la foi du moyen âge à nos jours," *Revue des sciences religieuses* 3 (1923), pp. 233–55, 328–57, esp. pp., 508–37.

188 The influence of other thinkers on Descartes is indisputable. For Bacon, see Appendix III below; A. Laland, "Sur quelques textes de Bacon et de Descartes," in *Revue de Métaphysique et de Morale* 9 (1911); Leon Roth, *Descartes' Discourse on Method* (Oxford: Clarendon Press, 1937), pp. 52–71; for Ramus, see Gaston Sortais, *La philosophie moderne depuis Bacon jusqu'à Leibniz* (Paris: Paul Lethielleux, 1920), pp. 12–33; for Scriptural references, see Vincent Carraud, "Les réfèrences scriptuaires du corpus cartésien," in Bulletin Cartésien, XVIII, *Archives de Philosophie*, 1990, 1; and Vincent Carraud with Jean-Luc Marion, "De quelques citations cartésiennes de l'Écriture Sainte," in *Bulletin Cartésien*, 24, *Archives de Philosophie*, 1996, 1.

189 For example, John Searle considers Descartes's *Meditations* to be the book of the Millennium. "The *Meditationes* is not the best book of philosophy of the past 1,000 years by any means . . . [but Descartes] set the agenda for the next 350 years." "International books of the year and the millennium," *Times Literary Supplement* (3 December 1999), p. 6.

For the reception and various "appropriations" of Descartes's philosophy, mainly in France, see François Azouvi's "Descartes," in *The Place of Memory*, Pierre Nora ed. (New York: Columbia University Press, 1996) and *Descartes et la France: Histoire d'une passion nationale* (Paris: Fayard, 2002). See also, Gaston Sortais, "Le Cartésianisme chez les Jésuites français au XVIIème siècle," in *Archives de Philosophie* 3 (1929); on the reception of Descartes's philosophy in England, see G.A.J. Rogers, "Descartes and the English," in *The Light of Nature. Essays in the History and Philosophy of Science Presented to A.C. Crombie*, J.D. North and J.J. Roche eds. (Dordrecht: Martinus Nijhoff Publishers, 1985), pp. 281–302; and J.E. Saveson, "Differing Reactions to Descartes among the Cambridge Platonists," in *Journal of the History of Ideas* (1960), pp. 560–656.

Appendix I

St. Thomas Aquinas

Summa Contra Gentiles

SAINT THOMAS

I T

1) Intellectus igitur et voluntas in Deo non sunt ut potentiae, sed solum ut actiones. Patet etiam ex praedictis quod multitudo actionum quae Deo attribuitur, ut intelligere, velle, producere res, et similia, non sunt diversae res . . .

***Summa Contra Gentiles*, II, 10.**

II T

1) Ex hoc autem ulterius habetur quod divina consideratio non est ratiocinativa vel discursiva. Tunc enim ratio cinativa est nostra consideratio quando ab uno considerato in aliud transimus, sicut syllogizando a principiis in conclusiones. Non enim ex hoc aliquis ratiocinatur vel discurrit quod inscipit qualiter conclusio ex praemissis sequatur, simul utrumque considerans.

***Summa Contra Gentiles*, I, 57.**

RENÉ DESCARTES

I D

1) Car c'est en Dieu une mesme chose de *voluerit & intellexerit, illas creavit,* sans que l'un précède l'autre, *ne quidem ratione.*

A Mersenne, 27 mai 1630. AT I, l. 27–28.

II D

1) Neque hic loquor de priorite temporis, sed ne quidem pruis fuit ordine, vel natura, vel ratione rationitata,[1] ut vocant, ita scilicet ut ista boni idea impulerit Deum ad unum potius quam aliud eligendum.

***Sextae Responsiones*, AT VII, 432.**

1 "But to avoid confusion, in article 60 of Part One of my *Principles of Philosophy* [AT VIIIA, 28; CSM I, 213] where I discuss it explicitly, I call it a conceptual distinction – that is, a distinction made by reason *ratiocinatae.* I do not recognize any distinction made by reason *ratiocinatis* – that is, one which has no foundation in reality – because we cannot have any thought without a foundation; and consequently in that article, I did not add the term *ratiocinatae.*" (See also CSMK III, 280, editor's footnote 2.) For Aquinas's use of "ratiocinatio," see *Summa Theologiae* 1. 58. 4; 79. 8 and 12; 85. 5 and 6; 116. 3; 51. 2.

SAINT THOMAS

I T

1) [I]intelligence and will are in God, not as powers, but only as actions. From the foregoing it is clear, also, that the multifarious actions attributed to God, as understanding, willing, producing things [*intelligere, velle, producere res*], and the like are not diverse realities, since each of these actions in God is His very being, which is one and the same.

***Summa Contra Gentiles*, II, 10, [1–2].**

II T

1) We thereby know that the divine consideration is not ratiocinative or discursive (*ratiocinativa vel discursiva*). Our consideration is ratiocinative when we proceed from the consideration of one thing to another, as when in syllogistic reasoning we proceed from principles to conclusions. For, when someone examines how a conclusion follows from premises and considers both together, he is not on this account reasoning or discoursing, since this takes place, not by arguing, but by judging the arguments.

***Summa Contra Gentiles*, I, 57, [1–2].**

RENÉ DESCARTES

I D

1) In God, willing, understanding and creating [*voluerit & intellexerit, illas creavit*] are all the same thing without one being *ne quidem ratione* [prior to the other].

To Mersenne, 27 May 1630. CSMK III, 25-26.

II D

1) I am not speaking here of temporal priority: I mean that there is not even any priority of order, or nature, or of *ratiocinativa* [rationally determined reason], as they [the Schoolmen] call it, such that God's idea of the good impelled Him to choose one thing rather than another.

***Sixth Set of Replies*, AT VII, 432. CSM II, 291.**

2) [S]equitur quod contraria horum principiorum Deus facere non possit : sicut quod genus non sit praedicabile de specie; vel quod lineae ductae a centro ad circumferentiam non sint aequales; aut quod triangulus rectilineus non habeat tres angulos aequales duobus rectis.

***Summa Contra Gentiles*, II, 25, [4].**

3) Hac autem positione facta, secundum rationem praedictam nihilominus sequitur Dei virtutem esse infinitam. Nam sive ex tempore, secundum nos, sive ab aeterno, secundum eos, res produxerit, nihil esse potest in re quod ipse non produxerit: cum sit universale essendi principium.

***Summa Contra Gentiles*, I, 43.**

2) Neque hic loquor de prioritate temporis, sed ne quidem prius fuit ordine, vel natura, vel ratione rationitata, ut cocant, ita scilicet ut ista boni idea impulerit Deum ad unum potius quam aliud eligendum. Nempe, exempli causa, non ideo voluit mundum creare in tempore, quia vidit melius sic fore, quam si creasset ab aeterno; nec voluit tres angulos trianguli aequales esse duobus rectis, quia cognovit aliter fieri non posse & c. Sed contra, quia voluit mundum creare in tempore, ideo sic melius est, quam si creatus suisset ab æterno . . .

***Sextae Responsiones*, AT VII, 432.**

III T

1) Adhuc, circa rerum originem duplex est positio: una fidei, quod res de novo fuerunt a Deo productæ in esse; et positio philosophorum, quod res æterno a Deo *fluxerunt*. Secundum autem utramque positionem; oportet dicere quod res conserventur a Deo in esse. Nam, si res a Deo productæ sunt in esse postquam non fuerunt, oportet quod esse rerum divinam voluntatem consequatur, et similiter non esse; quia permisit res non esse quando voluit, et fecit res esse quum voluit; tamdiu

III D

1) . . . ces veritez eternelles, lequelles ie ne conçoy point *émaner* de Dieu, comme les rayons du Soleil . . .

A Mersenne, 27 mai 1630. AT I, 152.

2) . . . God cannot make the contraries of those principles; He cannot make the genus not to be predictable of the species, nor lines drawn from a circle's center to its circumference not to be equal, nor the three angles of a rectilinear triangle not to be equal to two right angles.

***Summa Contra Gentiles*, II, 25, [14].**

3) For, whether God produced things in time, as we hold, or from all eternity, according to them, nothing can be in reality that God did not produce; for God is the universal source of being.

***Summa Contra Gentiles*, I, 43, [14].**
Cf. *Ibid.*, II, 23.

2) For example, God did not will the creation of the world in time because he saw that it would be better this way than if He had created it from eternity; nor did He will that the three angles of a triangle should be equal to two right angles because he recognized that it could not be otherwise, and so on. On the contrary, it is because He willed to create the world in time that it is better this way than if He had created it from eternity . . .

***Sixth Set of Replies*, AT VII, 432.**
CSM II, 291.

III T

1) Furthermore, there are two positions regarding the origin of things: one from faith, holding that things have been brought into being by God, at the beginning; and the position of certain philosophers, that things have *emanated* from God eternally. Now, in either position one has to say that things are preserved in being by God. For, if things are brought into being by God, after they were not existing, then the being of things, and similarly their non-being, must result from the

III D

1) I do not conceive them [eternal truths] as *emanating* from God like rays from the sun . . .

To Mersenne, 27 May 1630. CSMK III, 25.

igitur sunt quamdiu Deus eas esse vult; sua igitur voluntas conservatrix est rerum. Si autem res ab æterno a Deo fluxerunt, non est dare tempus aut instans in quo primo a Deo effluxerunt; aut igitur nunquam a Deo productæ sun, aut semper a Deo earum esse procedit quamdiu sunt; sua igitur operatione res in esse conservat.

***Summa Contra Gentiles*, III, 65 [8]**

divine will; for He has permitted things not to be, when He so willed. Hence, they exist just as long as He wills them to be. Therefore, His will is the preserver of things. But, if things have eternally emanated from God, we cannot give a time or instant at which they first flowed forth from God. So, either they never were produced by God, or their being is always flowing forth from God as long as they exist. Therefore, He preserves things in being by His operation.

***Summa Contra Gentiles*, III, 65 [8]**

Appendix II

St. Thomas Aquinas

Summa Theologica

SAINT THOMAS

I T

1) Quia cum voluntas sit boni vel apparentis boni, nunquam *voluntas in malum moveretur nisi id quod non est bonum aliqualiter rationi bonum appararet*: et propter hoc voluntas nunquam in malum tenderet, nisi cum aliqua ignorantia vel errore rationis.

***Summa Theologica,* Ia2æ. Q. 77, Art. 2, resp.**

2) Ad primum ergo dicendum quod malum dicitur esse praeter voluntatem, quia voluntas non tendit in ipsum sub ratione mali. *Sed qui aliquod malum est apparens bonum,* ideo voluntas aliquando appetit aliquod malum.

***Summa Theologica,* I2æ. Q. 74, Art. 2.**

3) Peccatum igitur in humanis actibus contingit quandoque, sicut ex defectu intellectus, puta *cum aliquis per ignoratiam peccat,* et ex defectu appetitus sensitivi, sicut cum aliquis ex passione peccat, ita etiam ex defectu voluntatis, qui est inordinatio ipsius. Est autem voluntas inordinata, quando minus bonum magis amat.

***Summa Theologica,* I2æ. Q. 78, Art.1.**

RENÉ DESCARTES

I D

1) Vous rejettez ce que i'ay dit, qu'il suffit de bien iuger pour bien faire; et toutefois il me semble que la doctrine ordinaire de l'école est que *voluntas non fertur in malum, nisi quatenus ei sub aliqua ratione boni repræsentatur ab intelluctu* (*la volonté ne se porte pas vers le mal, sinon en tant que l'entendement le lui représente sous quelque raison de bien*) d'où vient ce mot: *omnis peccans est ignorans;* en sorte que si iamais l'entendement ne representoit rien à la volonté comme bien, qui ne le fust, elle ne pourroit manquer en son élection. Mais il luy represente souvent diverses choses en mesme temps; d'où vient le mot video meliora proboque . . .

A Mersenne, 27 avril, 1637. AT I, 366. Cf. *Quintæ Responsiones,* AT VII, 378, l. 20–25.

SAINT THOMAS

I T

1) Because the object of the will is the good, or at least the apparent good, the will is never attracted by evil unless it appears to have an aspect of good about it, so that the will never chooses evil except by reason of ignorance or error.

***Summa Theologica,* Ia2æ. Q. 77, Art. 2, resp. vol. 25, p. 165.**

2) Evil is said to be outside the will in the sense that the will does not desire it under the aspect of evil. However, sometimes a thing that is evil in itself has the appearance of good so that in desiring it the will does desire evil.

***Summa Theologica,* I2æ. Q. 74, Art. 2. vol. 25, p. 165.**

3) When sin occurs in human behavior it comes either from a defect of intellect, e.g., as when one sins from ignorance; or from a defect of the sense appetite, e.g., as when one sins by reason of emotional disturbance; or from a defect of the will which is nothing but an inherent lack of order. Lack of order can be ascribed to the human will when it loves a lesser good too much.

***Summa Theologica,* I2æ. Q. 78, Art.1. vol. 25, pp. 190–91.**

RENÉ DESCARTES

I D

1) You reject my statement that in order to do well it is sufficient to judge well; yet it seems to me that the common scholastic doctrine is that *voluntas non fertur in malum, nisi quatenus ei sub aliqua ratione boni repræsentatur ab intellectu* (*the will does not tend toward evil except insofar as it is presented to it by the intellect under some aspect of goodness*) – that is why they say that: *omnis peccans est ignorans* (*whoever sins does so in ignorance*) – so that if the intellect never represented anything to the will as good without its actually being so, the will could never go wrong in its choice. But the intellect often represents different things to the will at the same time; and that is why they say *video meliora proboque . . .* (*I see and praise the better, but I follow the worse*) . . .

To Mersenne, 27 April, 1637. CSMK III, 56. Cf. *Fifth Set of Replies,* II, 260.

II T

1) *Sed haec omnia [intellectus, voluntas, vis] in Deo unum sunt.*

***Somme théologique*, Ia, Q. 19. Art. 5. Cf. Art. 2.**

2) Ideo enim Deus aliquid facit, quia vult: non tamen ideo potest, quia vult, sed quia talis est sua natura.

***Summa Theologica*, Ia, Q. 25, Art. 5, ad 1. Cf. 25, Art 3.**

II D

1) Sed praetera in Deo intelligimus absolutam immensitatem, simplicitatatem, unitatem omnia alia attributa complectentem.

***Secundae Responsiones.* AT VII, 137.**

III T

1) Sicut et concursus duorum servorum, licet sit causalis quantum ad eos, est tamen provisus a domino, qui eos scienter, sic ad unum locum mittit, ut unus de alio nesciat.

***Summa Theologiae*, Ia, Q. 22. Art. 2.**

III D

1) C'est pourquoy ie passe à la difficulté que votre Altesse propose touchant le libre arbitre, duquel ie tascheray d'expliquer la dependance & la liberté par une comparaison. Si un Roy qui a defendu les duels, & qui sçait tres-assurément que deux Gentils-hommes de son Royaume, demeurans en diverses villes, sont en querelle, & tellement animez l'un contre l'autre, que rien ne les sçauroit empecher de se battre s'ils se rencontre; si, dis-ie, ce Roy donne à l'un d'eux quelque commission pour aller à certain iour vers la ville où est l'autre, & qu'il donne aussi commission à cét autre pour aller au mesme iour vers le lieu où est le premier, il sçait bien assurément qu'ils ne manqueront pas de se rencontrer, & de se battre . . .

A Elizabeth, Janvier 1646. AT IV, 352–52.

II T

1) *But in God all three [intellect, will, power] are one.*

***Summa Theologica,* Ia, Q. 19. Art. 5. Cf. Art. 2.**

2) It is not the case that he [God] can [make them (i.e., the possibles) because he wills, but he can] because he is such in his own nature.

***Summa Theologica,* Ia, Q. 25, Art. 5, ad 1.**

II D

1) But in addition to this, our understanding tells us that there is in God an absolute immensity, simplicity and unity which embraces all other attributes . . .

***Secundae Responsiones.* AT VII, 137.**

III T

1) For instance, the meeting of two servants, although to them it appears a chance circumstance, has been fully foreseen by their master, who has purposely sent them to meet at the one place, in such a way that the one has no knowledge of the other.

***Summa Theologiae,* Ia, Q. 22. Art. 2.**

III D

1) I turn to Your Highness's problem about free will. I will try to give an illustration to explain how this is both dependent and free. Suppose that a king has forbidden duels, and knows with certainty that two gentlemen of his kingdom who live in different towns have a quarrel, and are so hostile to each other that if they meet, nothing will stop them from fighting. If this king orders one of them to go on a certain day to the town where the other lives, and orders the other to go on the same day to the place where the first is, he knows with certainty that they will meet, and fight, and thus disobey his prohibition; but he does not thereby compel them.

To Elizabeth, January 1646. CSMK III, 280.

Appendix III

John Duns Scotus

DUNS SCOTUS

I S

1) Ad primam instantiam primo excludendam dico quod philosophi non posucrunt infinitatem possibilem in causis essentialiter ordinatis, sed tantum in accidentaliter ordinatis, sicut patet per Avicennam sexto *Metaphysicae*, cap. v, ubi loquitur de infinitate individuorum in specie. Et ad propositurn melius ostendendum sciendum quae sunt causae essentialiter et accidentaliter ordinatae, ubi notandum quod aliud est loqui de causis per se et per accidens; et aliud est loqui de causis per se sive essentialiter et accidentialiter ordinatis, narn in prima est tantum operatio unius ad unum, scilicet causae ad causatum, et est causa per se quae secundum naturam propriam, et non secundum aliquid sibi accidens, causat ut subjectum est causa per se respectu suae propriae passionis et in aliis ut album disgregat et aedificator aedificat; sed causa per accidens econverso ut Polycletus aedificat. In secundo est comparatio duarum causarurn inter se in quantum ab eis est causatum.

Et differunt causae per se sive essentialiter ordinatae a causis per accidens sive accidentaliter ordinatis in tribus. Prima differentia est, quod in per se ordinatis secunda in quantum causa dependet a prima.

In per accidens non, licet in esse

RENÉ DESCARTES

I D

1) Nempe a quo essem? A me scilicet, vel a parentibus, vel ab aliis quibuslibet Deo minus perfectis; nihil enim ipso perfectius, nec etiam aeque perfectum, cogitari aut fingi potest. . . . Atqui, si a me essem . . . atque ita ipsemet Deus essem. . . . Quantum denique ad parentes attinet, ut omnia vera sint quae de illis unquam putavi, non tamen profecto illi me conservant, nec etiam ullo modo me, quatenu sum res cogitans, effecerunt; sed tantum dispositiones quasdam in ea materia posuerunt, cui me, hoc est mentem, quam solam nunc pro me accipio, in esse judicavi. Ac proinde hic nulla de iis difficultas esse potest; sed omnino est concludendum, ex hoc solo quod existam, quaedamque idea entis perfectissimi, hoc est Dei, in me sit, evidentissime demonstrari Deum etiam existere. Forte vero illud ens non est Deus, sumque vel a parentibus productus, vel a quibuslibet aliis causis Deo minus perfectis. Imo, ut jam ante dixi, perspicuum est tantumdem ad minimum esse debere in causa quantum est in effectu; & idcirco, cum sim res cogitans, ideamque quandam Dei in me habens, qualiscunque tandem mei causa assignetur, illam etiam esse rem cogitantem, & omnium perfectionum, quas Deo tribuo, ideam

DUNS SCOTUS[1]

I S

1) To exclude this first objection, I say that the philosophers do not assume the possibility of an infinity in causes essentially ordered, but only in causes accidentally ordered, as is evident from Avicenna's *Metaphysics*, BK. VI, c. v, where he speaks of an infinity of individuals in a species. To understand better what we have in mind, one should know that some causes are essentially ordered and others accidentally ordered. Here it should be noted that it is one thing to speak of incidental causes (*causae per accidens*) as contrasted with those which are intended by their nature to produce a given effect (*causae per se*). It is quite another to speak of causes which are ordered to one another essentially or of themselves (*per se*) and those which are ordered only accidentally (*per accidens*). For in the first instance we have merely a comparison one-to–one of the cause to that which is caused. A *per se cause* is one which

RENÉ DESCARTES

1 D

1) From whom, in that case, would I derive my existence? From myself presumably, or from my parents, or from some other beings less perfect than God; for nothing more perfect than God, or even as perfect, can be thought of or imagined. . . . Yet if I derived my existence from myself . . . I should have given myself all the perfections of which I have any idea, and thus I should myself be God. . . . Lastly, as regards my parents, even if everything I have ever believed about them is true, it is certainly not they who preserve me; and insofar as I am a thinking thing, they did not even make me; they merely placed certain dispositions in the matter which I have always regarded as containing me, or rather my mind, for that is all I now take myself to be.

But perhaps this being is not God, and perhaps I was produced either by my parents or by other causes less perfect than God. No, for as I have said before, it is quite clear that there

1. Literature on possible sources of Descartes' Scholastic vocabulary in the Third Meditation is rather scanty. However, there are several articles worthy of mention: Roland Dalbiez, "Les sources scolastiques de la théorie cartésienne de l'être objectif. A Propos du 'Descartes' de M. Gilson," in *Revue d'Histoire de la philosophie* 3, pp. 464–72; Calvin Normore, "Meaning and Objective Being: Descartes and His Sources," in *Essays on Descartes' Meditations*, Amélie Oksenberg Rorty ed. (Berkeley: University of California Press, 1986), pp. 223–43; Marco Forlivesi, "La distinction entre concept formèl et concept objectif: Suarez, Pasqualigo, Mastri," in *Les Études Philosophiques*, 1, 2002.

vel aliquo modo alio depend eat. Filius enim licet secundum esse dependeat a patre, non tamen in causando, quia patre mortua potest agere sicut ipso vivo. Differentia secunda est, quod in per se ordinatis est causalitas alterius rationis et alterius ordinis, quia superior est perfectior; in accidentaliter autem ordinatis non. Et differentia haec sumitur ex prima; nam nulla causa a causa ejusdem rationis dependet essentialiter in causando, quia in causatione alicujus sufficit unum unius rationis. Tertia est, quod omnes causae essentialiter et per se ordinatae simul necessario requiruntur ad causandum, alioquin aliqua causalitas essentialis et per se deesset effectui; in accidentaliter autem ordinatis non est sic, quia non requiritur simultas eorum in causando, quia quaelibet habet suam perfectam causalitatem sine alia respectu sui effectus. Sufficit enim quod successive causet una post aliam.

"De Esse Dei," ***Opus oxoniense,*** **I, dist. ii, q. i., pp. 153–55.**

Tum quarto, quia superior causa est perfectior in causando ex secunda differentia; ergo in infinitum superior est in infinitum perfectior; ergo [MS in] infinitae perfectionis. Et nuna talis est causans de virtute alterius quia quaelibet talis est imperfecte causans, quia est dependens incausando ab alia.

"De Esse Dei," ***Opus oxoniense,*** **I, dist. ii, q. i., p. 158.**

habere fatendum est. Potesque de illa rursus quaeri, an sit a se, vel ab alia. Nam si a se, patet ex dictis illam ipsam Deum esse, qiua nempe, cum vim habeat per se existendi, habet proculdubio etiam vim possendi actu omnes perfections quarum ideam in se habet, hoc est omnes quas in Deo esse concipio. Si autem sit ab alia, rursus eodem modo de hac altera quaeretur , an sit a se, vel ab alia, donec tandem ad causam ultimam deveniatur, quae erit Deus.

Med. III, AT VII, 48, 50–51, 49–50.

causes a given effect by reason of its very nature and not by reason of something incidental to it. For instance, the subject is a *per se* cause of its proper attributes. Other such instances are "white dilating" or "a builder building." On the contrary, "Polycletus building" would be an incidental cause. In the second instance, two causes are compared with each other in so far as they are causes of the same thing.

Per se or essentially ordered causes differ from accidentally ordered causes in three respects. The first difference is that in essentially ordered causes, the second depends upon the first precisely in its act of causation. In essentially ordered causes, the second depends upon the first precisely in its act of causation.[2]

In accidentally ordered causes this is not the case, although the second may depend upon the first for its existence or in some other way. Thus a son depends upon his father for existence but is not dependent upon him in exercising his own causality, since he can act just as well whether his father be living or dead.[3] The second difference is that in essentially ordered causes the causality is of another nature and order, inasmuch as the higher cause is more perfect.

must be at least as much in the cause as in the effect. And therefore whatever kind of cause is eventually proposed, since I am a thinking thing and have within me some idea of God, it must be admitted that what caused me is itself a thinking thing and possesses the idea of all the perfections which I attribute to God. In respect of this cause one may again inquire whether it derives its existence from itself or from another cause. If from itself, then it is clear from what has been said that it is itself God, since if it has the power of existing through its own might! then undoubtedly it also has the power of actually possessing all the perfections of which it has an idea – that is, all the perfections which I conceive to be in God.

Med. III, CSM, II, 33, 35, 33.

2. For Ockham's critique of Scotus's distinction between essential and accidental causality, see *Questiones in lib. I Physicorum*, Q. cxxxiv; English translation by Philotheus Boehner, in Ockham, *Philosophical Writings* (Indianapolis, Cambridge: Hackett, 1990), pp. 177 ff.
3. For Ockham's use of the same example ("quia filius generat patre mortuo sicut vivo"), see *Questiones in lib. I Physicorum*, Q. cxxxv, English translation, *ibid.*, p. 120.

Such is not the case, however, with accidentally ordered causes. This second difference is a consequence of the first, since no cause in the exercise of its causality is essentially dependent upon a cause of the same nature as itself, for to produce anything one cause of a given kind suffices. The third difference is that all *per se* and essentially ordered are simultaneously required to cause the effect, for otherwise some causality essential to the effect would be wanting. Incidentally ordered causes this is not so, because there is no need of simultaneity in causing inasmuch as each possesses independently of the others the perfection of causality with regard to its own effect. For it is enough that one cause after the other exercises causality successively.

Duns Scotus, pp. 40–42.

Then, fourthly, by reason of the second difference, the higher cause is more perfect in its causality; therefore what is infinitely higher is infinitely more perfect and hence of infinite perfection. Now nothing infinitely perfect can cause something only in virtue of another, because everything of this kind is imperfect in its causality since it depends on another in order to cause its effect.

Duns Scotus, p. 42.

II S

1) B probatur, scilicet quod infinitas in accidentaliter ordinatis sit impossibilis, nisi ponatur status essentialiter ordinatorum, quia infinitas accidentalis, si ponitur, hoc non est simul, patet, sed successive tantum, ut alterum post alterum, ita quod secundum aliquo modo fluit a priore, non tamen dependet ab ipso in causando. Potest enim causare, illo non existente, sicut illo existente; sicut filius generat, patre mortuo sicut ipso vivo. Talis infinitas successionis est impossibilis, nisi ab aliqua natura infinite durante, a qua tota successio et quidlibet ejus dependeat; nulla enim difformitas perpetuatur, nisi in virtute alicujus permanentis quod nihil est illius successionis, quia omnia successiva ill ius successionis sunt ejusdem rationis, et quia nulla pars successionis potest permanere cum tota successione eo quod tunc non esset pars ejus. Sed est aliquid prius essentialiter, quia quidlibet successionis dependet ab ipso, et hoc in alia ordinatione quam a causa proxima, quia est aliquid illius successionis. Omne igitur quod dependet a causa accidentaliter ordinata, dependet essentialius a causa per se et essentialiter ordinata.

[S]i primum haberet omnem causalitatem formaliter simul, licet non possent causabilia simul poni in esse, esset infinitum, quia simul, quantum est ex se, posset infinita producere, et posse plura simul concludit

II D

1) Nam proculdubio illae [idea] quae substantias mihi exhibent, majus aliquid sunt, atquae, ut ita loquar, plus realitatis objectivae in se continent, quam illae quae tantum modos, sive accidentia, repraesentant; & rursus illa per quam summum aliquem Deum . . . plus perfecto realitatis objectivae in se habet, quam illae per quas finitae substantia exhibentur.

Jam vero lumine naturali manifestum est tantumdem ad minimum esse debere in causa efficiente & totali, quantum in ejusdem causae effectu. Nam, quaeso, undenam posset assumere realitatem suameffectus, nisi a causa? Et quomodo illam ei causa dare posset, nisi etiam haberet? Hinc autem sequitur, nec posse aliquid a nihilo fieri, nec etiam id quod magis perfectum est, hoc est quod plus realitatis in se continet, ab eo quod minus. Atque hoc non modo perspicue verum est de iis effectibus, quorum realitas est actualis sive formalis, sed etiam de ideis, in quibus consideratur tantum realitas objectiva. Hoc est, non modo non potest, exempli causa, aliquis lapis, qui prius non fuit, nunc incipere esse, nisi producatur ab aliqua re in qua totum illud sit vel formaliter vel eminenter, quod ponitur in la-pide; nec potest calor in subjectum quod prius non calebat induci, nisi a re quae sit ordinis saltem aeque perfecti atque est calor, & sic de caeteris; sed praeterea etiam non potest in me

II S

1) Now B (namely, at an infinity of accidentally ordered causes is impossible unless we admit that the essentially ordered series has an end) is proved in this way. If we assume an infinity of accidentally ordered causes, it is clear that these causes do not exist simultaneously but only successively, one after the other, so that what follows flows in some way from what precedes. Still the succeeding cause does not depend upon the preceding for the exercise of its causality, for it is equally effective. A son in turn may beget a child just as well whether his father be dead or alive [cf. *De Primo Principio*, 3.14]. But an infinite succession of causes is impossible unless it exists in virtue of some nature of infinite duration from which the whole succession and every part thereof depends. For no change of form is perpetuated save in virtue of something permanent which is not a part of succession. And the reason for this is that everything of this succession which is in flux, is of the same nature and no part thereof can be coexistent with the entire series for the simple reason that it would no longer be a part of the latter. Something essentially prior to the series then exists, for everything that is part of the succession depends upon it[4]

Duns Scotus, p. 43.

II D

1) But insofar as different ideas [are considered as images which] represent different things, it is clear that they differ widely. Undoubtedly, the ideas which represent substances to me amount to something more and, so to speak, contain within themselves more objective reality than the ideas which merely represent modes or accidents. Again, the idea that gives me my understanding of a supreme God . . . that exist apart from him, certainly has in it more objective reality than the ideas that represent finite substances.

Now it is manifest by the natural light that there must be at least as much [reality] in the efficient and total cause as in the effect of that cause. For where, I ask, could the effect get its reality from, if not from the cause? And how could the cause give it to the effect unless it possessed it? It follows from this both that something cannot arise from nothing, and also that what is more perfect – that is, contains in itself more reality – cannot arise from what is less perfect. And this is transparently true not only in the case of effects which possess [what the philosophers call] actual or formal reality, but also in the case of ideas, where one is considering only [what they call] objective reality. A stone [see Scotus, *De primo principio*, 4.72],

4. For an analysis of the proof for the existence of God, see Olivier Boulnois, "Preuve de Dieu et structure de la métaphysique selon Duns Scotus," in *Revue des Sciences Philosophique et Théologiques*, vol. 83, No. 1 (January 1999).

majorem potentiam intensive; ergo si habet perfectius quam si haberet omnem causalitatem formaliter, magis sequitur infinitas intensiva. Sed habet omnem causalitatem cujuslibet rei secundum totum quod est in re ipsa eminentius quam si esset formaliter. . . . [T]um quia perfectiones totae secundum Aristotelem eminentius sunt in primo quam si ipsae formalitates earum sibi inessent, si possent inesse. Quod probatur, quia causa secunda proxima primae totam perfectionem suam causativam habet a sola prima; ergo totam perfectionem illam eminentius habet causa prima quam secunda causa habens ipsam formaliter. Consequentia patet, quia prima respectu illius causae secundae est causa totalis et aequivoca. Consimiliter quaeratur de tertia causa respectu secundae vel respectu primae. Si respectu primae, habetur propositum. Si respectu secundae, sequitur secundam eminenter continere perfectionem totalem quae est formaliter in tertia. Sed secunda habet a prima quod sic continet perfectionem tertiae, ex praeostensa; ergo prima eminent ius habet continere perfectionem tertiae quam secunda; et sic de omnibus aliis usque ad ultimam; quare [concluditur] primam causam habere eminenter totalem perfectionem causatuam omnium et perfectius quam si haberet causalitatem, si omnium formaliter, si esset possibile.

"De Esse Dei," ***Opus oxoniense*, I, dist. ii, q. i. pp. 159–60, 196–97.**

esse idea caloris, vellapidis, nisi in me posita sit ab aliqua causa, in qua tantumdem ad minimum sit realitatis quantum esse in calore vellapide concipio. Nam quamvis ista causa nihil desua realitate actuali sive formali in meam ideam transfundat non ideo putandum est illam minus realem esse debere, sed talem esse naturam ipsius ideae, ut nullam aliam ex se realitatem formalem exigat, praeter illam quam mutuatur a cogitatione mea, cujus est modus. Quod autem haec idea realitatem objectivam hanc vel illam contineat potius quam aliam, hoc profecto habere debet ab aliqua causa in qua tantumdem sit ad minimum realitatis formalis quantum ipsa continet objectivae. Si enim ponamus aliquid in idea reperiri, quod non fuerit in ejus causa, hoc igitur habet a nihilo; atqui quantumvis imperfectus sit iste essendi modus, quo res est objective in intellectu per ideam, non tamen profecto plane nihil est, nec proinde a nihilo esse potest.

Med. III, AT, VII, 40–41.

Nec etiam debeo suspicari, cum realitas quam considero in meis ideis sit tantum objectiva, non opus esse ut eadem realitas sit formaliter in causis istarum idearum, sed sufficere, si sit in iis etiam objective. Nam quemadmodum iste modus essendi objectivus competit ideis ex ipsarum natura, ita modus essendi formalis competit idearum causis, saltem

If the First Being at one and the same time formally possessed all causal power, even though the things which it could cause could not be given simultaneous existence, it would be infinite, because – as far as it is concerned – it has power enough to produce an infinite number at once, and the more one can produce simultaneously, the greater the power in intensity. But if the First Being possessed such power in even more perfect way than if it had it *formally* [as Avicenna, for instance, assumes], its intensive infinity follows *a fortiori*. But the full causal power that each thing may have in itself, the First Being possesses even more perfectly than if it were formally present. . . . Also, the First Being, according to Aristotle, contains all the perfections in a more perfect manner than if they were *formally* present, were this latter possible. The proof of this lies in the fact that the secondary cause closest to the first receives all of its causal perfection exclusively from the first. Consequently, the First Cause has the whole of this perfection in a more eminent way than the second cause, which possesses it formally. The consequence is evident, since the first is the total equivocal cause of the second. We can argue the same way regarding the relation of the third cause to the second or first cause. If we take it in relation to the first, we have the proposed conclusion. If we take it in relation to the for example, which previously did not exist, cannot begin to exist unless it is produced by something which contains, either formally or eminently everything to be found in the stone; similarly, heat cannot be produced in an object which was not previously hot, except by something of at least the same order (degree or kind) of perfection as heat, and so on. But it is also true that the idea of heat, or of a stone, cannot exist in me unless it is put there by some cause which contains at least as much reality as I conceive to be in the heat or in the stone. For although this cause does not transfer any of its actual or formal reality to my idea, it should not on that account be supposed that it must be less real. The nature of an idea is such that of itself it requires no formal reality except what it derives from my thought, of which it is a mode. But in order for a given idea to contain such and such objective reality, it must surely derive it from some cause which contains at least as much formal reality as there is objective reality in the idea. For if we suppose that an idea contains something which was not in its cause, it must have got this from nothing; yet the mode of being by which a thing exists objectively [or representatively] in the intellect by way of an idea, imperfect though it may be, is certainly not nothing, and so it cannot come from nothing.

Med. III, CSM II, 28–29.

primis & praecipuis, ex earum natura. Et quamvis forte una idea ex alia nasci possit, non tamen hic datur progressus in infinitum, sed tandem ad aliquam prim am debet deveniri, cujus causa sit instar archetypi, in quo omnis realitas formaliter contineatur, quae est in idea tantum objective. Adeo ut lumine naturali mihi sit perspicuum ideas in me esse veluti quasdam imagines, quae possunt quidem facile deficere a perfectione rerum a quibus sunt desumptae, non autem quicquam majus aut perfectius continere.

Atque haec omnia, quo diutius & curiosius examino, tanto clarius & distinctius vera esse cognosco. Sed quid tandum ex his concludam? Nempe si realitas objectiva alicujus ex meis ideis sit tanta ut certus sim eandem nec formaliter nec eminenter in me esse, nec proinde me ipsum ejus ideae causam esse posse, hinc necessario sequi, non me solum esse in mundo, sed aliquam aliam reem, quae istius ideae est causa, etiam existere. Si vero nulla talis in me idea reperiatur, nullum plane habebo argumentum quod me de alicujus rei a me diversae existential certum reddat; omnia enim diligentissime circumspexi, & nullum aliud potui hactenus reperire.

Med. III, AT VII, 40-42.

second, then it follows that the second cause contains the total perfection found formally in the third. But as we have shown, the second cause owes this all to the First Cause; therefore, the First Cause must contain the perfection of the third in an even more perfect way than does the second. And the same is true with all the other causes down to the very last. Therefore we conclude that the First Cause contains eminently the total causal power of perfection of all the other causes, and this is a way that is even more perfect than if it contained this causality formally, were it possible.

Duns Scotus, pp. 64–66.

And although the reality which I am considering in my ideas is merely objective reality, I must not on that account suppose that the same reality need not exist formally in the causes of my ideas, but that it is enough for it to be present in them objectively. For just as the objective mode of being belongs to ideas by their very nature, so the formal mode of being belongs to the causes of ideas – or at least the first and most important ones – by their very nature. And although one idea may perhaps originate from another, there cannot be an infinite regress here; eventually one must reach a primary idea, the cause of which will be like an archetype which contains formally [and in fact] all the reality [or perfection] which is present only objectively [or representatively] in the idea. So it is clear to me, by the natural light, that the ideas in me are like [pictures, or] images which can easily fall short of the perfection of the things from which they are taken, but which cannot contain anything greater or more perfect.

The longer and more carefully I examine all these points, the more clearly and distinctly I recognize their truth. But what is my conclusion to be? If the objective reality of any of my ideas turns out to be so great that I am sure the same reality does not reside in me, either formally or eminently, and hence that I myself cannot be its cause, it will necessarily follow that I am not

alone in the world, but that some other thing which is the cause of this idea also exists. But if no such idea is to be found in me, I shall have no argument to convince me of the existence of anything apart from myself. For despite a most careful and comprehensive survey, this is the only argument I have so far been able to find.

Med III, CSM II, 29.

Appendix IV

Francis Bacon

Bacon, like Moses, led us forth at last;
The barren Wilderness he past;
Did on the very Border stand
Of the blast promised Land;
And from the mountain Top of his Exalted Wit,
Saw it himself, and shew'd us it

But Life did never to one Man allow
Time to Discover Worlds, and Conquer too;
Nor can so short a Line sufficient be
To Fadome the vast depths of Nature's Sea.

Abraham Cowley

The most unusual and the best of his works is that which is today the least read and the most useless; I have in mind his *Novum scientiarum organum*. This is the scaffolding by which the new philosophy has been built; and when that edifice had been erected at least in part, the scaffolding was no longer of any use . . . [Francis Bacon] is the father of experimental philosophy.

Voltaire

Bacon, the illustrious sophist, who first brought philosophy out of the schools.

Baron d'Holbach

FRANCIS BACON

I B

1) Atque hic simul pars destruens Instaurationis nostrae claudi debet,[1] quae perficitur tribus redargutionibus: Humanae Rationis Nativae et sibi permissae; redargutione Demonstrationum; et redargutione Theoriarum, sive philosophiarum et doctrinarum quae receptae sunt[2]. . . . Quum enim in hoc primo Aphorismorum libro illud nobis propositum sit, ut tam ad intelligendum quam ad recipiendum ea quae sequuntur mentes hominum praeparentur; expurgata jam et abrasa et aequata mentis area, sequitur ut mens sistatur in positione bona, et tanquam aspectu benevolo, ad ea quae proponemus. Valet enim in re nova ad praejudicium, non solum praeoccupatio fortis opinionis veteris, sed et praeceptio sive praefiguratio falsa rei quae affertur. Itaque conabimur efficere ut habeantur bonae et verae de iis quae adducimus opiniones, licet ad tempus tantummodo, et tanquam usurariae, donec res ipsa pernoscatur.

***Novum Organum*, I, cxv.**

RENÉ DESCARTES

I D

1) Semel in vita esse evertenda, atque a primis fundamentis denuo inchoandum, si quid aliquando firmum & mansurum cupiam in scientiis stabilire. . . . Opportune igitur hodie mentem curis omnibus exsolvi, securum mihi otium procuravi, solus secedo, serio tandem & libere generali huic mearum opinionum eversioni vacabo. . . . Nec ideo etiam singulae erunt percurrendae, quod operis infinite; sed quia, suffossis fundamentis, quidquid iis superaedificatum est sponte collabitur, aggrediar statim ipsa principia, quibus illud omne quod olim credidi nitebatur.

Med. I. AT VII, 17–18.

1 Cf. I, cxxviii.
2 Cf. I, xxxix–xliv.

FRANCIS BACON

I B

1) And here likewise should close that part of my *Instauration*, which is devoted to pulling down: which part is performed by three refutations; first, by the refutation of the *natural human reason*, left to itself; secondly, by the refutation of the *demonstrations*; and thirdly, by the refutation of the *theories*, or the received systems of philosophy and doctrine.[3] . . . For whereas in this first book of aphorisms I proposed to prepare men's minds as well for understanding as for receiving what is to follow; now that I have purged and swept and leveled the floor of the mind,[4] it remains that I place the mind in good position and as it were in a favorable aspect toward what I have to lay before it. For in a new matter, it is not only the strong preoccupation of some old opinion that tends to create a prejudice, but also a false preconception or prefiguration of the new opinions as to the things I propose, although they are to serve only for the time, and by way of interest (so to speak), till the thing itself, which is the principle, be fully known.

***Novum Organum*, I, cxv.**

RENÉ DESCARTES

I D

1) I realized that it was necessary, once in the course of my life, to demolish everything completely and start again right from the foundations if I wanted to establish anything at all in the sciences that was stable and likely to last. . . . So, for the purpose of rejecting all my opinions, it will be enough if I find in each of them at least some reason for doubt. And to do this I will not need to run through them all individually, which would be an endless task. Once the foundations of a building are undermined, anything built on them collapses of its own accord, so I will go straight for the basic principles on which all my former beliefs rested.

Med. I. CSM II, 12.

3 Cf. I, xxxix–xliv.

4 ". . . all of which [idols – i.e., prejudices] must be renounced and put away with fixed and solemn determination, and the understanding thoroughly freed and cleansed; the entrance into the kingdom of man, founded on the sciences, being not much other than

2) [S]ed instauratio facienda est ab imis fundamentis, nisi libeat perpetuo circumvolvi in orbem, cum exili et quasi contemnendo progressu.

***Novum Organum*, I, xxxi.**

II B

1) Licet autem confutationum particularium nullus sit usus, de sectis tamen et generibus hujusmodi theoriarum nonnihil dicendum est; atque etiam paulo post de signis exterioribus, quod se male habeant; et postremo de causis tantae infelicitatis et diuturni et generalis in errore consensus; ut ad vera minus difficilis sit aditus, et intellectus humanus volentius expergetur et Idola dimittat.

***Novum Organum*, I, lxi.**

II D

1) Ad hoc autem non erit necesse, ut omnes esse falsas ostendam, sed . . . si aliquam rationem dubitandi in unaquaque repero. Nec ideo etiam singulae erunt percurrendae, quod operis esset infiniti; sed quia, suffossis fundamentis, quidquid iis superaedificatum est sponte collabitur, aggrediar statim ipsa principia, quibus illud omne quod olim credidi nitebatur.

Med I. AT VII, 18.

III B

1) Nemo adhuc tanta mentis constantia et rigore inventus est, ut decrevit et sibi imposuerit, theorias et notiones communes penitus abolere, et intellectum abrasum et aequum ad particularia de integro applicare. Itaque ratio illa humana quam habemus, ex multa fide et multo

III D

the entrance into the kingdom of heaven, whereunto none may enter except as a little child." *Novum Organum*, I, lxvii. For Bacon's refutation of the *Idols*, see *Novum Organum*, I, xxxviii ff.

2) We must begin anew from the very foundations, unless we would revolve for ever in a circle with mean and contemptible progress.

***Novum Organum*, I, xxxi.**

II B

1) But though particular confutations would be of no avail, yet touching the sects and general divisions of such systems I must say something; something also touching the external signs which show that they are unsound; and finally something touching the causes of such great infelicity and of such lasting and general agreement in error; that so the access to truth may be made less difficult, and the human understanding may the more willingly submit to its purgation and dismiss its idols.[5]

***Novum Organum*, I, lxi.**

II D

1) So, for the purpose of rejecting all my opinions, it will be enough if I find in each of them at least some reason for doubt. And to do this I will not need to run through them all individually, which would be an endless task. Once the foundations of a building are undermined, anything built on them collapses of its own accord, so I will go straight for the basic principles on which all my former beliefs rested.

Med. I. CSM II, 12. Cf. *Discourse on the Method*, II. CSM II, 117.

III B

1) No one has yet been found so firm of mind and purpose as resolutely to compel himself to sweep away all theories and common notions, and to apply the understanding, thus made fair and even, to fresh examination of particulars. Thus it happens that human knowledge, as we have it, is a mere medley and ill-

III D

5 Marin Mersenne in his *Certitude des Sciences* (1625) speaks of the four Idols as four buttreses of Bacon's philosophy.

etiam casu, nec non ex puerilibus quas primo hausimus notionibus, farrago quaedam est et congries.

Quod si quis aetate matura et sensibus integris et mente repurgata se ad experientiam et ad particularia de integro applicet, de eo melius sperandum est. Atque hac in parte nobis spondemus fortunam Alexandri Magni. . . . Atque simile etiam de nobis judicium futuris temporibus factum iri existimamus: nos nil magni fecisse, sed tantum ea quae pro magnis habentur minoris fecisse . . . non est spes nisi in regeneratione scientiarum; ut eae scilicet ab Experientia certo ordine excitentur et rursus condantur: quod adhuc factum esse aut cogitatum nemo (ut arbitramur) affirmaverit.

***Novum Organum*, I, xcvii.**

IV B

1) Etenim in ea opinione sumus; si justam Naturae et Experientiae Historiam praesto haberent homines, atque in ea sedulo versarentur, sibique duas res imperare possent; unam, ut *receptas opiniones et notiones* deponerent; alteram, ut mentem a generalissimis et proximis ab illis as tempus cohiberent; fore ut etiam vi propria et genuina mentis, absque alia arte, in formam nostram Interpretandi incidere possent.

***Novum Organum*, I, cxxx.**

1) Sed ingens opus esse videbatur, eamque aetatem expectabam, quae foret tam matura, ut capessendis disciplinis aptior nulla sequeretur. Quare tamdiu cunctatus sum ut deinceps essem in culpa, si quod temporis superest ad agendum, deliberando consumerem.

Med I. AT VII, 18.

IV D

1) Sed quia jam ratio persuadet, non minus accurate ab iis quae non plane certa sunt ataue indubitata. . . . Nempe quidquid hactenus ut maxime verum admisi, vel a sensibus, vel per sensus accepi; hos autem interdum fallere deprehendi,[6] ac prudentiae est nunquam illis plane confidere qui nos vel semel deceperunt.

Med. I. CSM II, 12.

6 "In the first place, the impressions of the senses itself are faulty, for the sense both fails us and deceives us." *Novum Organum*, I, lxix. Cf.*Valerius Terminus*, chap 15, vol. III, p. 244, and *Great Instauration*, "Plan of the Work," vol. IV, pp. 26–28.

digested mass, made up of much credulity and much accident, and also of the childish notions which we at first imbibed.

Now if any one of ripe age, unimpaired senses, and well-purged mind, apply himself anew to experience and particulars, better hopes may be entertained of that man. In which point I promise to myself a like fortune to that of Alexander the great. . . . And a like judgment I suppose may be passed on myself in future ages:[7] there is no hope except in a new birth of science; that is, in raising it regularly up from experience and building it afresh; which no one (I think) will say has yet been done or thought of.

***Novum Organum*, I, xcvii.**

1) But the task [of demolishing everything] looked an enormous one, and I began to wait until I should reach a mature enough age to ensure that no subsequent time of life would be more suitable for tackling such inquiries. This led me to put the project off for so long that I would now be to blame if by pondering over it any further I wasted the time still left for carrying it out . . . .

Med. I. AT IX, 13. Cf. *Discourse on the Method*, II. AT VI, 22; CSM I, 122.

IV B

1) For I am of opinion that if men had ready at hand a just history of nature and experience, and labored diligently thereon; and if they could bind themselves to two rules,– the

IV D

Reason now leads me to think that I should hold back my assent from opinions which are not completely certain and indubitable. . . . Whatever I have up till now accepted as

7 "I appear merely as a guide to point out the road, an office of small authority, and depending more upon a kind of luck than upon any ability or excellency" (*Preface to the Novum Organum*); and: "I come to set forth the true way for the interpretation of nature" (*Ibid.*). A reference to John the Baptist who came "to prepare the way"? If Bacon's philosophy was merely to "prepare the way," Cartesianism was the means of "salvation." Unlike the Schoolmen, Poisson writes in his *Commentaire* (1670, pp. 3–4), "Mr. Descartes believed that in the kingdom of Heaven there are only children, and because only the poor in spirit will enter there, one should indeed be very simple to enter the Kingdom of Reason; the truths one finds there should be treated with simplicity and without ornaments." Bernard Lamy in his *Entretiens sur les Sciences* (Lyon: Pierre Bruyset Ponthus, 1767), p. 276, says: "One needs to credit our Century & France because Descartes is the first to have opened up the true path for sciences."

V B

1) Nostra enim via inveniendi scientias exaequat fere ingenia, et non multum excellentiae eorum relinquit: cum omnia per certissimas regulas et demonstrationes transigat. . . . Nihil enim illis detrahitur, quum de via omnino quaestio sit. Claudus enim (ut dicitur[8]) in via anteverit cursorem extra viam. Etiam illud manifesto liquet, currenti extra viam, quo habilior sit et velocior, eo majorem contingere aberrationem.

***Novum Organum*, I, cxxii; I, lxi.**

V D

1) Le bon sens est la chose du monde la mieux partagée . . . et ainsi que la diversité de nos opinions ne vient pas de ce que les uns sont plus raisonnables que les autres, mais seulement de ce que nous conduisons nos pensées par diverses voyes, & ne considerons pas les mesmes choses. Car ce n'est pas asses d'avoir l'esprit bon, mais le principal est de l'appliquer bien . . . ceux qui ne marchent que fort lentement, peuvent avancer beacoup davantage, s'ils suivent toujours le droit chemin, que ne sont ceux qui courent, & qui s'en esloignent.

***Discours de la Méthode*, I. AT VI, 1–2.**

VI B

1) Meta autem scientiarum vera et legitima non alia est, quam ut dotetur vita humana novis inventis et copiis. . . . Neque enim negamus, postquam omnia omnium artium

VI D

1) Car elles m'ont fait voir qu'il est possible de parvenir a des connoissances qui soient fort utiles a la vie, & qu'au lieu de cette Philosophie speculative, qu'on enseigne dans les

8 The expression comes from St. Augustine's Sermon CLXIX.

first, to lay aside received opinions and notions; and the second, to refrain the mind for a time from the highest generalizations, and those next to them,– they would be able by the native and genuine force of the mind, without any other art, to fall into my form of interpretation.

***Novum Organum*, I, cxxx.**

most true I have acquired either from the senses or through the senses. But from time to time I have found that the senses deceive, and it is prudent never to trust completely those who deceived us even once.

Med. I. CSM II, 12.

V B

1) For my way of discovering sciences goes far to the level of man's wits, and leaves but little to individual excellence; because it performs everything by the surest rules and demonstrations. . . . For they are no wise disparaged – the question between them and me being only as to the way. For (as the saying is), the lame man who keeps the right road outstrips the runner who takes a wrong one. Nay it is obvious that when a man runs the wrong way, the more active and swift he is the further he will go astray.

***Novum Organum*, I, cxxii; I, lxi.**

V D

1) Good sense is the best distributed thing in the world . . . the diversity of our opinions does not arise because some of us are more reasonable than others but solely because we direct our thoughts along different paths and do not attend to the same things. For it is not enough to have a good mind; the main thing is to apply it well. The greatest souls are capable of the greatest vices as well as the greatest virtues; and those who proceed but very slowly can make much greater progress, if they always follow the right path, than those who hurry and stray from it.

***Discourse on the Method*, I. CSM I, 111.**

VI B

1) Now the true and lawful goal of the sciences is none other than this: that human life be endowed with new discoveries and powers. . . . For I, although I do not deny that when all the experiments of all the arts

VI D

1) For they opened my eyes to the possibility of gaining knowledge which would be very useful in life, and of discovering a practical philosophy which might replace the speculative philosophy taught in the

experimenta collecta et digesta fuerint atque ad unius hominis notitiam et judiciam pervenerint, quin ex ipsa traductione experimentorum unius artis in alias *multa nova inveniri possint ad humanam vitam et statum utilia*, per istam Experimentiam quam vocamus Literatam ; sed tamen minora de ea speranda sunt.

***Novum Organum*, I, lxxxi; I, ciii.**

2) Tertiam partem Medicinæ posuimus illam de *Prolongatione Vitæ*, quæ nova est, et *desideratur*; estque omnium nobilissima. Si enim tale aliquid inveniri possit, non versabitur tantum medicina in curationum sordibus, nec medici ipsi propter necessitatem solummodo honorabuntur; sed utique propter donum mortalibus ex terrenis quasi maximum, cujus poterint esse secundum Deum *disponatores et administri*. Licet enim Mundus homini Christiano ad Terram Promissionis contendenti tanquam Eremus sit, tamen in Eremo ipso proficiscentibus caceos et vestes (corpus scilicet nostrum, quod animæ loco tegminis est) minus atteri, Gratiæ Divinæ munus quoddam æstimandum. Hac de re, quia est ex optimis, eamque inter Desiderata posuimus, ex more nostro et Monita dabimus et Indicia et Præcepta.

***De Augmentis*, IV, ii, vol. II, p. 336.**

escholes, on peut trouver une pratique, par laquelle connoissant la force & les actions du feu, de l'eau, de l'air, des austres, des cieux, et de tous les autres cors qui nous environnent . . . nous les pourrions employer en mesme façon à tous les usages ausquels les sont propres, & *ainsi nous rendre comme maitres & possesseurs de la Nature*. Ce qui n'est pas seulement à desirer pour l'invention d'une infinité d'artifices . . . *mais principalement aussy pour la conservation de la santé.*

***Discours de la Méthode*, VI, AT VI, 61–62.**

shall have been collected and digested, and brought within one man's knowledge and judgment, the mere transferring of the experiments of one art to others may lead, by means of that experience which I term *literate*, to *the discovery of many new things of service to the life and state of man* . . .

***Novum Organum*, I, lxxx; *ibid.*, I, ciii.**

2) The third part of Medicine which I have set down is that which relates to the prolongation of Life, which is new, and deficient; and the most noble of all. For if such a thing may be discovered, the business of medicine will no longer be confined to humble cures, nor will physicians be honored only for necessity; but for a gift to men – of earthly gifts perhaps the greatest – of which, next to God, *they may become the dispensers and administrators*. For although to a Christian making for the Land of Promise the world is but a wilderness, yet even while we travel in the wilderness to have our shoes and garments (that is our bodies, which are the clothing of the soul) not worn out by the way, must be accounted as a gift of divine grace.

***De Augmentis*, Bk. IV, ii, vol. IX, p. 39.**

schools. Through this philosophy we could know the power and action of fire, water, air, the stars, the heavens and all the other bodies in our environment . . . and we could use this knowledge – as the artisans use theirs – for all the purposes for which it is appropriate, and thus *make ourselves, as it were, the lords and masters of nature*. This is desirable not only for the invention of innumerable devices . . . *but also, and most importantly, for the maintenance of health* . . .

***Discourse on the Method*, VI, CSM I, 142–43.**

3) Recuperet modo genus humanum jus suum in naturam quod ei ex dotatione divina competit, et detur ei copia: usum vero recta ratio et sana religio gubernabit.

Etenim in ea opinione sumus: si justam Naturae et Experientiae Historiam praesto haberent homines, atque in ea sedulo versarentur, sibique duas res imperare possent: unam, ut receptas opiniones et notiones deponerent; alteram, ut mentem a generalissimis et proximis ab illis ad tempus cohiberent: fore etiam vi propria et genuina mentis, absque alia arte, in formam nostram Interpretandi incidere possent. Est enim Interpretatio verum et naturale opus mentis, demptis iis quae obstant.

***Novum Organum*, I, cxxix, cxxx.**

VII B

1) Scientia aquarum similis est. Aquarum aliæ descendunt cœlitus, aliæ emanant e terra. Etiam Scientiarum primaria partitio sumenda est ex fontibus suis. Horum alli in alto siti sunt, alii hic infra. . . . Philosophiæ autem objectum triplex, Deus, Natura, Homo. . . . Convenit igitur partiri Philosophiam in doctrinas tres; Doctrinam de *Numine*, Doctrinam de *Natura*, doctrinam de *Homine*. Quoniam autem partitiones scientiarum non sunt

VII D

1) Ainsi toute la philosophie est comme un arbre, dont les racines sont la Metaphysique, le tronc est la Physique, & les branches qui sortent de ce tronc sont toutes les autres sciences . . .

***Principiorum Philosophia*e, AT IX, 14.**

3) Only let the human race recover that right over nature which belongs to it by divine bequest,[9] and let power be given it; the exercise thereof will be governed by sound reason and true religion.

For I am of the opinion that if men had ready hand a just history of nature and experience, and labored diligently thereon; and if they could bind themselves to two rules,– the first, to lay aside received opinions and notions; and the second, to refrain the mind for a time from the highest generalizations, and those next to them,– they would be able by the native and genuine force of the mind, without any other art, to fall into my form of interpretation.[10] For interpretation is the true and natural work of the mind when freed from impediments.

***Novum Organum*, I, cxxix, cxxx.**

VII B

1) The knowledge of man is as the waters. Some waters descend from above, and some spring from beneath; and in like manner the primary division of sciences is to be drawn from their sources; of which some are above in the heavens, and some here below. . . . The object of philosophy is threefold – God,

VII D

1) The whole of philosophy is like a tree. The roots are metaphysics, the trunk is physics, and the branches emerging from the trunk are all the other sciences . . .

***Principles of Philosophy* (Preface to the French Edition). CSM I, 186.**

9 Here Bacon has in mind the passage from Genesis I.

10 "That reason which is elicited from facts by a just and methodical process, I call Interpretation of Nature" (*Novum Organum*, I, xxvi.).

lineis diversis similes, quæ coëunt ad unum angulum; sed potius ramis arborum, qui conjunguntur in uno trunco (qui etiam truncus ad spatiam nonnullum integer est et continuus, antequam se partiatur in ramos); idcirco postulat res, ut priusquam prioris partitionis membra persequamur, constituatur una *Scientia Universalis,* quæ sit mater relinquarum, et habeatur in progressu doctrinarum tanquam portio viæ communis antequam viæ se separent et disjungant. Hanc Scientiam *Philosophiæ Primæ,* sive etiam *Sapientiæ* (quæ olim *rerum divinarum atque humanarum scientia* definiebatur), nomine insigimus. Huic autem scientiæ nulla alia opponitur; cum ab aliis scientiis potius limitibus intra quos continetur quam rebus et subjecto differat; fastiga scilicet rerum tantummodo tractans.

***De Augmentis Scientiarum,* Bk. III, 1.**
Vol. I, pp. 539–40.

2) Sunt enim Scientiæ instar pyramidum, quibus Historia et Experientia tanquam basis unica substernuntur; ac proinde basis Naturalis Philosophiæ est Historia Naturalis. Tabulatum primum a basi est *Physica;* vertici proximum Metaphysica; ad conum quod attinet et punctum verticale (*opus quod operatur Deus a principio usque ad finem*); summariam nempe naturæ legem),

Nature, and Man. . . . Philosophy may therefore be conveniently divided into three branches of knowledge: knowledge of God, knowledge of Nature, and knowledge of Man, or Humanity. But since the divisions of knowledge are not like several lines that meet in one angle; but are rather like branches of a tree that meet in one stem (which stem grows for some distance entire and continuous, before it divides itself into arms and boughs); therefore it is necessary, before we enter into the branches of the former division, to erect and constitute one universal science, to be as the mother of the rest. . . . This science I distinguish by the name of *Philosophia Prima*, primitive or summary philosophy; or Sapience, which was formerly defined as the knowledge of things divine and human.

***De Augmentis Scientiarum*, Bk. III, i. Vol. IV, pp. 336–37. For the corresponding passage in *The Advancement of Learning*, see vol. III, p. 346.**

2) For knowledges are as pyramids, whereof history and experience are the basis. And so of Natural Philosophy the basis is Natural History; the stage next the basis is Physic; the stage next the vertical point is Metaphysic. As for the cone and vertical point, *The work which God worketh from the beginning to the end* [Eccles. iii. II], namely, the summary law of nature, it may fairly be

hæstitamus merito, an humana possit ad illud inquisitio pertingere.

De Augmentis Scientiarum, **vol. I, p. 567.**

VIII B

1) Neque enim officimus, quin philosophia ista recepta, et aliæ id genus, disputationes alant, sermones ornent . . . atque non disputando adversarium, sed opere naturam vincere; denique, non belle et probabiliter opinari, sed certo et ostensive scire; tales, tanquam veri scientiarum fillii, nobis (si videbitur) se adjungant.

Præfatio, Novum Organum. **Vol. I, 154.**

VIII D

1) Et ie n'ay iamais remarqué non plus, que, par le moyen des disputes qui se pratiquent dans les escholes, on ait découvert aucune verité qu'on ignorast auparavant . . . en sorte que, selon que i'auray desormais la commodité d'en faire plus ou moins, i'avanceray aussy plus ou moins en la connoissance de la Nature. Ce que ie me prometois de faire connoistre, par le traité que i'avois escrit, & d'y monstrer si clairement l'utilité que le public en puet recevoir, que i'obligerois tous ceux qui desirent en general le bien des hommes, c'est a dire, tous ceux qui en effect vertueux, & non point par faux semblant, ny seulement par opinion, tant a me communiquer celles qu'ils ont desia faites, qu'a m'ayder en la recherche de celles qui restent a faire.

Discours de la Méthode, **VI. AT VI, 69, 65.**

doubted whether man's inquiry can attain to it.

De Augmentis Scientiarum, **Bk. III, 4. Vol. IV, p. 362. For the corresponding passage in** ***The Advancement of Learning*****, see vol. III, p. 356.**

VIII B

1) I do not object to the use of this received philosophy, or others like it, for supplying matter for disputations or ornaments for discourse,-for the professor's lecture. . . . [My purpose is] to overcome, not an adversary in argument, but nature in action; to seek, not pretty and probable conjectures, but certain and demonstrable knowledge;- I invite all such to join themselves, as true sons of knowledge.

Preface to the ***Novum Organum.***

VIII D

1) Nor have I ever observed that any previously unknown truth has been discovered by means of the disputations practiced in the schools. . . . And so the advances I make in the knowledge of nature will depend henceforth on the opportunities I get to make more or fewer of these observations. I resolved to make this known in the treatise I had written, and to show clearly how the public could benefit from such knowledge. This would oblige all who desire the general well-being of mankind – that is, all who are really virtuous, not virtuous only in appearance or merely in repute – both to communicate to me the observations they had already made and to assist me in seeking those which remain to be made.

Discourse on the Method**, VI. CSM I, 146, 144.**

IX B

1) Pervulgate est narratio, et in compluribus interponitur, de unico illo juramento, quo dii superi se obstringere solebant, cum pœnitentiæ locum sibi nullo modo relinqui volebant. Illud juramentum nullam majestatem cœlestem, nullum attributum divinum advocabat et testabatur; sed Stygem, fluvium quendam apud inferos, qui atria Ditis, multis spiris interfusus, cingebat. Hæc enim formula sacramenti sola, neque prætercam alia quæpiam, firma habita est et inviolabilis: scilicet incumbebat pœna perjurii, diis imprimis metuenda, ut qui fefellisset ad deorum convivia per certa annorum spatia non accederet. . . . Necessitas autem per Stygem eleganter repræsentatur, flumen fatale et irremeabile.

***De Sapientia Veterum, Styx, sive Fœdra,* vol. VI, pp. 633–34.**

IX D

1) Quod *vero ais tibi durum videri, statuere aliquid immutabile & æternum præter Deum,* merito sic videretur, si de re existente quæstio esset, vel tantum, si quid ita immutabile statuerem, ut ejus immutabilitas a Deo non penderet. Sed, quemadmodum Poëtæ fingunt a Iove quidem fata fuisse condita, sed postquam condita fuere, ipsum se iis servandis obstrinxisse; ita ego non puto effentias rerum, mathematicasque illas veritates quæ de ipsis cognosci possunt, esse independentes a Deo . . .

***Quinquæ Responsiones.* AT VII, 380.**

2) Que les verités mathematiques, lesquelles vous nommés eternelles, ont esteé establies de Dieu & en dependent entierement, aussy bien que tout le reste des creatures; C'est en effait parler de Dieu comme d'un Iuppiter ou Saturne, & l'ussuiettir au Stix & aus destinees, que de dire que ces verités sont independantes de luy.

A Mersenne, 15 avril 1630. AT I, 145.

IX B

1) It is a very common tradition that of the oath by which the gods bound themselves when they meant to leave no room for repentance; and finds a place in a great many fables. In that case they invoked in witness, not any majesty of heaven or any divine attribute, but Styx; a river in the infernal regions which with many windings encircled the palace of Diis. This form of oath alone, and no other, was held to be sure and inviolable: the penalty of breaking it being one which deities most dreaded,– namely that the breaker should for a certain period of years be excluded from the banquets of the gods. . . . Now Necessity is elegantly represented under the figure of Styx; the fatal river across which no man can return.

***The Wisdom of the Ancients, Styx; or Treaties*. Vol. VI, pp. 706-7. Cf. *De Augmentis Scientiarum*, Bk. II, xiii. Vol. I, pp. 521–24; English translation, vol. IV, pp. 318–21. Cf. IX M.**

IX D

1) You say that you think it is "very hard" to propose that there is anything immutable and eternal apart from God. You would be right to think this if I was talking about existing things, or if I was proposing something as immutable in the sense that its immutability was independent of God. But just as the poets suppose that the Fates were originally established by Jupiter, but that after they were established he bound himself to abide by them, so I do not think that the essences of things, and the mathematical truths which we can know concerning them, are independent of God.

***Fifth Set of Replies*, CSM II, 261.**

2) The mathematical truths which you call eternal have been laid down by God and depend on Him entirely, no less than the rest of his creatures. Indeed to say that these truths are independent of God is to talk of Him as if he were Jupiter or Saturn and subject Him to the Styx and the Fates.

To Mersenne, April 15, 1630. CSMK III, 23.

X B

1) Pessim enim omnium est augurium, quod ex consensu capitur in rebus intellectualibus. . . . Nihil enim multis placet nisi imaginationem feriat aut intellectum vulgarium notionum nodis astringat, ut supra dictum est.[11]

Novum Organum, **I, lxxvii.**

X D

1) La pluralité des voix n'est pas une preuve qui vaille rien pour les vérités un peu malaisées à découvrir, à cause qu'il est bien plus vraisemblable qu'un humme seul les ait rencontrées que tout un peuple.

Discours de la Méthode, **II. AT VI, 16.**

XI B

1) In rebus civilibus mutatio, etiam in melius, suspecta est, ob perturbationem; cum civilia auctoritate, consensu, fama et opinione, non demonstratione intantur. In artibus autem, tanquam in metalli fodinis, omnia novis operibus et ulterioribus progressibus circumstrepere debent.

Novum Organum, **I, xc.**

XI D

1) Il n'y aurait véritablement point d'apparence qu'un particulier fit dessein de réformer un Etat en y changeant tout dès les fondaments et en le renversant pour le redresser. . . . Ces grands corps sont trop malaisés à relever étant abattus, ou même à retenir étant ébranlés, et leurs chutes ne peuvent être que très rudes.

Discours de la Méthode, **II. AT VI, 13–14.**

XII B

1) Nos vero non Acatalepsiam, sed Eucatalepsiam meditamur et proponimus: sensui enim non derogamus, sed ministramus; et intellectum non contemnimus, sed regimus.

Novum Organum, **I, cxxvi.**

XII D

1) Non que j'imittasse pour cela les Sceptiques qui ne doutent que pour douter, et affectent d'être toujurs irrésolus; car au contraire tiut mon dessein ne tendait qu'à m'assurer et à rejeter la terre mouvante et le sable pour trouver le roc et l'argile.

Discours de la Méthode, **III. AT VI, 29.**

11 Seneca, *De vita beata,* 2: "Non tam bene cum rebus humanis agitur, ut meliora pluribus placeant; argumentum pessimi turba est."

X B

1) For the worst of all auguries is from consent in matters intellectual. . . . For nothing pleases the many unless it strikes the imagination, or binds the understanding with the bands of common notions, as I have already said.

***Novum Organum*, I, lxxvii.**

X D

1) And yet a majority vote is worthless as a proof of truths that are at all difficult to discover; for a single man is much more likely to hit upon them than a group of people.

***Discourse on the Method*, II. CSM I, 119.**

XI B

1) In matters of state a change even for the better is distrusted, because it unsettles what is established; these things resting on authority, consent, fame and opinion, not on demonstration. But arts and sciences should be like mines, where the noise of new works and further advances is heard on every side.

***Novum Organum*, I, xc.**

XI D

1) It would be unreasonable for an individual to plan to reform a state by changing it from the foundations up and overturning it in order to set it up again. . . . These large bodies are too difficult to raise up once overthrown, or even to hold up once they begin to totter, and their fall cannot but be a hard one.

***Discourse on the Method*, II. CSM I, 117–18.**

XII B

1) I maintain a sort of suspension of the judgment, and bring it to what the Greeks call Acatalepsia,- a denial of the capacity of the mind to comprehend truth. But in reality that which I mediate and propound is not Acatalepsia, but Eucatalepsia; not the denial of the capacity to understand, but provision for understanding truly.

***Novum Organum*, I, cxxvi.**

XII D

1) In doing this I was not copying the skeptics, who doubt only for the sake of doubting and pretend to be always undecided; on the contrary, my whole aim was to reach certainty – to cast aside the loose earth and sand so as to come upon rock or clay.

***Discourse on the Method*, III. CSM I, 125.**

XIII B

1) . . . omnis traditio et successio disciplinarum repræsentat et exhibet personas magistri et auditoris, non inventoris et ejus inventis aliquid eximum adjiciat. . . . Quin etiam, in primo nonnunquam quthore maxime vigent, et deinceps degenerant. . . . Vix enim datur authores simul et admirari, et superare: sed fit aquarum more quæ non altius ascendunt quam ex quo descenderunt.

Instauratio Magna, Præfatio, **vol. I, pp. 126, 128.**

2) Itaque maxima ingenia proculdubio per singulas ætates vim passa sunt; dum viri captu et intellectu non vulgares, nihilo secius existimationi suæ consulentes, temporis et multitudinis judicio se submiserint. Quamobrem altiores contemplationes si forte usquam emicuerint, opinionum vulgarium ventis subinde agitatæ sunt et extinctæ. Adeo ut Tempus, tanquam fluvius, levia et inflata ad nos devexerit, gravia et solida demerserit.

Instauratio Magna, Præfatio, **vol. I, p. 127.**

XIII D

1) Comme on voit aussy que presque iamais il n'est arrivé qu'aucun de leurs sectateurs les ait surpassez. . . . Ils sont comme le lierre qui ne tend point à monter plus haut que les arbres qui le soutiennent, & mesme souvent qui redescend aprés qu'il est parvenu iusques a leur faiste.

Discours de la Méthode, **VI. AT VI, 70.**

2) Et ie ne m'estonne aucunement des extravagances qu'on attribue a tous ces anciens Philosophes dont nous n'avons point les écrits, ny ne iuge pas pour cela que leurs pensées ayent esté fort déraisonables, veu qu'ils estaient des meilleurs esprits de leurs tems, mais seulement qu'on nous les a mal raportées.

Discours de la Méthode, **VI. AT VI, 70.**

XIII B

1) . . . all the tradition and succession of schools is still a succession of masters and scholars, not of inventors and those who bring to further perfection the things invented. . . . Nay, they sometimes flourish most in the hands of the first author, and afterwards degenerate. . . . For it is hardly possible at once to admire an author and to go beyond him; knowledge being as water, which will not rise above the level from which it fell.

***The Great Instauration*, Preface, vol. 4, pp. 14, 16.**

2) And therefore no doubt the greatest wits in each successive age have been forced out of their own course; men of capacity and intellect above the vulgar having been fain, for reputation's sake, to bow to the judgment of the time and the multitude; and thus if any contemplations of a higher order took light anywhere, they were presently blown out by the winds of vulgar opinions. So that Time is like a river, which has brought down to us things light and puffed up, while those which are weighty and solid have sunk.

***The Great Instauration*, Preface, vol. 4, p. 15.**

XIII D

1) We see too that it has almost never happened that any of their followers has surpassed them. . . . They are like ivy, which never seeks to climb higher than the trees which support it, and often grows downward after reaching the tree-tops.

***Discourse on the Method*, VI. CSM I, 147.**

2) I do not wonder at the absurdities attributed to all the ancient philosophers whose writings we do not possess; nor do I conclude from these attributions that their thoughts were highly unreasonable. As they were some of the best minds of their time, I conclude rather that their thoughts have been misreported.

***Discourse on the Method*, VI. CSM I, 146–47.**

XIV B

1) Pharmaca enim præscribunt medici, quæ morbis animæ persanandis inserviant, ut in curationibus maniæ et melanchiæ; quinentiam medicinas porrigunt ad animum exhilarandum, ad ingenium acuendum, ad memoriam robarandam, et similia. . . . Atqui radix omnium hujusmodi præceptionum (præter ipsam cæremoniam, et exercitum obedientiæ) in hac re consistit, de qua loquimur; nimirum, quod anima compatiatur corpori. . . . Quare apud poëtas, summa ratione, Musica cum medicina in Apollione conjungitur; quia similis fere sit utriusque artis Genius; atque in eo consistat plane medici officium, ut sciat humani corporis lyram ita tendere et pulsare ut reddatur concentus minime discors et insuavis. . . . *Desideratur* nimirum Philosophia Naturalis Vera et Activa, cui Medicinæ scientia inædificetur.

De Augmentis, **IV, i, ii. Vol. I pp. 584, 585, 584, 598.**

XIV D

1) Ce qui n'est pas seulement a desirer pour l'invention d'une infinité d'artifices qui feroient qu'on iouroit, sans aucune peine, des fruits de la terre & de toutes les commoditez qui s'y trouvent, mais principalement aussy pour la conservation de la santé, laquelle est sans doute le premier bien, & le fondament de tous les autres biens de cette vie: car mesme l'esprit dépend si fort du tempérement, & de la disposition des organes du corps, que s'il est possible de trouver quelque moyen qui rende communément les hommes plus sages et plus habiles qu'ils n'ont esté iusques icy, ie croy que c'est dans la Médicine qu'on doit le chercher. Il est vray que celle qui est maintenant en usage, contient peu de choses dont l'utilité soit si remarquable; mais, sans que i'aye aucun dessein de la mespriser, ie m'assure qu'il n'y a personne, mesme de ceux qui en sont profession, qui n'avouë que tout ce qu'on y sçait n'est presque rien, a comparaison de ce qui reste a y sçavoir, & qu'on se pourroit exemter d'une infinité de maladies, tant du cors que de l'esprit, & mesme aussy peutestre de l'affoiblissement de la viellesse, si on avoit assez de connoissance de leurs causes, & de tous les remedes dont la Nature nous a pourveus.

Discours de la Méthode, **VI. AT VI, 62.**

XIV B

1) For the physicians prescribe drugs to heal mental diseases, as in the treatment of frenzy and melancholy; and pretend also to exhibit medicines to exhilarate the mind, to fortify the heart and thereby confirm the courage, to clarify the wits, to corroborate the memory and the like. . . . The root and life of all which prescripts (besides the ceremony and the exercise of obedience) consists in that of which we are speaking, namely the sympathy of the mind with the state and disposition of the body. . . . And therefore the poets did well to conjoin music and medicine in Apollo; because the genius of both these arts is almost the same; for the office of the physicians is but to know how to stretch and tune this harp of man's body that the harmony may be without all harshness or discord. . . . Only there is one thing still remaining, which is of more consequence than all the rest;– namely, a true and active Natural Philosophy for the science of medicine to built upon. Medicine therefore (as we have seen) is a science which has been hitherto more professed than labored, and yet more labored than advanced, the labors spent on it having been rather in a circle, than in progression. . . . I will divide it into three parts, which I will term its three offices: the first whereof is the Preservation of Health, the second

XIV D

1) This [mastery of Nature] is desirable not only for the invention of innumerable devices which would facilitate our enjoyment of the fruits of the earth and all the goods we find there, but also, and most importantly, for the maintenance of health, which is undoubtedly the chief good and the foundation of all other goods in this life. For even the mind depends so much on the temperament and disposition of the bodily organs that if it is possible to find some means of making man in general wiser and more skillful than they have been up till now, I believe we must look for it in Medicine. It is true that medicine as currently practiced does not contain much of any significant use; but without intending to disparage it, I am sure there is no one, even among its practitioners, who would not admit that all we know in medicine is almost nothing in comparison with what remains to be known, and that we might free ourselves from innumerable diseases, both of the body and of the mind, and perhaps even from the infirmity of old age, if we had sufficient knowledge of their causes and of all the remedies that Nature has provided.

Discourse on the Method, **VI. CSM I, 143.**

XV B

1) Etenim cum, ex perpetua nostra cum natura consuetudine, majora de meditationibus nostris quam pro ingenii viribus speramus; tum poterunt ista veluti tabernaculorum in via positorum vice fungi, ut mens ad certiora contendens in iis paulisper acquiescat. Attamen testamur interim, nos illis ipsis, quod ex vera interpretandi forma non sint inventa aut probata, teneri minime velle. Istam vero judicii suspensionem non est quod exhorreat quispiam, in doctrina quæ non simpliciter nil sciri posse, sed nil nisi certo ordine et certa via sciri posse, asserit; atque interea tamen certos certitudinis gradus ad usum et levamen constituit, donec mens in causarum explicatione consistat.

Instauratio Magna, Distributio Operis, **vol.** I, p. **144.**

XV D

1) Et enfin, comme ce n'est pas assez, avant de commencer a retablir le logis ou on demeure, que de l'abattre, & de faire provision de materiaux & d'Architectes, ou s'exercer soymesme a l'Architecture, & outre cela d'en avior soigneusement tracé le dessein; mais qu'il faut aussy s'estre pouruû de quelque autre, où on puisse estre logé commodement pendant le tems qu'on y travaillera; ainsi, affin que ie ne demeurasse point irresolu en mes actions, pendant que la raison m'obligeroit de l'estre en mes iugemens, & que ie ne laissasse pas de vivre dés lors le plus hureusement que ie pourrois, ie me formay une morale par provision, qui ne consistoit qu'en trois ou quatre maximes. . . . Aprés m'estre ainsi assuré de ces maximes, & les avoir mises a part, avec les veritez de la foy, qui ont tousiours esté les premieres en ma creance, ie iugay que, pour tout le reste de mes opinions, ie pouvois librement entreprendre de m'en defaire.

Discours de la Méthode, **II. AT VI, 22, 28.**

Cure of Diseases, and the Third the Prolongation of Life.

De Augmentis, **IV, i, ii, vol. IV, pp. 377, 377, 380, 390, 383.**

XV B

1) For besides that I hope my speculations may in virtue of my continual conversancy with nature have a value beyond the pretensions of my wit, they will serve in the meantime for wayside inns, in which the mind may rest and refresh itself on its journey to more certain conclusions. Nevertheless I wish it to be understood in the meantime that they are conclusions by which (as not being discovered and proved by the true form of interpretation) I do not at all mean to bind myself. Nor need any one be alarmed at such suspension of judgment, in one who maintains not simply that nothing can be known except in a certain course and way; and yet establishes provisionally certain degrees of assurance, for use and relief until the mind shall arrive at a knowledge of causes in which it can rest.

***The Great Instauration*, Plan of the Work. vol. IV, pp. 31–32.**

XV D

1) Now, before starting to rebuild your house, it is not enough simply to pull it down, to make provision for materials and architects . . . and to have carefully drawn up the plans; you must also provide yourself with some other place where you can live comfortably while building is in progress. Likewise, lest I should remain indecisive in my actions while reason obliged me to be so in my judgments, and in order to live as happily as I could during this time, I formed for myself a provisional moral code consisting of just three or four maxims. . . . Once I had established these maxims and set them on one side together with the truths of faith, which have always been foremost among my beliefs, I judged that I could freely undertake to rid myself of all the rest of my opinions.

***Discourse on the Method*, II. CSM II, 122, 125.**

Francis Bacon and the Formation of Descartes's "First Philosophy"

The judgment that tarnished Bacon as a venal judge dishonors him less in our eyes than this painfully fraudulent job that he exercised on the Bible, to bend it to the most shameful speculations. Undoubtedly all sectarians have invoked it . . . but, up to Bacon, I did not know that materialism had called it to its assistance.

Joseph de Maistre, *An Examination of the Philosophy of Bacon Wherein Different Questions of Rational Philosophy Are Treated*

He [the ascetic] will regard such attempts to improve the human situation as laudable acts of humanity – for obviously nothing can be more humane, or more natural for a human being, than to relieve other people's sufferings, put an end to their miseries, and restore their *joie de vivre* . . .

Thomas More, *Utopia, Bk. II.*

The similarities between Bacon's and Descartes's philosophies have received little scholarly scrutiny, and those few passages in Descartes which scholars had identified as having their origin in Bacon's writings did not warrant more general conclusions about the dependence of Descartes's philosophy on his reading of Bacon's writings. The reason for ignoring Bacon as a plausible source for Descartes's philosophy is a tacit assumption about the incompatibility of Bacon's empirical-inductive method with Descartes's aprioristic-deductive system. Thus even when Bacon's influence seems obvious, it is never taken seriously into consideration.[1]

The passages I have collected in Appendix 3 demonstrate Descartes's familiarity with Bacon's *De Augmentis Scientiarum, Novum Organum,* and *De Sapientia Veterum.*[2] A glance at these passages suffices to discern at least five elements in Descartes that almost certainly come from Bacon: (1) the Styx metaphor; (2) the idea of "pulling down the foundations"; (3) the purification of one's mind of preconceived opinions (Idols); (4) the "provisional moral code" (see XVI); and (5) the idea of the Mastery of Nature.[3] The ancient story

1 In his edition of Descartes's works, Adam limits himself to the following remark: "Descartes avait au moins feuilleté Bacon, qu'il appelle Verulaminus" (AT XIII, 479). Nor does Gilson see any closer connections. See his "Francis Bacon," in *Modern Philosophy: Descartes to Kant,* É. Gilson, ed. (New York: Random House, 1963), pp. 25–44. Critical literature on Bacon and Descartes is very scanty. Among authors who devoted some space to the relationship between the two philosophers are: André Lalande, "Sur quelques textes de Bacon et de Descartes," *Revue de Métaphysique et de Morale* (1911), pp. 296–311; Marta Fattori, "Le Préface aux Passions de l'Âme: Remarques sur Descartes et Bacon," in *Archives de Philosophie* 61, 1998 (Bulletin Cartésien XXV), pp. 1–13; review-article of Descartes's *Opere filosofiche,* Ettore Lojacono ed. (Turin: UTET, 1994), in *Nouvelles de la Republique des Lettres,* 1995 (I), pp. 108–20; "'Nature Semplici' in Francesco Bacone," and "Francis Bacon e René Descartes: La Préface (Anonima) alle Passions de L'Âme," in Marta Fattori, *Linguaggio e Filosofia nel Seicento Europeo* (Rome: Leo S. Olschki, 2000), pp. 1–14, 227–48; Jean-Luc Marion, *Règles utiles et claires pour la direction de l'esprit dans la recherche de la vérité* (The Hague: Martinus Nijhoff, 1977).

2 André Lalande (*Ibid.,* pp. 296–311.) suggests that Descartes knew the manuscript of *Valerius Terminus.* Descartes personally knew William Boswell, the keeper of Bacon's papers (see AT XIII, 479). Descartes makes references to Bacon in two letters: "Ie vous remercie des qualitez que vous avez tirées d'Aristote; i'en avois desia une autre plus grande liste, partie tirée de Verulamio [Bacon], partie de ma teste." January 1630 (AT I, 109); and: "You once told me that you knew some people who were so dedicated to the advancement of science that they were willing to make every kind of experiment at their own expense. It would be very useful if some such person were to write the history of celestial phenomena in accordance with the method of Verulam [Bacon] and to describe the present appearances of the heavens." To Mersenne, May 10, 1632 (AT I, 251, CSMK III, 38).

3 See footnote 41.

of the Styx is an anti-metaphor of the Doctrine of Eternal Truths. Numbers (2) and (3) constitute the core of Descartes's methodology in the *Meditations*. (The very first paragraph of the First Meditation is a "transcription" of parts of the *Novum Organum*).[4] The "provisional moral code" is a temporary "lodging" where one lives after destroying the old philosophy before building a new one (see XVI). Finally, the "Project of the Mastery of Nature" crowns Descartes's considerations in the Sixth *Discourse on Method*.

Descartes's debt to Bacon is not limited to these borrowings alone. There is a deeper link, although it is harder to discern. It concerns the influence of Bacon's writings on the formation of Descartes's philosophy in general and his understanding of "metaphysics" in particular. The problematic nature of Cartesian metaphysics is fully documented in Jean-Luc Marion's *Descartes's Metaphysical Prism* (ch. I) and in Vincent Carraud's "Descartes appartient-t-il à l'histoire de la métaphysique?"[5] Étienne Gilson, commenting on the Baconian concept of the Mastery of Nature, states in his line-by-line commentary to the *Discours de la Méthode* that "that which inspires the philosophy of Bacon [mastery over Nature], inspires only the publication of the philosophy of Descartes [i.e., *The Discourse on the Method*]."[6] Gilson's contention is additionally strengthened by the fact that Descartes does not even allude to the idea of Mastery of Nature in the *Meditations*, published after the *Discourse*, or in the later *Principles of Philosophy* (1644).[7] Following the chronology of Descartes's works, Gilson did not feel that the speculative considerations of the *Meditations* are subsidiary to the practical aspect of his philosophy that the concept of the Mastery of Nature addresses.[8]

4 The passages in Appendix 3: I–IV contain all the essential elements in the first page of the First Meditation: 1) senses are deceptive, 2) one needs to empty one's mind from all previously acquired opinions; 3) since "particular confutations would be of no avail," one needs to undermine the whole edifice; one needs to get to the very foundations; 3) only a mature person can do it. Abbé Picot had pointed out to Descartes that "of all those who wrote before you, Chancellor Bacon had the best thoughts concerning the method that one needs to observe in order to develop physics to its perfection" (AT XI, 320).

5 In *Lire Descartes aujourd'hui*, O. Depré and D. Lories eds. (Louvain-Paris, Êditions de l'Institut Supérieur de Philosophie, 1997).

6 Étienne Gilson, *Discours de la Méthode. Texte et Commentaire* (Paris: Vrin, 1947), p. 444.

7 The best analysis of the role of the concept of the Mastery of Nature in Bacon and Descartes is Richard Kennington's "Descartes and Mastery of Nature," in *Organism, Medicine, and Metaphysics. Essays in Honor of Hans Jonas on His 75th Birthday*, ed. by Stuart F. Spicker (Dordrecht: D. Reidel Publishing Company, 1978). Cf. his "Descartes," in *History of Political Philosophy*, Leo Strauss and Joseph Cropsey eds. (Chicago: Rand McNally & Company, 1972).

8 Richard Kennington ("The 'Teaching of Nature' in Descartes' Soul Doctrine," *The*

Instead of the chronology, consider the order suggested by Descartes's famous image of philosophy as a tree, with metaphysics as its roots, physics as the trunk, and all other sciences as its branches. According to this metaphor, Descartes should have written his works in an order different from that in which they were published. The tree image implies that the *Meditations* – i.e., the *philosophia prima* (the roots) – were written first, and the *Discourse on the Method,* along with the three accompanying works (the trunk and the branches) only later. It appears that the concept of the Mastery of Nature, which crowns the *Discourse,* should be considered as the goal of a physics that stems from a specifically Cartesian conception of *philosophia prima,*[9] whose full account is the *Meditations.* Leon Roth in his minor and now forgotten classic, *Descartes' Discourse on Method,* makes the following observation:

> Because the *Discourse* was published in 1637 and the *Meditations* in 1641, we think of the *Meditations* as posterior to the *Discourse* in the same way that the *Principles,* published in 1644, is posterior to the *Meditations.* But the *Discourse* itself, as we saw, tells another story. The "true" date of the *Principles* is 1629–33. It follows that the *Discourse,* written in 1636, is far from being a preliminary manifesto worked out (or abandoned) in the later *Meditations* and *Principles.* It is the retrospective of a Descartes who has been through the stages of *Meditations* and *Principles* and now looks back on them. The Descartes of the *Discourse* is in full possession of himself. He is not sketching a program but summing up results. . . . The sixth chapter of the *Discourse,* far from being, as it is often thought to be, an otiose appendix to the whole, is thus Descartes' *confessio fidei.*[10]

Is Roth's claim tenable? I think it is. From the very beginning of his philosophical career, Descartes was working on one and the same project – the project of a Universal Science,[11] of which the Tree of Knowledge is a

Review of Metaphysics 26, no. 1 [1972], p. 95) rightly observes: "The goal of philosophy, which the quest for foundations [in the *Meditations*] subserves, must then be sought in the *Principles* and the *Discourse.*"

9 Bear in mind that the *Meditations* are a work on "First Philosophy" (subtitle), not on metaphysics. For the full analysis of the relationship between the traditional conception of *metaphysica* and Descartes's *philosophia prima,* see J.-L. Marion, *Sur le prisme métaphysique de Descartes* (Paris: PUF, 1991), ch. I.

10 Leon Roth, *Descartes' Discourse on Method* (Oxford: Clarendon Press, 1937), p. 73.

11 In the letter to Mersenne of 23 December 1630 (AT I, 194, CSMK III 29), Descartes writes: "I am sorry to hear that you have erysipelas and that M. M[ontas] is ill. Please

metaphor. This project comprises metaphysics, physics, medicine, and "related areas."[12] The goal of Descartes's Universal Science is to raise "our Nature to its Highest Degree of Perfection."[13] Each of Descartes's works addresses a different part of this Tree of Knowledge. Although the *Discourse* and the *Meditations* are self-contained works, they are not autonomous: they are parts of *Scientia Universalis Cartesiana*, and they should be read as constituent parts of the Cartesian Tree.

In a letter to Mersenne written in 1637, Descartes says that the *Discourse* contains only a "summary" of his metaphysics; he developed its complete formulation "at some length" in his "treatise on metaphysics."[14] We know that Descartes started his "Little Treatise" on God, the soul, and the "clear and distinct notions which are in us"[15] around July 1629, and expected to finish it in "two or three years," which means that he thought his metaphysics would be ready around July 1631 or, at the latest, July 1632.[16] Descartes seems to have advanced considerably by December the same year since on 18 December 1629,[17] five months later, and four months before he revealed to Mersenne the doctrine of the Eternal Truths, he wrote: "Thank you also for offering to take care of the little treatise that I have in hand." The expression "in hand" suggests that, at least as far as principal metaphysical notions are

look after yourself, at least until I know whether it is possible to discover a system of medicine which is founded on infallible demonstrations, which is what I am investigating at present." Medicine, which is a branch of the Cartesian Tree of Knowledge, is, as this letter shows, a part of the project on which Descartes was already working in 1630.

12 See Stephen Gaukroger, *Descartes, An Intellectual Biography* (Oxford: Clarendon Press, 1995), p. 222 ff. Cf. Daniel Garber, *Descartes' Metaphysical Physics* (Chicago: The University of Chicago Press, 1992, chap. 1.

13 "So that you may know what it is that I want to have printed, there will be four treatises, all in French, and the general title will be as follows: 'The Plan of a Universal Science which is capable of raising our Nature to its Highest Degree of Perfection. . . .'" To Mersenne, 1636 (AT I, 339; CSMK III, 51). The idea of perfection in Descartes is discussed by Emmanuel Faye, *Philosophie et perfection de l'homme: De la Renaissance à Descartes* (Paris: VRIN, 1998), pp. 289–350.

14 Letter to Mersenne of 27 February 1637 (AT I, 350; CSMK III, 53).

15 *Principles of Philosophy, Preface to the French edition* (AT IXB, 14; CSMK I, 186).

16 "I expect to put you to some trouble when I complete a little treatise that I am starting. I would not have told you it was under way unless I feared that the length of time it needs would make you forget your promise to correct it and give it the finishing touches; for I do not expect to complete it within two or three years, and perhaps in the end I shall decide to burn it, or at least not to let it out of my hands or those of my friends without giving it careful scrutiny. If I am not clever enough to produce something worth while, I shall at any rate try to be astute enough not to publish my shortcomings." To Gibieuf, 18 July 1629 (AT I, 17; CSMK III, 5–6).

concerned (divine attributes, the conception of the soul, clear and distinct ideas[18]), the "Little Treatise" had been more or less worked out by the end of 1629. But only the *Meditations* contain the full account of Descartes's metaphysics; the *Discourse*, by Descartes's own admission, contains only a "summary." It would therefore seem that the *Meditations* is a rough version of the work that Descartes is referring to in the letter of 1637,[19] and should be read in place of its abbreviated form, the Fourth Discourse.

André Lalande, Jean-Luc Marion, and Marta Fattori have demonstrated Bacon's presence in Descartes's earliest work, the *Regulæ*.[20] Leslie J. Beck, in turn, in his *The Method of Descartes. A Study of the Regulæ*, offers an interesting comparison between the rules of the *Regulæ* and the rules in the *Discourse on the Method*. I reproduce this list here.

Regulæ	*Discourse on the Method*
Circa illa tantum objecta oportet versari, ad quorum certam et indubitabam cognitionem nostra ingenia videntur sufficere (Rule 2, AT X, 362: 2–4)	Primum erat, ut nihil unquam veluti verum admitterem nisi quod certo et evidenter verum esse cognoscerem; hoc est, ut omnem praecipitantiam atque anticipationem in judicando diligentissime vitarem; nihilque amplius conclusione complecterer, quam quod tam clare et distincte rationi pateret, ut nullo modo in dubium possem revocare.
Circa objecta proposita, non quid alii senserint, vel quid ipsi suspicemur, sed quid clare et evidenter possimus intueri, vel certo deducere quaeren-	Alterum, ut difficultates quas essem examinaturus, in tot partes dividerem, quot expediret ad illas commodius resolvendas.

17 To Mersenne, December 18, 1629 (AT I, 85; CSMK III, 14).

18 *Principles of Philosophy*, Preface to the French edition (AT IXB, 14; CSMK I, 186).

19 One needs to note, however, that the complete account of the proof for the existence of God had not been worked out in 1637: "It is true that I have been too obscure in what I wrote about the existence of God in this treatise on Method, and I admit that although the most important, it is the least worked out section in the whole book. This is partly because I did not decide to include it until I had nearly completed it and the publisher was becoming impatient." To Vatier, 22 February 1638 (AT I 560; CSMK III, 85–86).

20 The term "simple natures" comes from Bacon. For its meaning and application, see,

Regulæ	*Discourse on the Method*
dum est: non aliter scientia acquiritur (Rule 3, 366: 11–14)	
Tota methodus consistit in ordine et dispositione eorum ad quae mentis acies est convertenda, ut aliquam veritatem inveniamus. Atque hanc exacte servabimus, si propositiones involutas et obscuras ad simpliciores gradatim reducamus, et deinde ex omnium simplicissimarum intuitu ad aliarum omnium cognitionem per eosdem gradus ascendere tentemus (Rule 5, 379: 15–21)	Tertium, ut cogitationes omnes quas veritati quaerendae impenderem, certo semper ordine promoverem: incipiendo scilicet a rebus simplicissimis et cognitu facillimis, ut paulatim et quasi per gradus ad difficilliorum et magis compositarum cognitionem ascenderem; in aliquem etiam ordinem illas mente disponendo, quae se muto ex natura sua non praecedunt.
Ad scientiae complementum oportet omnia et singula, quae ad institutum nostrum pertinent, continuo et nullibi interrupto cogitionis moto perlustrare, atque illa sufficienti et ordinata enumeratione complecti (Rule 7, 387: 10–13)	Ac postremum, ut tum in quaerendis mediis, tum in difficultatum partibus percurrendis, tam perfecte singula enumerarem et ad omnia circumspicerem, ut nihil a me omitti essem certus.

In commenting on the comparison of the rules in the two works, Beck, following Gilson, considers them as "essentially the same."[21] Leon Roth traces Descartes's rules to Bacon (see next page).

"Of these rules," Roth says, "the first and second of Bacon correspond to the two parts of the first rule of Descartes; the last rule of both is in intention much the same. Descartes's third rule, the so-called rule of 'order,' may fair-

for example, *Novum Organum*, II, v. For other references, see André Lalande, "Sur quelques textes de Bacon et de Descartes," in *Revue de Métaphysique et de Morale* (1911); and, especially, Marta Fattori, "'Nature Semplici' in Francesco Bacone," in *Linguaggio e Filosofia nel Seicento Europeo*, *op. cit.*, pp. 1–14. For other parallels between Bacon and the *Regulae*, see Jean-Luc Marion, *Règles utiles et claires pour la direction de l'esprit dans la recherche de la vérité* (The Hague: Martinus Nijhoff, 1977).

21 *The Method of Descartes. A Study of the Regulæ* (Oxford: Clarendon Press, 1970), p. 151. Cf. É. Gilson, *Commentaire*, *op. cit.*, p. 196: "La méthode a donc été dès le début, quant à l'essentiel, ce qu'elle devait toujours demeurer."

BACON	DESCARTES
1. To lay aside received opinions.	1. (a) To accept nothing as true which I did not clearly recognize to be so.
2. To refrain the mind for a time from the highest generalizations.	(b) carefully to avoid precipitation and prejudice in judgments.
3. To muster instances before understanding.	2. To divide up each of the difficulties which I examined into as many parts as possible.
4. To arrange them in tables.	
5. To review the instances all and each.	3. To carry on my reflections in due order, commencing with objects which were the most simple in order to rise by degrees to knowledge of the most complex.
	4. To make enumerations so complete and review so general that I should be certain of having omitted nothing.

ly be held to be included in the 'arrangement' of instances in 'tables' which constitutes Bacon's fourth rule, though, as we shall see, Descartes's 'order' is of a very peculiar and highly significant kind. The central difference between the two sets of rules lies, therefore, in Descartes's second, the so-called rule of division, as against Bacon's third which is one of addition or accumulation. Thus we come, through comparison with Bacon, to a conclusion, which is so far from novel as to be that asserted by Descartes himself. Rule 3 of the *Discourse* is Rule 5 and 6 of the *Regulae*. Of the former Descartes writes: 'In this alone lies the sum of all human endeavor, and he who would approach the investigation of truth must hold to this rule as closely as he who enters the labyrinth must follow the thread which guided Theseus.'"[22]

Thanks to Marta Fattori's work "'Nature Semplici' in Francesco Bacone," we know that the term "natura simplex" appears in Bacon's two works: *Novum Organum* and *De Augmentis Scientiarum*.[23] "Simple nature" is one of the key terms in Descartes's earliest work, the *Regulæ*, which he composed in

22 Roth, *Ibid.*, pp. 69–71.

23 "'Nature Semplici' in Francesco Bacone," *op. cit.*, pp. 13–14. The passages from Bacon collected by Lalande (see Appendix 3: XI–XVI) come from these two works.

1628–29. This means that Descartes read *Novum Organum* or *De Augmentis* (or both) before 1628–29. Are there any traces of Bacon's more general influence on Descartes?

In Book III of his *De Augmentis Scientiarum*, Bacon is concerned with the division of the sciences. He begins with the water and tree metaphors (see Appendix 3: VIII). The first division runs through Divinity and Philosophy. Philosophy is divided into Divine Philosophy (or Natural Theology; Bk. III, i, vol. IV, p. 341), Natural Philosophy, and Human Philosophy, or the Philosophy of Humanity. Natural Philosophy, again, is divided into Speculative or Theoretical (which is concerned with the Inquisition of Causes) and Operative (which is concerned with the Production of Effects; Bk. IV, iii, vol. IV, p. 343). Finally, Speculative Philosophy is divided into Physics, which is concerned with efficient and material causes, and Metaphysics, which is concerned with final and formal causes.

Next, Bacon moves to the "universal science," which is the same as "philosophia prima, primitive or summary philosophy, or sapience" (Bk. IV, i, vol. IV, p. 337). He also calls it the "mother" of Divine, Natural, and Human Philosophy. *Philosophia prima* deals with the Adventive Conditions of Essences or Transcendentals, such as "Much, Little, Like, Unlike, Possible, Impossible; likewise Being and Non-Being, and the like" (Bk. IV, i, vol. IV, p. 339). "It appears by that which has been already said, that I intend Primitive or Summary Philosophy and Metaphysics, which heretofore have been confounded as one, to be two distinct things. . . . It may fairly therefore now be asked, what is left remaining for Metaphysics? Certainly nothing beyond nature; but of nature itself much the most excellent part." And he adds: "It follows that the true difference between them [Physics and Metaphysics] must be drawn from the nature of the causes that they inquire into" (Bk. IV, iv, vol. IV, p. 346).

At first glance, Bacon's Tree of Knowledge (with *philosophia prima* as the trunk and Divine, Natural, and Human Philosophy as the branches) does not appear to correspond to Descartes's division. (For one thing, Bacon's Tree seems to lack roots). Nor does the object of Bacon's philosophy – God, Nature, and Man – seem to correspond to that of Descartes, who at the opening of the *Meditations* announces (following St. Augustine) that philosophy has a twofold object: God and soul. However, the differences are only apparent. The object of Bacon's inquiry in Book Four of his *De Augmentis* is Human Philosophy or Philosophy of Humanity: it consists of knowledge of the body and of the mind or soul.[24] One of its considerations is "the nature of man

24 Like Descartes, Bacon often uses the terms "mind" and "soul" interchangeably. See, for example, Bk. IV, i, vol. 4, p. 373.

undivided [between body and soul] and the other regarding the bond and connection between the mind and the body; whereof I will term the doctrine concerning the Person of Man, the second the doctrine concerning the League" (Bk. IV, i, vol. IV, pp. 373–74), or "Impression," because it is concerned with "how and how far the humors and temperament of the body alter and work upon the mind; or again, how and how far the passions or apprehensions of the mind alter and work upon the body" (Bk. IV, i, vol. IV, p. 377).[25] The doctrine of the League or Impression is also called the doctrine of the "Common Bond between the soul and body," because it answers the question of "how these two . . . disclose the one to the other, and how they work the one upon the other" (Bk. IV, i, vol. IV, p. 375).

As for the rational soul, one of the two elements of the doctrine of the League, Bacon says the following: "The first part of the general doctrine concerning the human soul I will term the doctrine concerning the Breath of Life. . . . For since the substance of the soul in its creation was not extracted or produced out of the mass of heaven and earth, but was immediately inspired from God; and since the laws of heaven and earth are the proper subjects of philosophy; how can we expect to obtain from philosophy the knowledge of the substance of the rational soul? It must be drawn from the same divine inspiration, from which that substance first proceeded" (Bk. IV, iii, vol. IV, pp. 397–98). Accordingly, neither knowledge of God nor knowledge of the soul can be part of metaphysics, which in Bacon's classification of sciences is the study of Nature.[26] What is left as the object of Baconian science is man "undivided" (i.e., the human body), who is the subject matter of the Third Part of medicine "which relates to the Prolongation of Life, which is new, and deficient; and most noble of all. For if such a thing may be discovered, the business of medicine will no longer be confined to humble cures, nor will physicians be honored only for necessity; but for a gift to men – of earthly gifts perhaps the greatest – of which, next to God, they may become dispensers and administrators" (Bk. IV, ii, vol. 4, p. 390; cf. Appendix 3: XVD).

25 For the corresponding, if slightly different passage in *The Advancement of Learning*, see Bk. II, vol. I, p. 239. There Bacon remarks that in the past the Doctrine of the League "hath been inquired and considered as a part and appendix of Medicine, but much more as a part of Religion or Superstition." Bacon's own explanation of the bond between Mind and Body is through and through "scientific." This is the beginning of the Modern **cap?** reduction of all explanations to purely "rational" or "scientific" phenomena.

26 According to Bacon, the impediment to the progress of the sciences, or, "a great improficience in the sciences," as he calls it, lies in the confounding of final causes with "the rest in physical inquiries." *The Advancement of Learning*, Bk. II, vol. III, p. 357–58.

The task of medicine is to counteract "the Miseries of the human race," (Bk. IV, i, vol. 4, p. 374), or, as he says in the *Novum Organum*, I, lxxiii, "to relieve and benefit the condition of man."

In the Sixth Meditation, Descartes seems to espouse the Baconian doctrine of the League or Bond between mind and body or the Doctrine of Impression that concerns itself with the question of "how and how far the humors and temperament of the body alter and work upon the mind. . . . For I could never be separated from [the body]," Descartes says, "as I could from other bodies, and I felt all my appetites and emotions in, and on account of, this body; and finally, I was aware of pain and pleasurable ticklings in parts of this body, but not in other bodies external to it. But why should that curious sensation of pain give rise to a particular distress of mind, or why should a certain kind of delight follow on tickling sensation? Again, why should that curious tugging in the stomach which I call hunger tell me that I should eat, or dryness of the throat tell me to drink, and so on?"[27] Bacon's doctrine of the Person, of which the Third Part of Medicine is a part, rests on the implicit assumption that the human body, insofar as it is a body, does not need a rational soul to operate. Because the nature of the soul cannot be known by the light of nature, Bacon relegated it to the realm of Revealed Theology (the excerpt cited above), which in his division of Sciences seems to be nothing but a dustbin littered with metaphysical and religious items.

According to Joseph de Maistre, Bacon's Doctrine of the Breath is only a smokescreen for his atheistic materialism. In commenting on this Doctrine, de Maistre says:

> The origin of the first [rational soul], [Bacon] says, is related to these words of Scripture: "He formed man from the slime of the earth and breathed into his face the breath of life," so that this first soul is born immediately from the divine breath. The origin of the second [sensitive soul] is announced in other words: "Let the waters bring forth! Let the earth bring forth!" From this we see what was drawn from earthly wombs. One is astonished, and even irritated, to see the audacity with which a consummate falsifier thus abuses Holy Scripture, and torments it to force it to say what he wants. In the first places in the first chapter of Genesis where Moses says: "Let the waters bring forth! Let the earth bring forth!" it is not at all a question of man. Moses begins by revealing to us the creation of the world, for this is what is meant by the heavens and earth. . . . Man is created separately; he does not say a word

27 Sixth Med. (AT VII, 76; CSM II, 52–53).

> about living soul or animal life; man is declared purely and is simply image of God, that is to say intelligence. . . . However, Bacon is absolutely determined to get rid of this intelligent soul that embarrasses him. . . . he means that the doctrine of breath should be reserved for theology. . . . Bacon was, one can be very sure, far removed from having the least sentiment of the astonishing absurdity that escapes him here; but his mind rejects nothing that could distract man from every spiritual idea.[28]

De Maistre may ultimately be right in claiming that materialism in Bacon leads to atheism,[29] but Descartes's own case shows that even if one retains the doctrine of the rational soul as part of Natural Theology, the practical effects are the same.[30]

Descartes defined the nature of the soul as *res cogitans* and the material world as *res extensa.* Cartesian Philosophy introduced a chasm between body and soul, but it also set man's body free from the Scholastic "substantial union" with the soul. Cartesian man in the Sixth Meditation is not a being whose soul is the form of the body (*anima corporis forma*), as the Scholastics would have it.[31] Cartesian man is a mechanical man. The rational soul or mind is unnecessary for explaining how the human body functions – it func-

28 Joseph de Maistre, *An Examination of the Philosophy of Bacon Wherein Different Questions of Rational Philosophy Are Treated,* translated and edited by Richard A. Lebrun (Montreal: McGill-Queen's University Press, 1998), pp. 172–74.

29 For example, in *De Augmentis*, Bk. III, ii, (vol. IV, p. 342), Bacon is concerned with the nature of angels. After a relatively lengthy comment on them, he concludes: "But this part of knowledge touching angels and spirits I cannot note as deficient," and, in his usual way, he drops the question. Passages such as this may indeed raise doubts about "sincerity" of his treatment. In all likelihood, Bacon's purpose in discussing theological and metaphysical "items," which he includes as part of Revealed Theology, is to point out their incompatibility with philosophy as he understands it. Several decades later, Hobbes seems to have completed the Baconian "project" of ridding philosophy of all notions that cannot be known by "natural reason." In his *Elements of Philosophy* 1, no. 8 (published in 1655), he openly declares that philosophy excludes the doctrines of angels, God, "knowledge that [is] acquired by Divine inspiration," "the doctrine of God's worship," but also of history, including natural and political, since it is based on "authority, and not on ratiocination."

30 On different appropriations of Descartes's philosophy by the materialistic-atheistic Enlightenment thinkers, see my *Cartesian Theodicy*, pp. 151–62.

31 As I argue in "Is Descartes' Doctrine of the Soul Orthodox?" *Revue de Metaphysique et de Morale,* January 2000, pp. 39–55, Descartes tried to redefine the official Catholic conception of the soul as *anima corporis forma* to render it consistent with the demands of his philosophy.

tions in the same way as the animal body, which does not have a rational soul. Thus, as Descartes says in the Sixth Meditation,[32]

> I might consider the body of a man as a kind of machine equipped with and made up of bones, nerves, muscles, veins, blood, and skin in such a way that, even if there were no mind in it, it would still perform all the same movements as it now does in those cases where movement is not under the control of the will or, consequently, of the mind.[33]

Once the separation of the (rational) soul from the body has been accomplished – in Bacon as a result of the "Doctrine of the Breath"; in Descartes as a result of the Universal Doubt – the Scholastic substantial union between body and mind was broken.[34] The soul of the Cartesian mechanical man from the Sixth Meditation is not the *mens, sive animus, sive intellectus* of the Cartesian man from the Second Meditation but the life-giving blood that flows in the veins of a body composed of bones, muscles, and nerves, which Descartes describes in much more scientific detail in his *Treatise on Man.*[35]

The greater part of the Fifth Discourse, which follows Descartes's summary of his metaphysics in the Fourth Discourse, is devoted to blood circulation. This is because blood, one of the things alluded to in the above excerpt from the Sixth Meditation, was traditionally considered to be the seat of the soul, the animating principle of bodies. The Fifth Discourse begins precisely

32 Cf. *Treatise on Man* (AT XI 120; CSM I, 99).

33 AT 84; CSM II, 58. In *The Passions of the Soul*, 17, Descartes says: "Having thus considered all the functions belonging solely to the body, it is easy to recognize that there is nothing in us that we must attribute to our soul except our thoughts."

34 In "How to Read Descartes' First Meditation," *The Southern Journal of Philosophy*, 1997, XXXV, pp. 324ff, I argue that the Universal Doubt is linked with Descartes's Doctrine of the Eternal Truths. As I claim in my "Is Descartes' Doctrine of the Soul Orthodox?" *Revue de Metaphysique et de Morale*, January 2000, pp. 47–48, this doctrine is incompatible with the Scholastic idea of the substantial union between the soul and a body.

35 One of Descartes's "accomplishments" here is the elimination of the Aristotelian-Scholastic conception of the vegetative and sensitive soul. At the very end of his *Treatise on Man* (AT XI, 202: CSM I, 108), Descartes writes: "In order to explain these functions, then, it is not necessary to conceive of this machine as having any vegetative or sensitive soul or other principle of movement and life." Iin his speech on May 7, 1796, Mercier opposed the idea of transferring Descartes's remains to the Pantheon on the grounds that Descartes created a philosophy that inspired in man a spirit of abstraction that led to the reign of Terror during the French Revolution: "Disastrous philosophy, which sought to animalize man!" For details, see François Azouvi, "Descartes," in *Realms of Memory: The Construction of the French Past*. Vol. III: Symbols, edited by Pierre Nora (New York: Columbia University Press, 1998), esp., pp. 489–95.

where the Sixth Meditation ends – with the analysis of how blood *animates* the body:

> These functions are just the ones in which animals without reason may be said to resemble us. But I could find none of the functions that, depending on thought, are the only ones that belong to us as men; although I do find all these later on, once I had supposed that God created a rational soul and joined it to this body in a particular way that I described.
>
> But so that you might see how I dealt with this subject, I shall give my explanation of the movement of the heart and the arteries.[36]

The human body, insofar as it is a mechanism, is subject to deterioration and in need of repair. "Things are preserved and continued in two ways," Bacon writes in *De Augmentis*, Bk. IV, ii (vol. IV, p. 392). "Either in their own identity, or by repair. . . . Now he that seeks to effect the prolongation of life must use both methods . . . and the human body must be preserved as bodies inanimate . . . and lastly to a certain degree as things mechanical are preserved."

In the Sixth Discourse, Descartes addresses the Baconian doctrine of Man undivided, that is, man reduced to his bodily operations, and, like Bacon, suggests the Mastery of Nature as the remedy for man's earthly miseries: illnesses and brevity of life. Also in the *Discourse*, just after invoking the concept of Mastery over Nature, Descartes explains in the same breath that the goal of his philosophy, in contradistinction to the old speculative philosophy "taught in the Schools," is to free man "from innumerable diseases, both of the body and of the mind, and perhaps even from the infirmity of old age."[37] The Baconian doctrine of Man undivided – which in Descartes grew out of Augustinian metaphysics that divides Man into two substances – naturally culminates in a program of the Mastery of Nature. The human body is a mechanism, and, like every mechanism, is subject to the laws of Nature. Thus (Modern) philosophy's concern is not "forms" but "laws" of Nature.

The idea that the business of philosophy is the knowledge of the laws of Nature, rather than "Forms," is the most fundamental shift away from the Ancient Aristotelian-Platonic idea of contemplation as the highest good for man,[38] to the association of philosophy with power that can be used in the

36 *Discourse on the Method*, V (AT VI, 46; CSM I, 134).

37 *Discourse on the Method*, VI (AT VI, 62; CSM, I, 143).

38 See Aristotle, *Nicomachean Ethics*, X, 7, and Plato, *Republic*, VII. In the Sixth Discourse (AT VI, 62, CSM I, 143) Descartes juxtaposes his philosophy with the "speculative philosophy taught in the schools." The stress here is on the word "speculative." Richard

service of man.[39] "The true and lawful goal of the sciences is," Bacon writes, "none other than this: that human life be endowed with new discoveries and powers" (*Novum Organum*, I, lxxxi). A similar idea is expressed by Thomas Hobbes, who in his *Elements of Philosophy* (I, 6; cf. I, 7, 6) makes this point even more explicit: "The end of knowledge is power." And he adds: "Now, the greatest commodities of mankind are the arts. . . . By which sciences, how great benefits men receive is more easily understood than expressed. . . .we may produce the like effects of those we conceive in our mind, as far forth as matter, strength, and industry, will permit, for the commodity of human life." Once philosophy was identified with the knowledge of the laws of Nature and knowledge with power, man could declare himself to be the "dispenser and administrator" (Bacon) or "lord and master" (Descartes) of Nature.[40]

The shift from the Old (Ancient) to the New (Modern) philosophy is starkly exhibited in the juxtaposition of the following aphorisms from Bacon's *Novum Organun*.

> *Ancient Way*: For the form of inquiry and discovery that was in use among the Ancients is by themselves professed, and appears on

Kennington, in discussing Bacon's criticism of the Ancients, "Bacon's Critique of Ancient Philosophy," *op. cit.*, p. 237, notes: "Of course, we do not often think of Bacon as contemplative philosopher, but that is because the term (and its near equivalent *speculative*) has become dominated by the meaning stamped on it by the great tradition of Platonic and Aristotelian philosophy, ancient and medieval." (For Bacon's conception of contemplation, see pp. 237–45.) One may wonder whether the Bacon's notion of "contemplatio" could not be extended to Descartes. If so, it would seem that much of Bacon's critique of the Ancients could be ascribed to Descartes who does not offer a systematic criticism of the Ancients.

39 Two centuries later Friedrich Engels, a thinker of a very different provenance, writes in his *Anti-Düring*, I, XI: "Freedom does not consist in the dream of independence of natural laws, but in the knowledge of those laws and in the possibility thus afforded of making them work systematically towards definite ends." It is not at all surprising that Engels defines freedom in terms almost identical to those used by the seventeenth-century philosophers. After all, the future socialist society was supposed to be built according to "scientific," that is, "rational" in the 17th-century sense, principles. Cf. also *The Communist Manifesto*. On Engels's account of Nature, see Leszek Kolakowski, *Main Currents of Marxism. Its Rise, Growth and Dissolution*, vol. 1, *The Founders* (Oxford: Clarendon Press, 1978), chap. XV, "The Dialetic of Nature."

40 Descartes's famous expression in the Sixth Discourse "to make men lords and masters of Nature" was probably inspired by Bacon: "For if such a thing may be discovered, the business of medicine will no longer be confined to humble cures, nor will physicians be honored only for necessity; but for a gift to men – of earthly gifts perhaps the greatest – of which, next to God, they may become dispensers and administrators." *De Augmentis Scientiarum*, Bk. IV, ii, vol. IV, p. 390.

> the very face of their writings. And that form was simply this. From a few examples and particulars (with addition of common notions and perhaps of some portion of the received opinions which have been most popular) they flew at once to the most general conclusions, or first principles of science: taking the truth of these as fixed and immovable, they proceeded by means of intermediate propositions to educe and prove from them the inferior conclusions, and out of these they framed the art. After that, if any new particulars and examples repugnant to their dogmas were mooted and adduced, either they subtly molded them into their systems by distinctions or explanations of their rules, or else coarsely got rid of them by exceptions; while to such particulars as were not repugnant they labored to assign causes in conformity with those of their principles. (*Novum Organum*, I, cxxv.)
>
> *Modern Way*: The rule of the axiom for the transformation of bodies is of two kinds. The first regards a body as a troop or collection of simple natures. In gold for example, the following properties are met. It is yellow; heavy up to a certain weight; malleable or ductile to a certain degree of extension; it is not volatile and loses none of its substance by the action of fire; it turns into a liquid with a certain degree of fluidity; it is separated and dissolved by particular means, and so on for the other natures which meet in gold. This kind of axiom, therefore, deduces the thing from the forms of simple natures. For he who knows the forms of yellow, weight, ductility, fixity, fluidity, solution, and so on, and the methods for superinducing them, and their gradation and modes, will make it his care to have them joined together in some body, whence may follow the transformation of that body into gold. (*Novum Organum*, II, v.)

In another of his aphorisms the indisputable originator of the idea of the Mastery of Nature gives the gist of what the Modern Way consists:

> The human understanding is of its own nature prone to abstractions and gives a substance and reality to things which are fleeting.[41] But to resolve nature into abstractions is less to our purpose than to dissect her into parts. . . . Matter rather than forms should be the object of our attention, its configurations and changes of configuration, and simple action, and law of action or motion, for

41 "For it being the nature of the mind of man (to the extreme prejudice of knowledge) to delight in the spacious liberty of generalities, as in a champion region, and not in the inclosures of particularity." *The Advancement of Learning*, Bk. II, vol. IIII, p. 359.

> forms are figments of the human mind, unless you will call those laws of action forms.[42] (*Novum Organum*, I, li.)

This aphorism (cf. *Ibid.*, I, lxxxii) contains the germ of everything that is necessary for understanding Modern philosophy. (1) Mastery of Nature: Nature is not a collection of objects each of which is a material representation of eternal forms which we come to know by contemplation; physical objects are composed of smaller elements; they can be taken apart and put together in different configurations.[43] (2) The relationship between Speculative and Practical Philosophy: because the object of philosophy is "dissection," the Old philosophy's concern with "forms," which can be known only through contemplation, is an idle activity. Thus the object of "metaphysics" should be material and efficient causes.[44] (3) The vocabulary of traditional philosophy should be retained (out of prudence), but its meaning should be changed.[45]

42 Cf. I, 55, II, 17. For Hobbes' short discussion of the problematic nature of "formal causality," see his *Elements of Philosophy*, X, 7.

43 Note that Bacon is not an atomist; he denies the existence of atoms: see *Novum Organum*, II, 8. He is a "corpuscularist." According to Bacon, body is a "troop, a collection of simple natures," *Novum Organum*, II, v. Richard Kennington, "Bacon's Critique of Ancient Philosophy" [in *Nature and Scientific Method*, Studies in Philosophy and the History of Philosophy, vol. 22, Daniel Dahlstrom, ed. (Washington, D.C.: The Catholic University of America Press, 1991)], pp. 246 ff.) discusses this issue in relation to Bacon's conception of "form."

44 The Baconian shift from the Old to New "metaphysics" is well illustrated in the following passages: "It appeareth likewise that Natural Theology, which heretofore hath been handled confusedly with Metaphysics, I have enclosed and bounded by itself. It is therefore now a question, what is left remaining for Metaphysic. . . . Physic should contemplate that which is inherent in matter and therefore transitory, and Metaphysic that which is abstracted and fixed." "In the same manner to enquire the Form of a lion, of an oak, of gold, nay of water, of air, is a vain pursuit: but to enquire the Forms of sense, of voluntary motion, of vegetation, of colors, of gravity and levity, of density, of tenuity, of heat, of cold, and all other natures and qualities, which like an alphabet are not many, and of which the essences (upheld by matter) of all creatures do consist; to enquire the *true forms* of these, is that part of metaphysic which we now define of. Not but that Physic doth make inquiry and take consideration of the same natures: but how?" *The Advancement of Learning*, Bk. II, vol. III, pp. 353, 355–56.

45 "Natural Science or Theory is divided into Physic and Metaphysic: wherein I desire it may be conceived that I use the word Metaphysic in a differing sense from that that is received: and in like manner I doubt in this and other particulars, wheresoever my conception and notion may differ from the ancient, yet I am studious to keep the ancient terms." *The Advancement of Learning*, Bk. II, vol. III, p. 352. A similar technique was adopted by Descartes. In the letter to Regius of January 1642 (AT III, 491–92; CSMK III, 205), Descartes writes: "I should like it best if you never put forward any new opinions, but retained all the old ones in name, and merely brought forward new

Why did the idea of the Mastery of Nature as the goal of Descartes's philosophy escape the attention of Étienne Gilson and of the later generations of Cartesian scholars? Considered separately, the *Meditations* are Descartes's chef-d'œuvre on the basis of which readers traditionally formed their views on Descartes's philosophy. Besides, Descartes does not mention Mastery of Nature in the *Meditations* published after the *Discourse*. One needs to bear in mind that the *Meditations* are subsidiary to a project of a Universal Science of which the tree image is the metaphor. As the trunk (physics) grows from the roots (metaphysics), so the *Meditations* logically precede the *Discourse*, which ends with the announcement of the Mastery of Nature: "Just as it is not the roots or the trunk of a tree from which one gathers the fruit, but only the ends of the branches," Descartes writes in the Preface to the French edition of *The Principles of Philosophy*, "so the principal benefit of philosophy depends on those parts of it which can only be learnt last of all."[46]

To appreciate fully the structure of *Scientia Universalis Cartesiana*, one should read Descartes's works in the following order: Discourse I–III,[47] Meditation I–III, the Doctrine of the Eternal Truths (i.e., Divine Freedom)[48] contained in Descartes's three letters to Mersenne of 1630, Meditation IV (i.e., Descartes account of Human Freedom, which is a consequence of Divine Freedom), Meditations V–VI, Discourse V[49]–VI (and the accompanying sci-

arguments. This is a course of action to which nobody could take exception, and yet those who understood your arguments would spontaneously draw from them the conclusions you had in mind."

46 The same idea is expressed in a slightly different language in Bacon's *Novum Organum*, I, lxxiii: "From all these systems of the Greeks and their ramifications through particular sciences, there can hardly after the lapse of so many years be adduced a single experiment which tends *to relieve and benefit the condition of man* . . . as in religion we are warned to show our faith by works, *so in philosophy by the same rule the system should be judged of by its* fruits, *and pronounced frivolous if it be barren.*"

47 If Beck and Roth are right that the *Discourse* contains the rules of the *Regulæ*, Descartes's decision not to publish them was probably due to the fact that he thought the *Discourse* superseded the *Regulæ*.

48 As I suggest in the Commentary, if the Doctrine of Human Freedom presented in the Fourth Meditation springs from the Doctrine of the Eternal Truths (expressed in the three famous letters to Mersenne of 1630), the Doctrine should be read before the Fourth Meditation. Thus the complete account of Descartes's metaphysics is the *Meditations* and the Doctrine of the Eternal Truths.

49 One can profitably read *The World* and *Treatise on Man* in place of the first part of the Fifth Discourse (i.e., AT VI, 40–46; CSM I, 131–34), before the discussion on blood circulation. At the beginning of the Fifth Discourse (AT VI, 41; CSM I, 131–32), Descartes makes the following disclaimer: "I endeavored to explain the most important of these truths in a treatise which certain considerations prevent me from publishing, and *I know of no better way to make them known than by summarizing the contents.*"

entific writings). Only then can the Project of the Mastery of Nature be seen to be Descartes's *cofessio fidei*, as it is for Bacon's.

* * * * *

Mastery of Nature may be the end of both Bacon's and Descartes's philosophies. Yet these two philosophies provide us with two very different accounts of reality. To the empirically oriented Bacon, the light of nature extends neither to God nor to the rational soul. The atheism of which de Maistre accused Bacon seems to be an inevitable consequence of his empiricism.[50] Descartes, on the other hand, by choosing an extreme form of skepticism as the point of departure for his philosophy,[51] built a philosophia prima that makes the knowledge of one's soul and the existence of God possible, and a science that explains natural phenomena independent of the Scholastic metaphysica that is concerned with essences of things.[52] The (Augustinian) dualism of soul and body which is an incurable defect of Descartes's philosophy, paradoxically, proves to be the cornerstone of his physics and medicine.[53]

* * * * *

The above remarks on the relationship between Bacon's and Descartes's

50 Bacon himself need not have been an atheist, but his system does not offer any defense against it. The knowledge of God, writes Bacon in *The Advancement of Learning*, Bk. II, vol. III, pp. 349, "may be obtained by the contemplation of his creatures. . . .The bounds of this knowledge are, that it sufficeth to convince atheism, but not to inform religion." Descartes, by casting doubt on the existence of the world, excluded the possibility of inferring any knowledge of God's existence by contemplating Nature.

51 "The certainty and evidence of my kind of argument for the existence of God cannot really be known without distinctly recalling the arguments which display the uncertainty of all our knowledge of material things; and these I wished to be intelligible in part even to women while providing matter for thought for the finest minds." To Vatier, 22 February 1638 (ATI, 560; CSMK III, 86).

52 On Thomas Aquinas' First Philosophy, see John F. Wippel, "'First Philosophy' According to Thomas Aquinas," in *Metaphysical Themes in Thomas Aquinas* (Washington, D.C.: The Catholic University of America Press, 1984), pp. 55–67.

53 Cartesian medicine is part of physics, or more precisely of mechanics. For an excellent analysis of Descartes's medical views, see Vincent Aucante's most recent edition of Descartes's medical writings: *Descartes. Êcrits physiologiques et médicaux*, Paris: PUF, 2000.

Note that in the English language a "medical doctor" is called a "physician." "Physic (taking it according to the derivation, and not according to our idiom for Medicine,) is situated in a middle term or distance between Natural History and Metaphysic." *The Advancement of Learning*, Bk. II, vol. III, p. 354.

philosophies have an immediate bearing on the chronology of Descartes's reading of the Augustinian corpus. First, if the *Discourse* is posterior to the "Little Treatise" (that is, a rough version of the *Meditations*), and if a major part of Descartes's metaphysics had been worked out by around 1631–32, then it would seem that Descartes read most, or all, of Augustine's writings referred to in the Index before 1631–32. His decision not to publish the *Meditations* before the time was ripe was, as I suggest in the Commentary, almost certainly caused by the attacks against Guillaume Gibieuf and the growing animosity between the Jesuit-Molinists and Augustinians. Second, the metaphor of the rays emanating from the Sun, which most likely comes from Aquinas' *Summa Contra Gentiles* (see Appendix 1: III), further suggests that Descartes had read the *Summa* before he formulated the Eternal Truths Doctrine in 1630. His reading of Suarez most likely goes back to his student years at La Flèche. When did Descartes read Bacon? The reference to the famous metaphor of the Styx (See Appendix 3: X), which we find in Descartes's letter to Mersenne of 1630, most likely comes from Bacon's *De Sapientia Veterum*. This suggests that he read this work before 1630. If the *Discourse* contains the rules from the *Regulae*, composed in 1628–29, which Descartes found in *De Augmentis Scientiarum* and the *Novum Organum*, Descartes must have read them before composing the *Regulae*.

Post Scriptum

As I remark at the opening of the Commentary, the title of Descartes's *Meditations* is without precedent in the history of philosophy. But the title of Descartes's *opus magnum* is not the only Cartesian title that causes the reader to ponder its significance. The same question can be asked with respect to *Le Monde, ou Traité de la Lumière*. Why "The World or the Treatise on Light"? In the Book of Genesis, I, 3, we read: "in principium fecit Deus cælum et terram, ut, quod dixit Deus: fiat lux" (*in the beginning God made heaven and earth and He said: let there be light*). The creation of the world is simultaneous with God's saying *fiat lux*. "*Le Monde, ou Traité de la Lumière*" is almost certainly a reference to this line in the Bible.[54] Like the Biblical Creator, Descartes is creating a new world (*fiat lux*), according to new principles described in the *Principles of Philosophy*. Why six Meditations and six parts of the *Discourse*? Again, God created the world in six days. So there are six parts of the *Discourse* and six Meditations. God created man on the sixth day. In the Sixth

54 I owe this insight to Professor Hans Aarsleff of the English Department at Princeton University.

Meditation, we witness the birth of the modern (mechanical) man whose life is not animated by a rational soul but is propelled by the blood that flows through his veins according to the laws of Nature. *The Passions of the Soul* may be a reference to the heading of Section 713 of Bacon's *Sylva Sylvarum*: *Experiments in consort touching the impressions which the passions of the mind make upon the body.*[55] Finally, the metaphor of the Tree in the *Principles*[56] is an allusion to the Tree of the Knowledge of Good and Evil from the Biblical Garden of Eden.

55 *Sylva Sylvarum* was not translated into Latin until 1648. As Marta Fattori pointed out to me, Descartes's friend Beeckman read this work. Mersenne, according to Claudio Buccolini, was translating parts of the *Sylva*. However, we have no proof that Descartes knew the *Sylva Sylvarum* before writing the *Passions*. The title of the *Passion of the Soul* may be a reference to the sentences from *De Augmentis* that I quote in the text. On Beeckman and *Sylva Sylvarum*, see Benedino Gemelli, *Aspetti dell'atomismo classico nella filosofia di Francis Bacon e nel Seicento* (Florence: Leo S. Olschki editore, 1966).

56 For possible sources of the structure and title of the *Principles*, see J.-L. Marion's *Sur le prisme métaphysique de Descartes* (Paris: PUF, 1991), pp. 12–13, 45.

Appendix V

Montaigne

When I quote others I do so in order to express my own ideas more clearly. . . . For I make others say what I am unable to say so well myself, now for want of words, now for want of understanding. I do not number my borrowings, I weigh them. And if I had wished to raise their value by number, I could have laden myself with twice as many. There are all, or very nearly all, of so famous and ancient names, that I think they reveal themselves sufficiently without my naming them. . . . What I retain of them I no longer recognize as another's.

"Of the Education of Boys," I, xxvi, vol. I, 145; "Of Books," II, x, 397; "Of Presumption," I, xvii, vol. I, 102.

MONTAIGNE

I M

1) Somme, pour revenir à moy, ce seul par où je m'estime quelque chose, c'est ce en quoy jamais homme ne s'estima deffaillant: ma recommendation est vulgaire, commune et populaire, car qui a jamais cuidé avoir faute de sens? . . . Il ne fut jamais crocheteur ny femmelette qui ne pansast avoir assez de sens pour sa provision. Nous reconnoissons ayeséement ès autres l'avantage du courage, de la force corporelle, de l'experience, de la disposition, de la beauté; mais m'advantage du jugement, nous ne le cedons à personne. . . . On dit communément que le plus juste partage que nature nous aye fait de ses graces, c'est celuy du sens: car il n'est aucun qui ne se contente de ce qu'elle luy en a distribué. . . . Cette capacité de tirer le vray, quelle qu'elle soit en moy, et cett'humeur libre de n'assubjectir aisément ma creance, je la dois principalement à moy: car les plus fermes imaginations que j'aye, et generalles, sont celles qui, par maniere de dire, nasquirent avec moy.

"De la præsumption," II, xvii, V: vol. III, 656–57, PL: 640–41, EG: vol. I, 60.

RENÉ DESCARTES

I D

1) Le bon sens est la chose du monde la mieux partagée: car chacun pense en estre si bien pouruû, que ceux mesme qui sont les plus difficiles a contenter en toute autre chose, n'ont point coustume d'en desirer plus qu'ils en ont. En quoy il n'est pas vraysemblable que tous se trompent; mais plustot cela tesmoigne que la puissance de bien iuger, & distinguer le vray d'avec le faux, qui est proprement ce qu'on nomme le bon sens ou la raison, est naturellement esgale en tous les hommes.

***Discours de la Méthode*, I. AT VI, 1–2.**

MONTAIGNE

I M

1) In fine, to return to myself, the only quality for which I take some credit to myself is that in which no man ever thought himself deficient. My self approbation is common and vulgar, and shared by all; for what man ever has imagined he was lacking in Sense. . . . There never was a street-porter or any little woman who did not think they had enough sense for their needs. We are ready enough to acknowledge others to have the advantage over us in courage, bodily strength, experience, agility, beauty; but the advantage in judgment we yield to none. . . . It is commonly said that the fairest portion of her favors that Nature has given us is that of Sense, for there is no man who is not contented with his share of it. . . . This capacity which I have, whatever it may be worth, for sifting the truth, and my independence in not readily subjecting my belief, I owe chiefly to myself. For the most abiding and general ideas I have are those which, so to say, were born with me; they are natural and entirely my own.

"Of Presumption," II, xvii, T: vol. I, 107–9; S: 745–47.

RENÉ DESCARTES

I D

1) Good sense is the best distributed thing in the world: for everyone thinks himself so well endowed with it that even those who are the hardest to please in everything else do not usually desire more of it than they possess. In this it is unlikely that everyone is mistaken. It indicates rather that the power of judging well and of distinguishing the true from the false – which is what we properly call "good sense" or "reason" – is naturally equal in all men.

***Discourse on the Method,* I. AT VI, 1–2, CSM I, 111.**

II M

1) Il [l'escholier] practiquera, par le moyen des histoires; ces grandes ames des meilleurs siecles. . . . Il se tire une merveilleuse clarté, pour le jugement humain, de la frequentation du monde. . . . Ce grand monde, que les uns multiplient encore comme espaces soubs un genre, c'est le miroüer où il nous faut regarder pour nous connoistre de bon biais. Somme, je veux que ce soit le livre de mon escholier. Tant d'humeurs, de sectes, de jugemens, d'opinions, de loix sainement des nostres, et apprennent nostre jugement à reconnoistre son imperfection et sa naturelle foiblesse. . . . A cette cause, le commerce des hommes y est marveilleusement propre, et la visite des pays estrangers. . . . Quant il portoit le busc de son pourpoint entre les mamelles, il maintenoit par vives raisons qu'il estoit en son vray lieu; quelques années après, le voylà avalé jusques entre les cuisses: il se moque de son autre usage, le trouve inepte et insuportable.

"De l'institution des enfens," I, xxvi, V, vol. I, 156–58, 296, PL: 155, 156, 157, 152; EG: vol., I, 167–68, 163; "De Coustumes Anciennes," I, xlix, PL: 285; EG: vol. I, 329.

II D

1) Ie ne laissois pas toutefois d'estimer les exercices, ausquels on s'occupe dans les escholes . . . la lecture des bons livres est comme une conversation avec les plus honnestes gens des siecles passez, qui en ont esté les autheurs. . . . Car c'est quasi le mesme de converser avec ceux des autres siecles, que de voyager. Il est bon de sçavoir quelque chose des meurs de divers peuples, affin de iuger des nostres plus sainement, & que nous ne pensions pas que tout ce qui est contre nos modes soit ridicule, & contre raison. . . . C'est pourquoy, sitost que l'aage me permit de sortir de la suietion de mes Precepteurs, ie quittay entierement l'estude des lettres. Et me resoluant de ne chercher plus d'autre science, que celle qui se pourroit trouver en moymesme, ou bien dans le grand livre du monde, i'employay le reste de ma ieunesse à voyager, a voir des cours & des armées, a frequnter des gens de diverses humeurs & conditions, a recueillir diverses experiences . . . et depuis [le College], en voyasgeant, ayant reconnu que tous ceux qui ont des sentiments fort contraire aux nostres, ne sont pas, pour cela, barbares ny sauvages . . . iusques aux modes de nos habits, la mesme chose qui nous a plû a dix ans, & qui nous plaira peutestre encore avant dix ans, nous semble maintenant extravagante & ridicule.

***Discours de la Méthode*, I et II. AT VI, 5–6, 9, 16.**

II M

1) Through the medium of histories he [the pupil] will hold converse with the great souls of the best ages.[1] . . . Mixing with society has a marvelous effect in clearing up a man's judgment. . . . This great world, which some yet multiply as a species under one genus, is the mirror wherein we are to behold ourselves, in order to know ourselves from the right point of view. In a word, I should wish it to be my pupil's book. So many ways of looking at things, so many sects, teach us to form a sound estimate of our own, and teach our judgment to discover its own imperfection and its natural feebleness. . . . To this end human intercourse is marvelously well adapted, as well as travel in foreign countries. . . . When it was the fashion to wear the busk of the doublet as high as the chest, he [Laesilus, the Roman] would maintain with heated arguments that it was in its proper place, a few years after behold it slipping down as low as the thighs, then he laughs at the other fashion, finding it absurd and intolerable.

"Of the Education of Boys," I, xxvi, T: vol. I, 155; S: 175–76 (Cf. "Of Presumption," II, xvii, T: vol. II, 110), 156–57, 151; "Of Ancient Custom," I, xlix, T: vol. I, 289; S: 331.

II D

1) I did not, however, cease to value the exercises done in the Schools . . . the reading good books is like having a conversation with the most distinguished men of the past ages. . . . For conversing with those of past centuries is much the same as traveling. It is good to know something of the customs of various peoples, so that we may judge our own more soundly and not think that everyone contrary to our own ways is ridiculous and irrational. . . . That is why, as soon as I was old enough to emerge from the control of my teachers, I entirely abandoned the study of letters. Resolving to seek no knowledge other than that which could be found in myself or else in the great book of the world, I spent the rest of my youth traveling, visiting courts and armies, mixing with people of diverse temperaments and ranks . . . and since then [my college years] I have recognized through my travels that those with views quite contrary to ours are not on that account barbarians or savages . . . even in our fashions of dress, the very thing that pleased us ten years ago, and will perhaps please us again ten years hence, now strikes us as extravagant and ridiculous.

***Discourse on the Method*, I and II. CSM I, 113–14, 115, 119.**

1 "Whether it be perhaps that my continual intercourse with the habits of mind of ancient writers, and the picture I have formed of those richly-endowed minds of the past . . ." "Of Presumption," II, xvii, T: vol. I, 110; S: 748; PL: 642; EG: vol. II, 62.

III M

1) Qui ignore Aristote, selon eux [les sçavans] s'ignore quand et quand soy-mesme. . . . Le monde regarde tousjours vis à vis; moy, je replie ma veue au dedans, je la plante, je l'amuse là. Chacun regarde devant soy; moy, je regarde dedans moy: je n'ay affaire qu'à moy, je me considere sans cesse, je me conterolle, je me gouste. . . . Quel que soit donq le fruict que nous pouvons avoir de l'experience, à peine servira beacoup à nostre institution celle que nous tirons des examples estrangers, si nous faisons si mal nostre profficit de celle que nous avons de nous mesme, qui nous est plus familiere, et certes suffisantes à nous instruire de ce qu'il nous faut. . . . Je m'estudie plus qu'autre subject. C'est ma metaphysique, c'est ma physique. . . . En fin, toute cette fricassée que je barbouille icy n'est qu'un registre des essais de ma vie . . .

"De la Præsumption," II, xvii, V: vol. II, 656–57, PL: 640-641; EG: vol. II, 61; "De l'Experience," III, xiii, PL: 1050, 1056; EG: vol. II, 525, 532.

III D

1) Mais aprés que i'eu employé quelques années a estudier ainsi dans le livre du monde, & a tascher d'acquerir quelque experience, ie pris un iour resolution d'estudier aussy en moymesme. . . . Ainsi mon dessein n'est pas d'enseigner icy la Method que chascun doit suivre pour bien conduire sa raison, mais seulement de faire voir en quelle sorte i'ay tasché de conduire la miene.

***Discours de la Méthode*, I. AT VI, 4, 10.**

III M

1) According to them [the scholars], the man who is ignorant of Aristotle is at the same time ignorant of himself. . . . The world always looks over the other way; I turn my eyes inwards. There I fix them and keep them fixed. Every one looks in front of him; I look within myself. I have no business but with myself, I continually reflect upon myself, examine and analyze myself. . . . Whatever then may be the fruit of experience, that which we derive from foreign examples will make us little wiser if we profit so little from that which we have of ourselves, which is more familiar to us, and certainly sufficient to tell us what we need. I study myself more than any other subject; that is my Metaphysics, that is my Physics. . . . In fine, all this farrago that I am scribbling here is nothing but a record of the experiences of my life.

"Of Presumption," II, xvii, T: vol. II, 108-109; S: 746-47; "Of Experience," III, xiii, T: vol. II, 549, 556; S: 1217, 1224.

III D

1) But after I had spent some years pursuing these studies in the book of the world and trying to gain some experience, I resolved one day to undertake studies within myself. . . . My present aim, then, is not to teach the method which everyone must follow in order to direct his reason correctly, but only to reveal how I have tried to direct my own.

***Discourse on the Method,* I. CSM I, 116, 112.**

IV M

1) Il n'est chose en quoy le monde soit si divers qu'en coustumes et loix. Telle chose est icy abominable, qui apporte recommendation ailleurs. . . . Au demeurant, si c'est de nous que nous tirons le reglement de nous meurs, à quelle confusion nous rejettons nous! Car ce que nostre raison nous y conceille de plus vraysemblables, c'est generalement à chacun d'obeir aux loix de son pays, comme l'advis de Socrates inspiré, dict-il, d'un conseil divin. Et par là que veut elle dire, sinon que nostre devoir n'a autre regle que fortitude? . . .

Mais on decouvre bien mieux ses effets aux estranges impressions qu'elle fait en nos ames, où elle [la coustume] ne trouve pas tant de resistance. Que ne peut elle nos jugements et en nos creances. . . . Mais le principal effet da sa puissance, c'est de nous saisir et empieter de telle sorte, qu'à peine soit-il en nous de nous r'avoir de sa prinse et de r'entrer en nous, pour discourir et raisonner de ses ordonnances. . . . Qui voudra se desfaire de ce violent prejudice de la coustume, il trouvera plusieurs choses receues d'une resolution indubitable, qui n'ont appuy qu'en la barbe chenue et rides de l'usage qui les accompaigne; mais, ce masque arraché, rapportant les choses à la verité et à la raison, il sentira son jugement comme tout boulversé, et remis pourtant en bien plus seur estat.

IV D

1) Il est vray que, pendant que ie ne faisois que considerer les meurs des autres hommes, ie n'y trouvois gueres de quoy m'assurer, & que i'y remarquois quasi autant de diversité que i'avois fait auparavant entre les opinions des Philosophes. En sorte que le plus grand profit que i'en retirois, estoit que, voyant plusieurs choses qui, bien qu'elles nous semblent fort extravagants & ridicules, ne laissent pas d'estre communement receuës & approuvées par d'autres grans peuples, i'apprenois a ne rien croyre trop fermement de ce qui ne m'aviot esté persuadé que par l'exemple & par la coustume; et ainsi ie me delivrois peu a peu de beaucoup d'erreurs, qui peuvent offusquer nostre lumiere naturelle, & nous rendre moins capables d'entendre raison. . . . Comme, en effect, i'ose dire que l'exact observation de ce peu de precepts que i'avois choisis, me donna telle facilité a demesler toutes les questions ausauelles ces deux sciences s'estendent . . . outre que ie sentois, en la pratiquant, que mon esprit s'accoustumoit peu a peu a convevoir plus netement & plus distinctement ses obiets . . .

***Discours de la Méthode*, I. AT VI, 10, 20–21.**

IV M

1) There is nothing in which the world varies so much as in customs and laws. Many a thing is abominable here that is commended elsewhere. . . . Moreover, if we ourselves determine the rule of our conduct, into what confusion we are thrown! For the counsel that our reason is most likely to give us is that every man generally shall obey the laws of his country, which was the advise of Socrates, inspired, as he says, by divine counsel. And what does reason mean thereby, if not that our duty is only guided by chance? . . .

But the effects of custom are far better discovered in the strange impressions she makes on our minds, where she meets with less resistance. What can she not impose on our judgments and beliefs? . . . But the principal effect of the force of custom is to seize and grip us so firmly, that we are scarce able to escape from its grasp, and to regain possession of ourselves sufficiently to discuss and reason out its commands. . . . He who would rid himself of this violent prejudice of custom will find that many things are accepted with undoubting resolve, which have no support but in the hoary beard and wrinkles of the usage which attends them; but, the mask once torn away, if he will refer

IV D

1) It is true that, so long as I merely considered the customs of other men, I found hardly any reason for confidence, for I observed in them almost as much diversity as I had found previously among the opinions of philosophers. In fact the greatest benefit I derived from these observations was that they showed me many things which, although seeming very extravagant and ridiculous to us, are nevertheless commonly accepted and approved in other great nations; and so I learned not to believe too firmly anything of which I had been persuaded only by example and custom.[2]

Thus I gradually freed myself from many errors which may obscure our natural light and make us less capable of heeding reason. . . . In fact, I venture to say that by strictly observing the few rules I had chosen, I became very adept at unraveling all the questions which fall under these two science. . . . Moreover, as I practiced the method I felt my mind gradually become accustomed to conceiving its objects more clearly and distinctly.

***Discourse on the Method*, I. CSM I, 115–16, 121.**

2 For Montaigne's descriptions of customs, see *Apology for Raymond Sebond*, II, xii, T: vol. II, 27 ff. and "Of Custom, and That an Established Law Is Not Lightly To Be Changed," I, xxiii, T: vol. I, 106–10.

***Apologie de Raymond Sebond*, II, xii, PL: 564, 562, EG: vol. I, 652, 650; "De la coustume et de ne changer aisément une loy receüe," I, xxiii, PL: 109, 114, 116; EG: vol. I, 115, 121, 123.**

V M

1) Car c'est la regle des regles, et general loy des loix, que chacun observe celles du lieu où il est. . . . Il y a grand doubte, si'il se peut trouver si evident profit au changement d'une loy receue, telle qu'elle soit, qu'il y a de mal à la remuer, d'autant qu'une police, c'est comme un bastiment de diverses pieces jointes ensemble, d'une telle liaison, qu'il est impossible d'en esbranler une que tout le corps ne s'en sente. . . .

Je suis desgousté de la nouvelleté, quelque visage qu'elle porte, et ay raison, car j'en ay veu des effets très-dommageables. . . .

"De la coustume et de ne changer aisément une loy receüe," I, xxiii, V: vol. I, 118–19, PL: 117–18; EG: vol. I, 125–26.

V D

1) La premiere [maxime] estoit d'obeir aux lois & aux coustumes de mon païs, retenant constanment la religion en laquelle Dieu m'a fait la grace d'estre instruit dés mon enfance, & me gouvernant, en toute autre chose, suivant les opinions les plus moderées, & les plus esloignées de l'excés, qui fussent communement receuës en pratique par les mieux sensez de ceux avec lesquels i'aurois a vivre. . . .

C'est pourquoy ie ne sçaurois aucunement approuver ces humeurs brouillonnes & inquietes, qui, n'estant appelez, ny par leur naissance, n'y par leur fortune, au maniement des affairs publiques, ne laissent pas d'y faire tojours, en idée, quelque nouvelle reformation.

***Discours de la Méthode*, III et II. AT VI, 22–23, 14–15.**

the matter to truth and reason, he will feel his judgment turned as it were topsy-turvy, and yet restored to a condition of greater sureness.

***Apology for Raymond Sebond*, II, xii, T: vol. II, 27, 25; S:654, 652. "Of Custom, and that an Established Law Is Not Lightly to Be Changed," I, xxiii, T: vol. I, 106, 111, 113; S: 125, 130, 132.**

V M

1) [F]or it is the rule of rules, and universal law of laws, that every man shall observe those of the place wherein he lives. . . . It is much to be doubted whether the manifest advantage of changing an established law, be it ever so bad, outweighs the evil involved in the removing of it, inasmuch as a government is a structure of various parts so closely joined together, that it is impossible to shake one part without the whole body feeling the concussion. . . .

I dislike innovation in any disguise whatever, and have reason to do so, for I have witnessed its very injurious effects . . .

"Of Custom, and that an Established Law Is Not Lightly to Be Changed," I, xxiii, T: vol. I, 115; S: 133–34.

V D

1) The first [maxim] was to obey the laws and customs of my country, holding constantly to the religion in which by God's grace I had been instructed from my childhood, and governing myself in all other matters according to the most moderate and least extreme opinions – the opinions commonly accepted in practice by the most sensible of those with whom I should have to live.

I cannot by any means approve of those meddlesome and restless characters, called neither by birth nor by Fortune to the management of public affairs, are yet forever thinking up some new reform.

***Discourse on the Method*, III and II. CSM I, 122, 118.**

VI M

1) Par ce que ès choses humaines, à quelque bande qu'on panche, il se presente force apparences qui nous y confirment . . . de quelque costé que je me tourne, je me fournis toujours assez de cause et de vray-semblance pour m'y maintenir. Ainsi j'arreste chez moi le doubte et la liberté de choisir, jusques à ce que l'occasion me presse. Et lors, à confesser la verité, je jette le plus souvent la plume au vent, comme on dict, et m'abandonne à la mercy de la fortune: une bien legere inclination et circonstance m'emporte. . . . L'incertitude de mon jugement est si également balancée en la pluspart des occurrences, que je compromettrois volontiers à la decision du sort et des dets . . .

"De la Præsumption," II, xvii, PL: 637–38, 639; EG: vol. II, 57–58.

VI D

1) Ma seconde maxime estoit d'estre le plus ferme & le plus resolu en mes actions que ie pourrois, & de ne suivre pas moins constanement les opinions les plus douteuses, lorsque ie m'y serois une fois determiné, que si elles eussent esté tres assurées. . . . Et ainsi, les actions de la vie ne souffrant souvent aucun delay, c'est une verité tres certaine que, lorsqu'il n'est pas en nostre pouvoir de discerner les plus vrayes opinions, nous devons suivre les plus probables; et mesme, qu'encore nous ne remarquions point davantage de probabilité aux unes qu'aux autres, nous devons neamoins nous determiner a quelques unes, & les considerer aprés, non plus comme douteuses, en tant qu'elles se rapportent a la prattique, mais comme tres vrayes & tres certaines, a cause que la raison qui nous y a fait determiner, se trouve telle.

***Discours de la Méthode*, III. AT VI, 25.**

VII M

1) A faute d'avoir assez de fermeté pour souffrir l'importunité des accidents contraires ausquels nous sommes subjects, les affaires, je nourris autant que je puis en moy cett'opinion, m'abandonnant du tout à la fortune, de prendre doucement et patiemment. C'est à cela seul

VII D

1) Ma troisieme maxime estoit de tascher tosiours plutost a me vaincre que la fortune, & a changer mes desirs que l'ordre du monde; et generamement, de m'accoustumer a croire qu'il n'y a rien qui soit entierement en nostre pouvoir, que nos pensées, en sorte qu'aprés que nous

VI M

1) For in human affairs, to whatever side we lean, we are confronted by many probabilities which confirm our opinions . . . so, whichever way I turn, I can always provide myself with grounds and probabilities enough to keep me there. Hence I hold myself in suspense, with freedom to choose, until the occasion urges me. And then, to confess the truth, I most often throw the feather into the wind, as the saying goes, and commit myself to the mercy of Fortune. . . . The uncertainty of my judgment is so evidently balanced on most occasions, that I could readily decide it by a throw of the dice . . .

"Of Presumption," II, xvii, T: vol. II, 105; S: 743.

VI D

1) My second maxim was to be as firm and decisive in my action as I could, and to follow even the most doubtful opinions, once I had adopted them, with no less constancy than if they had been quite certain . . . since in everyday life we must often act without delay, it is a most certain truth that when it is not in our power to discern the truest opinions, we must follow the most probable. Even when no opinions appear more probable than others, we must still adopt some; and having done so we must then regard them not as doubtful, from a practical point of view, but as most true and certain, on the grounds that the reason which made us adopt them is itself true and certain.

***Discourse on the Method,* III. CSM I, 123.**

VII M

1) Why should we, contrary to the laws of reason and nature, make our contentment subject to another's power? To anticipate, moreover, the accidents of fortune[3]; to deprive ourselves of the good things we possess,

VII D

1) My third maxim was to try always to master myself rather than fortune, and change my desires rather than the order of the world. In general I would become accustomed to believing that nothing lies entirely

3 Cf. "Of Presumption," II, xvii, T: vol. II, 93–94, and "Of Solitude," I, xxxix, T: vol. I, 240.

que je travaille, et le but auquel j'achemine tous mes discours . . .

[L]e sage doit au dedans retirer son ame de la presse, et la tenir en liberté et puissance de juger librement des choses; mais, qunt au dehors, qu'il doit suivre entierement les façons et formes receues. Le societé publique n'a que faire de nos pensées . . .

"De la Præsumption," II, xvii, V: vol. II, 644, vol. I, 118, PL: 627; EG: 45–46 (Cf. I, xxxix, PL: 238); "De la coustume et de ne changer aisément une loy receüe," I, xxiii, PL: 117; EG: vol. I, 125.

avons fait nostre mieux, touchant les choses qui nous sont exterieures, tout ce qui manque de nous reussir est, au regard de nous, absolument impossible. . . . Mais i'avouë qu'il est besoin d'un long exercise, & d'une meditation souvent reïterée, pour s'ccoustumer a regarder de ce biais toutes les choses; et ie croy que c'est principalment en cecy que consistoit le secret de ces Philosophes, qui ont pû autrefois se soustraire de l'empire de la Fortune, & malgré les douleurs & la pauvreté, disputer de la felicité avec leurs Dieux. Car s'occupant sans cesse a considerer les bornes qui leur estoient prescrites par la Nature, ils se persuadoient si parfaitement que rien n'estoit en leur pouvoir que leurs pensées, que cela seul estoit suffisant pour les empecher d'avoir aucune affection pour d'autres choses.

***Discours de la Méthode,* III. AT VI, 25–26.**

VIII M

1) Qu'il luy face tout passer par l'estamine et ne loge rien en sa test par simple authorité et à credit; les principes d'Aristote ne luy soyent principes, non plus que ceux des Stoiciens ou Epicuriens.

"De l'institution des enfens," I, xxvi, V: vol. I, 151, PL: 150; EG: vol. I, 161.

VIII D

1) Le premier estoit de ne recevoir iamais aucune chose pour vraie, que ie ne la connusse évidemment estre telle.

***Discours de la Méthode,* II. AT VI, 18.**

as many have done from religious motives, and some philosophers in accordance with the dictates of reason . . .

[T]he wise man should, in respect of his inward thoughts and opinions, withdraw his mind from the common crowd,[4] and keep it at liberty and with power to judge freely of things; but, in respect of his exterior, that he should wholly follow accepted forms and fashions. Society in general has no business with our thoughts . . .

"Of Solitude," I, xxxix, T: vol. I, 240; S: 273; "Of Custom, and that an Established Law Is Not Lightly To Be Changed," I, xxiii, T: vol. I, 114–15; S: 133.

within our power except our thoughts, so that after doing our best in dealing with matters external to us, whatever we fail to achieve is absolutely impossible so far as we are concerned. . . . But I admit that it takes long practice and repeated meditation[5] to become accustomed to seeing everything in this light. In this, I believe, lay the secret of those philosophers who in earlier times were able to escape from the dominion of fortune and, despite suffering and poverty, rival their gods in happiness. Through constant reflection upon the limits prescribed for them by nature, they [the Stoics][6] became perfectly convinced that nothing was in their power but their thoughts, and this alone was sufficient to prevent them from being attracted to other things.

***Discourse on the Method,* III. CSM I, 123–24.**

VIII M

1) We must let him [the pupil] pass everything through a sieve, and store nothing in his head on mere authority and trust. To him Aristotle's principles should be no

VIII D

1) The first [rule] was never to accept anything as true if I did not have evident knowledge of its truth . . .

***Discourse on the Method,* II. CSM I, 120.**

4 See Montaigne, "Of Solitude," I, xxxix, T: vol. I, 234ff.

5 "The idea of those who seek solitude from religious motives, filling their hearts with the certainty of the divine promises in the next life, is much more consistent with sanity. They keep God before their eyes, as an object infinite in goodness and power, there the soul has the wherewithal to satisfy its desires in all freedom . . ." "Of Solitude," I, xxxix, T: vol. I, 242.

6 See letters to Princess Elizabeth in which Descartes refers to the Stoics.

IX M

IX D

1) Il m'a toujours semblé qu'à un homme Chrestien cette sorte de parler est pleine d'indiscretion et d'irreverance: Dieu ne pas mourir, Dieu ne se peut desdire, Dieu ne peut faire cecy ou cela. Je ne trouve pas bon d'enfermer ainsi la puissance divine soubs les loix de nostre parolle. . . .. Voyez comment on se prevaut de cette sorte de parler pleine d'irreverence. . . . Et, enfin que cette sociétté de l'homme à Dieu s'accouple encore par des examples plaisans, il ne peut faire que deux fois dix ne soyent vingt. Voilà ce qu'il dict, et qu'un Chrestien devroit eviter de passer par sa bouche, là où, au rebours, il semble que les hommes recerchent cette fole fierté de langage, pour ramener Dieu à leur mesure,

Cras vel atra
Nube polum pater occupato,
Vel sole puro; non tamen irritum
Quodcumque retro est, efficet, neque
Diffinget infectumque reddet
Quod fugiens semel hora vexit

Horace, *Odes*, III, xxix, 43–48

Que Jupiter demain étale au ciel
Unnoir nuage ou bien un soleil pur!
Mais il ne peut revenir sur le temps.

more principles than those of the Stoics and Epicureans.

"Of the Education of Boys," I, xxvi, vol. I, 149.

IX M

IX D

1) It has always seemed to me that it is altogether unwise and irreverent in a Christian to say this sort of thing: "God cannot die, God cannot go back from His word; God cannot do this, God cannot do that." I cannot approve of the divine power being thus confined by the laws of our speech. . . . See how the people revel in that most irreverent way of speaking! . . . And, that this association of man and God may be coupled with some absurd examples, he cannot make twice not to be twenty.' That is what he [Pliny the Elder in his *Historia Naturalis*, II, 23] says, and what a Christian should take heed not to allow his lips to utter. Whilst, on the contrary, men seem to study this foolish arrogance of speech, to bring God to their stature:

Let Jove to-morrow, if he will,
With blackest clouds the welkin fill,
Or flood it all with sunlight pure;
Yet from the past he cannot take
Its influence, for that is sure;
Nor can he mar or bootless make
Whate'er of rapture and delight
The hours have borne us in their flight

Horace, *Ode* III, xxix, 43–48.

. . . Whence are bred all the delusions

Il ne peut pas reprendre et annuler
Ce qu'à jamais ravit l'heure qui fuit!

. . . Et de là s'engendrent toutes les reseries et erreurs desquelles le monde se trouve saisi. . . . Combien insolemment rebroüent Epicurus les Stoïciens sur ce qu'il tient l'estre veritablement bon et heureux n'appartenir qu'à Dieu, et l'homme sage n'en avoir qu'un ombrage et similitude! Combien temeraiment ont ils attaché Dieu à la destinée (à la mienne volonté, qu'aucuns du surnom de Chrestiens ne le facet pas encore!) et Thales, Platon et Pythagoras l'ont asservy à la necessité!

***Apologie pour Raymond Sebond*, II, xii, V: vol. II, 527–28, PL: 507–9; EG: vol. I, 587–89.**

1) Que les verités mathematiques, lesquelles vous nommés eternelles, ont esteé establies de Dieu & en dependent entierement, aussy bien que tout le reste des creatures; C'est en effait parler de Dieu comme d'un Iuppiter ou Saturne, & l'ussuiettir au Stix & aus destinees, que de dire que ces verités sont independantes de luy.

A Mersenne, 15 avril 1630. AT I, 145.

and errors with which the world is possessed, when we reduce and weigh on our scales things so far above our measure. . . . How arrogantly the Stoics reprehended Epicurus when he maintains that a truly good and happy existence belongs to God alone, and that the wise man has but a shadow and semblance of it! How airly they bind God to Destiny (let no man that calls himself a Christian do it again with my consent!), and Thales, Plato, and Pythagoras make him a slave to Necessity![7]

***Apology for Raymond Sebond,* II, xii, T: vol. I, 525, 527–28; S: 590–92. Cf. Bacon's mention of the metaphor: XB.**

1) The mathematical truths which you call eternal have been laid down by God and depend on Him entirely no less than the rest of his creatures. Indeed to say that these truths are independent of God is to talk of Him as if he were Jupiter or Saturn and subject Him to the Styx and the Fates.

To Mersenne, April 15, 1630. CSMK III, 23.

7 See Seneca, Letter 92: 275.

Montaigne, Descartes, and the Discovery of the Self

The passages from the writings of Montaigne and Descartes collected in Appendix 3[1] can be grouped around the five following points: (1) criticism of Aristotelian philosophy, (2) custom, (3) authority, (4) skepticism, and (5) relativism. These five points do not do justice to the richness of Montaigne's thought; they do show, however, *how* Descartes read Montaigne and *what* he found in the *Essays* to be of philosophical importance.

The presence of Montaigne can be detected already in the opening paragraph of the *Discourse on the Method* (CSM I, 111):

> Good sense is the best distributed thing in the world... the diversity of our opinions does not arise because some of us are more reasonable than others but solely because we direct our thoughts along different paths and do not attend to the same things. For it is not enough to have a good mind; the main thing is to apply it well. The greatest souls are capable of the greatest vices as well as the greatest virtues; and those who proceed but very slowly can make much greater progress, if they always follow the right path, than those who hurry and stray from it.[2]

It has been known to Cartesian scholars that the term "sense" comes from Montaigne's *Apology for Raymond Sebond*, II, xii.[3] What has not been noticed, however, are the anti-Aristotelian connotations of this notion. The term "sense" appears in the *Essays* in the context of Montaigne's criticism of the old way of learning and of the Aristotelian conception of knowledge. "And then, for whom do you write?" Montaigne asks.

1 For Montaigne's influence on *The Passions of the Soul* see Michael G. Paulson, *The Possible Influence of Montaigne's* Essais *on Descartes'* Treatise on The Passions, (Lanham, Md.: University of America Press, 1988).

2 The first paragraph of the *Discourse* is a "collage" from the works of three authors: Montaigne ("Of Presumption," II, xvii, T: vol. I, 107–9), Bacon (*Novum Organum*, I, cxxii), and St. Augustine (Sermon, 109):

> [Montaigne:] It is commonly said that the fairest portion of her favors that Nature has given us is that of Sense, for there is no man who is not contented with his share of it. [Bacon:] For my way of discovering sciences goes far to the level of man's wits, and leaves but little to individual excellence; because it performs everything by the surest rules and demonstrations. For they are no wise disparaged – the question between them [the Ancients] and me being only as to the way. For [as St. Augustine says in Sermon 109 – Z.J.], the lame man who keeps the right road outstrips the runner who takes the wrong one. Nay it is obvious that when a man runs the wrong way, the more active and swift he is the further he will go astray.

3 Étienne Gilson, *Discours de la méthode: Texte et commentaire* (Paris: Vrin, 1967), pp. 82–83.

4 *Apology for Raymond Sebond*, II, xii, T: . . . S: 746.

> The scholars, to whom it falls to sit in judgment on books, value them only for their learning, and will admit no procedure in the mind but along the lines of art and erudition. If you have mistaken one of the Scipios for the other, can you say anything worth saying?" And he adds: "According to them [the scholars], the man who is ignorant of Aristotle is at the same time ignorant of himself.[4]

Learning, as the scholars understand it, is the pedantic acquisition of knowledge. The supreme form of knowledge is the knowledge of Aristotle's natural philosophy; ignorance of Aristotle equals ignorance of oneself. A few paragraphs later, Montaigne says that knowledge does not lie in knowledge of the external world, but in the knowledge of oneself: "The world always looks over the other way. . . . I turn my eyes inwards. There I fix them and keep them fixed. . . . I revolve in myself" (II, xvii, T: vol. II, 109; S: 747). In conclusion to his *Essays*, Montaigne writes: "I study myself more than any other subject; that is my Metaphysics, that is my physics" (III, xiii, T: vol. II, 549; S: 1217)

Descartes's decision to open the *Discourse* with the notion of "sense" can hardly be accidental, and it must have invoked an array of anti-Aristotelian associations in his readers, beginning with Montaigne's criticism of the scholars' notion of knowledge, to his ironic remark that the proper object of physics and metaphysics is not the external world, but the *self*.

Montaigne's criticism of Aristotelianism is not autonomous, however. Montaigne never directly concerns himself with the content of Aristotle's thought; he criticizes "the monarch of modern science" for the paralyzing effects his authority has had on man's ability to form a judgment, which is according to Montaigne the primary goal of education.

> We do not ask if Galen said anything worth saying, but whether he said thus or otherwise... The god of the scholastic knowledge is Aristotle; to question his laws is as profane as it was to question those of Lycurgus at Sparta. We accept his teaching as if it were magisterial law, when it is perhaps as wrong as any other. (II, xii, T: vol. I, 540; S: 605)

"A good education," in Montaigne's view, "changes one's judgment and character." (II, xvii, T: vol. II, 12; S: 750). "[Our educational system's aim, on the other hand] has been to make us not good and wise, but learned; and it has succeeded" (II, xvii, T: vol. II, 111; S: 749). An illustration of the effects of the traditional educational method is the following story: "At Pisa I had a private interview with a worthy man, but such an Aristotelian that the most

5 *Apology for Raymond Sebond*, II, xii, T: vol. I, 476–77; S: 537–38.

universal of his dogmas was: 'That the touchstone and measure of all sound opinions and of every truth is conformity to the teaching of Aristotle; that outside of that there is nothing but chimeras and foolishness. That he had seen all and said all'" (I, xxvi, T: vol. I, 149; S: 170). Right after telling this story, Montaigne says that the student should pass "everything through a sieve, and store nothing in his head on mere authority and trust" (I, xxvi, T: vol. I, 149; S: 170). What in Montaigne is a piece of educational advice becomes in Descartes a procedural rule in philosophy: "never to accept anything as true if I did not have evident knowledge of its truth" (*Discourse*, II. CSM I, 120).

"Custom" has a similar effect to that of authority in education, which made Montaigne's interlocutor at Pisa confuse truth with Aristotelian philosophy. It makes us think that *our* idea of beauty, *our* laws, and *our* way of life express an objective point of view. Montaigne gives a number of examples showing his skepticism as to whether human reason is capable of discovering universal norms:

> With regard to the beauty of the body. . . it is probable that we have little idea of what beauty in Nature and in general is, since to our human beauty we ascribe so many different forms. . . . The Indians paint it black and dusky, with big swollen lips, a broad and flat nose. . . . In Peru the largest ears are the most beautiful. . . . By the Mexicans a small forehead is regarded as a sign of beauty. . . . The Italians' idea of beauty is big and massive, that of the Spaniards is gaunt and hollow. With us, one likes it fair, the other dark... Just as the preference in beauty is given by Plato to the spherical figure, the Epicureans give it rather to the pyramidal or the square. . . . But, however that may be, Nature has not privileged us in that any more than in any other respect, above her common laws.[5]

As for the law,

> During my lifetime I have known the laws of our neighbors the English to change and change back again three or four times... Here at home I have known a thing to become lawful which used to be a capital offense.[6]

Or morality,

> The murder of infants, the murder of fathers, community of wives,

6 *Apology for Raymond Sebond*, II, xii, T: vol. II, 25; S: 653.

7 *Apology for Raymond Sebond*, II, xii, T: vol. II, 27; S: 654–65.

> traffic in robberies, license in all sorts of pleasures, nothing in short is so outrageous but it may be allowed by the custom of some nation or other.[7]

In conclusion to his considerations, Montaigne rhetorically asks:

> What kind of truth can that be that is bounded by these mountains, and that becomes a lie to the people on the other side of them? But those people amuse me who, to give some certainty to laws, say that there are some that are fixed, perpetual and immutable, which they call the laws of Nature, and which by the very condition of their being, are imprinted in humankind . . .[8]

And:

> What can custom not impose on our judgments and beliefs? . . the principal effect of the force of custom is to seize and grip us so firmly, that we are scarce able to escape from its grasp, and to regain possession of ourselves sufficiently to discuss and reason out its commands. . . . He who would rid himself of this violent prejudice of custom will find that many things are accepted with undoubting resolve, which have no support but in the hoary beard and wrinkles of the usage which attends them.[9]

Does this mean that man can never know the truth, or, what is worse, that there is no truth? On the one hand Montaigne says that man's ability to arrive at an objective judgment has been completely destroyed: "We are all convention," he writes in "Of Presumption" (II, xvii, T: vol. II, 80; S: ...); and in "The Apology for Raymond Sebond" (II, xii, T: vol. II, xxvii) he adds: "I can quite believe that there are laws of Nature, such as we may observe in other creatures; but in us they have vanished..." In "Of Custom . . ." (I, xxiii, T: vol. I, 111; S: 130) he goes so far as to claim that "The laws of conscience, which we say are born of Nature, are born of custom." On the other hand Montaigne seems to believe that only if one could free oneself from the enslaving power of custom, one might be able to see reality as it is: "the mask once torn away, if he will refer the matter to truth and reason, he will feel his judgment turned as it were topsy-turvy, and yet restored to a condition of greater sureness." Again, following Montaigne, Descartes admits that the diversity of customs gives one "hardly any confidence"; but he also believes

8 *Apology for Raymond Sebond*, II, xii, T: vol. II, 26; S: 653–64.

9 *Apology for Raymond Sebond*, II, xii, T: vol. II, 27, 25; "Of Custom, and that an Established Law is not Lightly to be Changed," I, xxiii, T: vol. I, 106, 111, 113.

10 Montaigne says: "with greater sureness." See Appendix 3, IV M.

that the purification of the mind from "preconceived ideas" will gradually lead us to "conceiving objects clearly and distinctly."[10] Thus Descartes begins his *Meditations* with the rejection of all preconceived opinions (or Idols, as Bacon calls them) that "obscure natural light."

To be sure, there is no physics or metaphysics properly speaking in Montaigne. The *Essays* are not a work in philosophy; they are a record of the life of a French gentleman who had neither a thorough knowledge of philosophy nor patience for scholarly quibbles. "Philosophy is a hollow bone with no flesh on it." What was of philosophical importance in the *Essays* for Descartes was Montaigne's deep skepticism regarding the possibility of the universality of values. The Medieval idea of harmony toppled under the pressure of the discovery of new cultures, and Montaigne captured this with unspeakable force in his *Essays*. One could still philosophize in the old way, but only in a cell in a monastery of a religious order; however, the world around Descartes looked more like the one that Montaigne described in his *Essays*. This was a world in which, after the discovery of the Americas, people had learned that eating one's father is a form of piety and natural affection (II, xii, T: vol. II, 27; S: 655); it was a world where one no longer believed in the objective character of law; finally, it was a world where even religious certainties and the authority of the Church magisterium were crumbling.[11]

The discovery of the texts of the Ancient Skeptics[12] and the Epicureans furnished additional philosophical arguments for those whose faith in the objectivity of European norms had already been weakened by the discovery of other cultures. The last part of the *Apology for Raymond Sebond* is devoted for

11 "I have observed that in Germany Luther had left as many divisions and disputes concerning the uncertainty of his beliefs, and more, as he raised concerning the Holy Scriptures" ("Of Experience, III, xiii, T: vol. II, 545; S: 1213). And: "Now, what seems to me to bring so much trouble to our conscience, in these times of religious commotion, is the way in which the Catholics surrender their beliefs. They imagine themselves to be acting the part of moderate and intelligent men when they cede to their opponents some of the articles in their dispute. . . . Either we must submit wholly to the authority of our ecclesiastical polity, or entirely dispense with it. It is not for us to determine what portion of obedience we owe to it" ("It Is Folly to Measure the True and the False by Our Own Capacity," T: I, xxvii, vol. I, 182). One can say, however, that his criticism is inconsistent. "Obedience," as he says, "is never pure and simple in one who talks and argues" (*Apology for Raymond Sebond*, II, xvii, T: vol. II, 107).

12 For the influence of skepticism and the formation of the "method of doubt" in Montaigne, see Roger Duhamel, *Lecture de Montaigne* (Ottawa: Éditions de l'Université d'Ottawa, 1965), pp. 155–56.

13 See T: vol. II, 35–50. It appears that Descartes (cf. Med. III; AT VII, 39, CSM II, 27) took

the most part to Epicurean philosophy. Here Descartes could have learned that according to the Epicureans "all knowledge is conveyed to us through the senses: they are our masters" (T: vol. II, 35; S: 663).[13] And:

> The schools that deny that we can know anything ground their denial chiefly on the uncertainty and weakness of the Senses. For, since all knowledge comes to us by and through them, if they fail in their report, if they alter and corrupt what they convey to us from without, if the light which through them shines into our soul be obscured on the way, we have nothing else to go by. (T: vol. II, 38, S: 667).

Finally:

> Should it be true that what the Epicureans say, namely, "That we have no knowledge if the senses represent things falsely"; and also true what the Stoics say, "That the senses represent things so falsely, that they cannot furnish us with any manner of knowledge," we shall arrive at the conclusion, to the cost of these two great Dogmatic schools, That there is no such thing as knowledge.[14] (T: vol. II, 40; S: 669).

Such was the cultural and philosophical climate in the first few decades of the seventeenth century, and there is little doubt that the general impact behind Descartes's quest for certitude came from Montaigne's *Essays*.

Read against Montaigne, Cartesianism is an attempt to raise science from the shambles of skepticism and relativism into which Montaigne had thrown it. In other respects Montaigne's influence is limited to a few points, albeit important ones. The three maxims of the Provisional Moral Code were clearly inspired by Montaigne, although the expression itself comes from Francis Bacon.[15] Next, Descartes's personal odyssey about the discovery of the method written in an essayistic form was also inspired by Montaigne. *The Essays* (or "attempts," "trials") are "nothing but a record of the experiences of my life," says Montaigne ("Of Experience," III, xiii, T: vol. II, 556; S: 1224).

some examples from Montaigne: "That the sun is no bigger than it appears to our sight," T: vol. II, 39.

14 "Seeing that the Senses cannot decide our dispute, being themselves full of uncertainty, we must have recourse to Reason; there is no reason but must be built upon another reason: so here we are retreating backwards to all eternity" (T: vol. II, 49).

15 It is also probable that Descartes learned some of Montaigne's themes from Bacon, as Montaigne exercised considerable influence on the English philosopher. See Pierre Villey, *Montaigne et François Bacon, 1913* (Geneva: Slatkine Reprints, 1973).

16 "Mixing with society has a marvelous effect in clearing up a man's judgment," "Of the

But they are also the first version of a modern "physics and metaphysics," which is the study of the *self* – a treasure house, as it were, built out of the content of one's experiences such as travels, conversations,[16] and analysis of customs.[17]

As is well-known, Montaigne invented the literary genre known as the essay. As it appears from the reading of his chef-d'œuvre this particular form of writing was in Montaigne's eyes particularly suited for the exploration of the self. One should bear in mind, however, that the question behind the exploration of the self, and thus behind the essay, was Phyrron's dictum *Que sais-je?* (*What do I know?*), which Montaigne has ordered to be engraved on his medallion in 1576.[18] The influence of Montaigne's maxim and his literary style is felt in the literary style of the *Discourse*. After giving the account of his travels, readings, conversations, Descartes writes: "After I had spent some years pursuing these studies in 'the book of the world,'" an expression which he borrows from Montaigne, "and trying to gain some experience, I resolved one day to undertake studies within myself. . . . My present aim . . . is to reveal how I have tried to direct my own [mind]" (*Discourse*, I. CSM I, 116, 112). Descartes could well have entitled his *Discourse on the Method, The Essay on the Method*; if he did not, it was only because, in France, as Pierre Villey notes, the essay remained the personal property of Montaigne.[19] "For works of personal psychology and on morals which were not strictly didactic and technical, in France, one generally uses the term *discours, traité, réflexions, considérations*, and even *dialogue*."[20] Descartes's decision to use the word *discours* for his work on the method in sciences was in keeping with the idea that *discours*, like Montaigne's *essai*, was reserved for an account of personal experiences.

Montaigne, following the ancient Skeptics, discovered the self by "turning away" from the external world. However, this discovery was not without consequences. To Montaigne the self stands in opposition to the external world, as the "science" of the self stands in opposition to the science of Nature. This opposition in Montaigne is real, and we can know ourselves only at the expense of the knowledge of the external world.[21] "While

Education of Boys," I, xxvi, T: vol. I, 156; S: 176.

17 "Apology for Raymond Sebond," II, xvii, T: vol. II.

18 Pierre Villey discusses this issue in his *Les Essais de Michel de Montaigne* (Paris: Librarie Nizet, 1946), pp. 61 ff. Cf. Roger Duhamel, *Lecture de Montaigne*, pp. 31–44.

19 Pierre Villey, *ibid*. pp. 149ff.

20 Gustave Lanson, *Les Essais de Montaigne* (Paris: Librairie Mellottée, 1927), p. 326.

21 "For, to sum it up, I know that there is medicine, jurisprudence, four parts of mathematics, and roughly, what these aim at, and perhaps I know besides how much the sciences in general have helped us in our lives; but as to diving deeper, as to biting my

Montaigne had dissociated metaphysics from science and by the same token liberated science from metaphysics, Descartes linked them anew, and subordinated science to metaphysics. . . . Montaigne had shown that the question did not concern the construction of *ars demonstrandi* but of organizing a *ratio sciendi*. . . . Descartes will jump over the ditch before which Montaigne stopped. Descartes will identify *scire* and *demonstrare* . . ."[22]

nails in the study of Aristotle, the monarch of modern science, or stubbornly pursuing some particular branch of knowledge, I have never done it . . ." "Of the Education of Boys," I, xxvi, T: vol. I, 143; S: 163–64.

22 Gustave Lanson, *ibid.*, pp. 282, 281.